KEY POINTS BOXES P9-CRU-284

FIVE WAYS TO USE
POCKET KEYS FOR SPEAKERS

Pocket Keys for Speakers makes it easy for you to find information quickly. Here are five convenient ways to locate the information you need:

1. Color-Coded Pages
Blue sections cover speaking issues from getting started to delivery.

Red sections cover sentence-level concerns such as style, grammar, and usage.

2. Contents
The Key to the Book (inside front cover) is a directory to the book's fourteen parts.

Detailed Tables of Contents (on the back of each part divider) allow you to scan easily for the exact topic you are seeking.

Complete Table of Contents (inside back cover) shows the book at a glance.

3. Indexes
The Main Index (p. 313) provides a complete alphabetical list of topics, terms, and words such as *it's* and *its, who* and *whom, toasts, anxiety, gestures,* and *eye contact.*

4. Lists
Key Points Boxes (see list on pp. i–iii) give quick answers to quick questions.

Correction and Editing Marks (p. 325) shows common symbols, with cross-references to related coverage in the book.

5. Glossaries
Glossary of Speaking Terms (p. 282) defines common communication and speaking terms, and provides cross-references to related coverage throughout the book.

Glossary of Usage (p. 295) clarifies the use of commonly confused words such as *affect/effect* and *lie/lay.*

Glossary of Grammatical Terms (p. 303) defines helpful terms and provides cross-references to related coverage in the book.

Pocket Keys
for
SPEAKERS

Pocket Keys
for
SPEAKERS

ISA ENGLEBERG

*Prince George's Community College,
Largo, Maryland*

ANN RAIMES

*Hunter College,
City University of New York*

WADSWORTH
CENGAGE Learning·

Australia • Brazil • Japan • Korea • Mexico • Singapore
Spain • United Kingdom • United States

WADSWORTH
CENGAGE Learning™

Pocket Keys for Speakers
Isa Engleberg and Ann Raimes

Senior sponsoring editor: Mary Finch

Associate editor: Kristen LeFevre

Senior project editor:
Rachel D'Angelo Wimberly

Editorial assistant: May Jawdat

Senior production/design coordinator:
Jill Haber

Senior designer: Henry Rachlin

Manufacturing manager:
Florence Cadran

Marketing manager: Barbara LeBuhn

Cover image: © The Image Bank

For product information and technology assistance, contact us at
Cengage Learning Customer & Sales Support, 1-800-354-9706

For permission to use material from this text or product, submit all requests online at
www.cengage.com/permissions
Further permissions questions can be e-mailed to
permissionrequest@cengage.com

Library of Congress Catalog Card Number: 2002100899

ISBN-13: 978-0-618-23046-4

ISBN-10: 0-618-23046-7

Wadsworth Cengage Learning
20 Davis Drive
Belmont, CA 94002-3098
USA

Cengage Learning is a leading provider of customized learning solutions with office locations around the globe, including Singapore, the United Kingdom, Australia, Mexico, Brazil, and Japan. Locate your local office at **www.cengage.com/global**

Cengage Learning products are represented in Canada by Nelson Education, Ltd.

To learn more about Wadsworth, visit **www.cengage.com/wadsworth**

Purchase any of our products at your local college store or at our preferred online store **www.cengagebrain.com**

Printed in China
3 4 5 6 15 14 13 12

Table of Contents

Why and How You Should Read and Use Pocket Keys for Speakers

A Multipurpose Handbook

Are you a college student taking a variety of courses? Do you work part-time, full-time, or even over-time? Are you active in social and community groups? Do you want to feel confident and competent whenever you interact with others? If your answer is *yes* to any of these questions, much of your success depends on your ability to prepare and deliver effective presentations.

Pocket Keys for Speakers is a presentation speaking handbook. Unlike the many public speaking books that describe *what* to do when making a presentation, *Pocket Keys for Speakers* describes *how* to do it. For example, rather than telling you "Make sure you speak loud enough," we explain *how* to increase your volume, *how* to speak with or without a microphone, and *how* to adjust your voice to different surroundings. In addition to providing a variety of ways to organize a presentation, we also explain *how* to use specific organizational strategies that will help you achieve your purpose. Learning *how* goes well beyond *what* because it empowers you to draw upon a variety of effective communication strategies and skills for a multiplicity of speaking occasions.

Pocket Keys for Speakers focuses on *presentation* speaking. As we see it, presentation is a broad term that covers many different kinds of speaking: public speaking, classroom speaking, professional speaking, social event speaking, and community-based political speaking. Most of you will make many presentations but few public speeches. If you decide to run for office or become a community activist, you will have to speak in front of many public audiences. If you become famous, you will be invited to speak at public appearances. But in general, you are much more likely to be asked to make presentations in smaller, private settings.

Presentations are much more common than public speeches. They occur at school, at work, at community events, and at social and family gatherings. Generally, a public speech is also more formal than a presentation. Usually, presentations are delivered from notes rather than written out and delivered word for word from manuscript. Given the workplace setting of most presentations, you are also more likely to use visual aids during a presentation. Such settings also allow and even encourage more interaction between the speaker and the audience. Both the speaker and the audience members may question each other. On the other hand, in public speaking, the speaker speaks, the audience listens, and questions usually come after the speech is finished. As you read this handbook, always remember that presentations are more common and less formal than public speeches and they are more important to teachers, employers, and community members.

College classrooms, businesses, and community groups need good presenters, not public orators. When employers are asked about skills they are looking for in new employees, public speaking is not at the top of their lists. What does emerge, however, is a strong preference for communication skills, including the ability to present ideas and information to colleagues and clients.

Peggy Noonan, who was one of President Ronald Reagan's speech writers, notes, "As more and more businesses become involved in the new media technologies, as we become a nation of fewer widgets and more web sites, a new premium has been put on the oldest form of communication: the ability to stand up and say what you think in front of others."[1] Throughout your lifetime, your ability to prepare and deliver effective presentations will benefit you academically, professionally, publicly, and personally.

Academic Benefits

Regardless of whether you are giving a team presentation in a marketing course, explaining a proof in mathematics, or critiquing a novel in your English class, your ability to speak in front of the class will have a significant effect on your academic success. Successful students must be able to write and speak with clarity. So declares the prestigious Carnegie Foundation[2] as well as your professors. Many students find themselves in academic difficulty because they have not mastered the ability to write *and* speak. Both skills are indispensable. A student who can write a good report may not be able to explain its arguments or conclusions in an effective oral presentation. A student who thrives on classroom discussions and presentations may become paralyzed when required to put those same thoughts in a written report. *Pocket Keys for Speakers* bridges both skill areas by offering strategies and skills in speaking *and* writing.

Students derive an added benefit from learning how to speak and write effectively. They also acquire valuable academic skills—critical thinking, effective listening, research techniques, cultural sensitivity, organizational ability—necessary for enhancing learning and academic success.

Professional Benefits

Your ability to make effective presentations impacts your professional growth and career success. Good speakers are more likely to get a job, keep a job, and advance in their careers. Study after study emphasizes that employers seek applicants who have the ability to present ideas clearly and persuasively to others. Effective speakers are viewed more positively; poor speakers may find themselves trapped in dead-end career positions. The 21st century executive will have to be able to speak in front of small and large groups in both corporate and public settings. Learning to speak is not a luxury: it is a necessity in most careers.

Public Benefits

The survival of democracies depends on whether citizens are ready, willing, and able to speak in public. The First Amendment guarantees our right to free speech. Exercising that right depends on your ability to prepare and deliver effective presentations. Most of us will not become famous public figures or elected officials. All of us, however, can become advocates for important social issues in our communities. Your ability to speak effectively at a school board hearing, rally of faith communities, political candidate's forum, and community celebration can influence the prosperity, vitality, and well-being of the community in which you and your family live.

Personal Benefits

Effective presentation speaking can boost your personal confidence as well as your perceived competence and popularity. As you become a more effective speaker, you will also become more skilled at expressing your thoughts. Most listeners admire a speaker who can express ideas clearly, justify opinions logically, and share feelings eloquently. Effective speakers derive enormous personal satisfaction from their speaking experiences. As they become more competent, their confidence, self-esteem, and success grows.

A Two-Part Handbook

Pocket Keys for Speakers has two color-coded parts. Part I (blue) focuses on the presentation speaking strategies and skills. The primary source for Part I is Isa Engleberg and John Daly's textbook, *Presentations in Everyday Life*, published by Cengage Learning. Part II (red) focuses on writing strategies and skills, most of which also support effective speaking. The source for Part II is Ann Raimes' *Pocket Keys for Writers*, also published by Cengage Learning.

For readers seeking to improve their presentation speaking skills but who are strong, confident writers, the strategies and skills in Part II may be second nature. But for readers who are less confident writers, Part II provides valuable information about basic writing techniques.

Parts I and II are separate because speaking and writing are not the same. Writing for readers is not the same as speaking to listeners. The major difference is that a reader can go back and reread a written message, whereas a listener cannot go back and rehear a presentation unless it has been taped or distributed in written form. In most speaking situations, a listener is required to "get the message" as it is spoken. Once it's out of the speaker's mouth, it's gone. You must consider this unique "now you hear it, now you don't" quality of presentation speaking in every decision you make about a presentation. If you load your talk with technical details (something perfectly acceptable in a written report), your listeners may struggle to understand what you are saying. If you use long, complicated sentences (also perfectly acceptable in formal writing), you run the risk of losing the audience's attention and interest. If you speak too softly or too quickly (qualities irrelevant to a reader), your listeners cannot turn up the volume or reduce your speed as you speak.

Writing for readers and speaking to an audience also require some different skills. Certainly good writing is a prerequisite for becoming a good speaker. Most good speakers are often good writers. The key is knowing what *kind* of writing is best for readers and what kind is best for speaking. Most listeners have difficulty and become frustrated when a presentation is little more than someone reading a written report. The speaker would be better off giving everyone a copy of the report and letting everyone read it silently.

Even though speaking and writing are different kinds of skills, they are not unrelated. Just the opposite. Both speakers and writers must know the rules of good grammar and style. Although speakers often break grammatical rules on purpose—using sentence fragments, slang expressions, contractions—in order to achieve a more informal speaking style, their decision to do so is purposeful. However, a speaker who unwittingly says "Him and me went. . ." runs the risk of appearing uneducated and losing credibility.

Part II of *Pocket Keys for Speakers* includes writing strategies and skills that can help a speaker craft an appropriate and effective presentation. It also helps speakers who must transform parts of or an entire presentation into written form. Although oral and written styles may differ, speakers and writers should know which style or mixture of styles is best suited for a particular presentation or written document.

A Nonlinear Handbook

Developing and then delivering an effective presentation is not a linear process. Effective speakers know that every decision they make has an impact on previous and upcoming decisions. For example, whereas the purpose of a presentation influences the kind and amount of research needed, the results of research can, in turn, change the purpose and even the topic of a presentation. Just as audience analysis affects decisions about persuasive strategies, the strength of persuasive arguments can change a presentation's organizational plan. While effective speaking involves discovering and organizing ideas, it also requires the ability to modify decision and revise plans.

As a nonlinear process, preparing and delivering a presentation cannot be mastered by following a fixed set of step-by-step rules. Effective speaking depends on your ability to think critically and make strategic decisions throughout the process.

Pocket Keys for Speakers includes frequent cross-references to previous or upcoming portions of the handbook to help you understand the interdependence of its components. Frequently, you will see cross-references such as (See **20b** for storytelling techniques) or (See **19** for ways to develop eloquent and memorable language) or (See **30** for impromptu speaking strategies). Thus, in a section on methods for concluding a presentation, "Tell a Story" is suggested and illustrated with an example. A cross-reference is provided to a larger section explaining *how* to tell a story—regardless of whether it's used in the introduction, body, or conclusion of a presentation.

A Universal Handbook

Pocket Keys for Speakers is designed for many purposes and types of speakers. If you are a student required to present a team report with a group of classmates or to make a presentation on your own, the handbook's seven basic principles of effective speaking can guide you through the entire process. If your job requires that you prepare and deliver a briefing, report, training presentation, or strategic proposal, *Pocket Keys for Speakers* can help you choose appropriate communication strategies and techniques. If you take on the challenge of representing the needs and concerns of your community to decision makers in front of a public audience, major sections of the handbook can help you choose an appropriate goal, adapt your message to your audience, select effective and interesting supporting material, and deliver your presentation with conviction.

    Pocket Keys for Speakers has a title that suggests its function. Like the pocket keys you carry with you, *Pocket Keys for Speakers* should be a faithful companion every time you face the prospect of making a presentation. And, like your personal keys, *Pocket Keys for Speakers* has the potential to unlock doors that can enhance your academic, professional, public, and personal success.

Notes

[1] Peggy Noonan, *Simply Speaking: How to Communicate Your Ideas with Style, Substance, and Clarity* (New York: HarperCollins, 1998).

[2] Ernest L. Boyer, *College: The Undergraduate Experience in America* (New York: Harper, 1987), p. 73.

Pocket Keys
for
SPEAKERS

Unit 1

Keys to Effective Speaking

Part 1

Getting Started as a Speaker

3

1   Begin the Speechmaking Process

No matter what you do now or in the future, no matter where you live or work, you will be invited or required to make presentations in front of colleagues, friends, family members, and public audiences. Learning to speak is a wise personal investment. Since you *will* make presentations, be prepared to do them well.

This introductory section of *Pocket Keys for Speakers* previews basic speaking and listening principles. The sections that follow further develop these principles into the specific strategies and techniques that you will use to become a more effective speaker.[1]

1a The benefits of speechmaking

In addition to sharing a message, an effective presentation allows your knowledge, abilities, talents, and opinions to stand out from the crowd. The person who speaks well is more likely to be noticed, believed, respected, and remembered.

The benefits of learning how to speak well extend far beyond the few minutes you stand before an audience. Effective speaking skills also offer personal, professional, and public benefits.

Personal Learning how to prepare and present effective presentations will help you develop self-awareness, self-confidence, and critical thinking ability. It will also teach you valuable skills that you can call upon throughout your lifetime — how to choose and narrow a topic, adapt to other people, research and structure a message, use informative and persuasive strategies, employ memorable language, and enlist your voice and body to compel attention.

Professional Almost everything you do in a career involves some form of communication. For many years, the Business–Higher Education Forum, in affiliation with the American Council on Education, has conducted a study that asks employers to identify the skills college students need for the world of work.[2] Oral communication skills have always topped the list. When the National Association of Colleges and Employers surveys ask employers to list, in rank order, the top ten skills they seek in college graduates, oral communication comes in first again—well ahead of other basic skills such as writing and computer literacy.[3]

Employers seek job applicants who can present ideas and information to colleagues and clients. They value employees who know how to analyze, adapt, and appeal to a wide variety of audiences. Learning to develop and deliver effective presentations greatly improves your chances of getting a job, keeping it, and advancing in your chosen career.

Public The ability to present your views in public is the right and privilege of every citizen, as guaranteed by the First Amendment to the U. S. Constitution. Learning how to make effective presentations will help you participate in the development of public policies at all levels of government. It will also help you become a critical listener who can understand, analyze, and critique the speeches of government officials, corporate executives, and media spokespersons.

1b Determine why you are speaking

By the time you are facing an audience, it is too late to decide what you want to say and how you want to say it. As soon as you know you may have to speak, you should begin to craft a message that will benefit both you and your audience. The very first step requires you to understand *why* you are speaking.

Before you begin to prepare a speech—whether it's a major address to an audience of thousands or a presentation to five colleagues at work—you will need to make a critical decision. Ask yourself these questions: *Should I speak, or should I write? Could a detailed report accomplish the same purpose? Would a memo be just as good? Could a brochure have the same effect?*

In many cases, a well-written message may be more appropriate and more effective than a well-prepared speech. For example, if a user-friendly manual effectively explains how to assemble a new computer system, a speech on that same topic may not be necessary. Teaching someone how to use a job-specific software program, however, may require the presence of a live instructor who is skilled at helping listeners navigate a new system.

Before you invest much time and effort, be sure that making a presentation is the best way to communicate your message. The answers to four questions can help you decide whether a speech is necessary.

 KEY POINTS

Deciding Whether to Speak or Write

1. Is a presentation required?
2. Is immediate action needed?
3. Is the topic controversial?
4. Will *you* make a difference?

Is a presentation required?   You may be asked to present a major report at a staff meeting or conference, offer a toast at a wedding or retirement dinner, or introduce a guest speaker. In such cases, not only does the nature of the event *require* a speech; the audience also expects certain qualities in the presentation—clarity and brevity in a report, good cheer at a celebration, and background information about a speaker in an introduction.

Is immediate action needed?   If an audience must be made aware of a problem in order to take immediate action, there may not be time to write a memo or publish a report. Making a presentation may be the best way to respond. For example, President George W. Bush was initially criticized for *not* speaking to the American public immediately after the September 11 tragedy. At that time, a shocked nation sought assurance that its government and president were responding to the crisis.

Is the topic controversial?   Responding to a controversy in writing can often lead to more, not fewer, problems and misunderstandings. Responding with a speech, however, gives a speaker the opportunity to explain the controversy, correct misunderstandings, and answer questions. Audience members can listen, ask questions, and challenge ideas. Although this kind of speaking can be difficult, speakers can use this face-to-face opportunity to gauge audience reactions to the controversy.

Will you make a difference?   It is much easier to ignore an email, memo, or report than it is to ignore someone who is talking to you. A presentation can be the most effective form of communication simply because *you are there.* The emotion in a speaker's voice and the physical energy of a presentation are difficult to capture in written messages. Audiences will appreciate the risks you are taking when you put yourself and your message in front of them rather than communicating through the safety and distance of a written message. The more your message depends on *you,* the more you need to make a presentation.

2 Understand the Seven Basic Principles of Effective Speaking

The first and most important step in developing an effective speech relies on your ability to make seven critical decisions about your presentation. By applying the following seven basic principles, you will be able to make effective decisions about what to say, explain the reasons why your decisions make sense, and evaluate the success of your presentation.

 KEY POINTS

The Seven Basic Principles of Effective Speaking

1. Purpose
2. Audience
3. Logistics
4. Content
5. Organization
6. Credibility
7. Performance

2a Purpose: Why are you speaking?

Purpose raises the following questions about the outcome of your speech: What do you want audience members to know, think, believe, or do as a result of hearing your presentation? Given your purpose, how do you focus and narrow your topic? How will you *and* your audience benefit if you achieve your purpose? (See **Part 2**: sections **6–7** for an in-depth discussion of purpose and topic.)

2b Audience: How will you adapt to your audience?

Understanding your audience requires answers to several questions: How do the characteristics of your audience—such as their demographics, interests, and attitudes—affect the way you develop your presentation? How can you learn more about your audience? How can you adapt to your audience in order to improve your speech? (See **Part 3**: section **8** for audience analysis and adaptation strategies.)

2c   Logistics: Where and when will you be speaking?

Logistics raise the following questions: Why are you speaking to this group at this time and in this place? How can you plan and adapt to the logistics (audience size, facilities, equipment, time) of the place where you will be speaking? Does the occasion require special adaptations? (See **Part 3**: section **9** for keys to adapting to the setting and occasion of a presentation.)

2d   Content: What ideas and information should you include?

When searching for and selecting the content for your presentation, consider these questions: Where and how can you find good ideas and information? How much and what kind of supporting material do you need? Have you found the best sources? (See **Part 4**: sections **10–11** for research gathering and selection guidelines.)

2e   Organization: How should you arrange your content?

Sharing your **content** with an audience requires good **organization.** Ask these questions: Is there a natural order to the ideas and information you want to include in your presentation? What are the most effective ways to organize your presentation in order to adapt it to your purpose, the people in your audience, the place where you will be speaking, and the content you want to include? How should you begin and end your presentation? (See **Part 5**: sections **13–17** for how to organize, outline, begin, and end a presentation.)

2f   Credibility: Are you believable?

An effective presentation has the potential to enhance your **credibility.** Consider these questions: How can *you* become associated with your message in a positive way? What can you do to demonstrate your expertise and trustworthiness? (See **Part 6**: sections **18–20** for strategies designed to enhance your believability and generate audience interest.)

2g　Performance: How should you deliver your speech?

Performance raises the following questions: What forms of vocal and physical delivery are appropriate for your purpose, audience, and setting? What delivery techniques will make your presentation more effective? How much and what should you practice? (See **Part 7**: sections **21–24** for the keys to achieving effective vocal, physical, and mediated delivery.)

Remember, the seven principles of effective speaking cannot produce a successful presentation—only *you* can. These principles are designed to serve as a road map: guiding you, helping you avoid mistakes, and getting you to your communication destination as efficiently and effectively as possible.

3　Reduce Your Speaking Anxiety

What is your number one fear? Is it fear of heights, death, snakes, or financial ruin? If you are like most Americans, speaking in front of groups is right at or near the top of your list. You know the feeling—upset stomach, shaky voice and hands, sense of panic, confused thoughts, dizziness. Whether it's called *stage fright, presentation anxiety, communication apprehension,* or *talking terror,* the thought of giving a speech makes almost everyone nervous. Even people who regularly appear in front of large audiences experience some degree of stage fright.

Fortunately, communication researchers and psychologists have studied this common but often terrifying experience, and have identified strategies to help you understand and reduce your nervousness. They also recognize that a speaker's level of **presentation anxiety** can vary with either real (delivering the speech) or anticipated (worrying about the speech) communication to a particular group of people or audience.

3a　Understand the sources of your nervousness

One of the keys to reducing speaking anxiety is to understand the sources of your nervousness. Although everyone has his or her own personal reasons for feeling anxious, there are several key fears that underlie or cause most stage fright. See if you can recognize yourself in any of the following scenarios.

Fear of failure   Just about everyone fears failure, especially public failure. Speakers may be anxious because they can imagine all the things that might go wrong. In all probability, however, everything will be okay; nothing will go wrong. Too often, an unrealistic fear of failure puts speakers in an unnecessary state of panic.

Fear of the unknown   For many inexperienced speakers, speechmaking is an unfamiliar activity. Therefore, the more they practice and the more they speak, the more comfortable they will become. Practice turns the unknown into the well known.

Fear of the spotlight   Audience members focus their attention on everything a speaker says and does. As a result, speakers often find it difficult to concentrate on their message.

Fear of breaking the rules   Many speakers experience stage fright because they are burdened with too many rigid rules and misconceptions about public speaking. Keep in mind that most rules are generalizations, and some rules are wrong. As you learn the "rules" of speechmaking, make sure that they come from an expert source. And remember that no two presentations or audiences are alike, so it's okay to bend or even break some of the rules.

Fear of fear   Anxiety can grow upon itself. If, for example, a speaker feels a slight tremor of fear, he or she may become more conscious of that feeling, and that awareness can generate even more anxiety. Once the fear cycle begins, it can be difficult to stop.

3b Build your confidence

Successful speakers know two very important facts about stage fright: They know that it's very common, and they know that it's usually not visible to audience members.

Remember that most speakers experience some level of anxiety. This means that most audience members will understand your feelings, wouldn't want to trade places with you, and might even admire your courage.

Also, remember that in most cases your anxiety is invisible. The audience cannot see or hear your fear—they cannot see your pounding heart, upset stomach, cold hands, or worried thoughts. They don't even notice small changes in your voice or appearance. In fact, most speakers who describe themselves as being nervous actually appear very confident and calm to their audiences.

3c Use anxiety-reducing techniques

One positive side effect of speech anxiety's universality is that many effective methods have been developed to help nervous speakers cope. Several of the following strategies may work for you.

Prepare   Preparation is critical. Know your topic. If you don't, the audience will sense that you are bluffing. Learn as much as you can about your audience and setting. Prepare your material in advance. When you know what you want to say and how you are going to say it, you will feel less anxious.

Practice   When you have practiced your presentation—out loud, of course—you have less reason to be nervous. Since many speakers are most nervous at the very beginning of a presentation, consider memorizing the first thirty seconds of your speech in order to cope with this initial anxiety. If you're worried about your ability to memorize, practice your introduction multiple times until you feel very comfortable with your opening. That way, you will begin with confidence, and that good feeling will see you through the rest of your presentation.

 KEY POINTS

Tips for Practicing Your Presentation

- Review your notes, but practice *out loud.*
- Schedule several practice sessions rather than one long rehearsal.
- Schedule at least three, but no more than five, complete run-through sessions.
- Practice sections of your presentation (introduction, individual key points, conclusion) separately and repeatedly.
- Don't practice in front of a mirror if you find doing so distracting and unnatural.
- Take frequent breaks to refresh your voice and mind.

Think positively   The power of positive thinking really does work for speakers. Don't talk yourself into being nervous: "This is going to be awful!" or "What if I make a fool of myself?" Instead, tell yourself you'll do a great job: "What an opportunity this is!" or "I know my material and will convince my audience." Remember the personal, professional, and public benefits of effective speaking. (See section **1a**.) Use your nervous energy to animate your presentation and give it power. If you visualize yourself succeeding, you're more likely to see that vision come true.

Relax   Simple relaxation techniques can minimize the symptoms of speaker anxiety. Practicing deep breathing techniques, tensing and releasing your stomach or shoulder muscles, or inhaling and exhaling while thinking "relax" or "calm down" can lower your pulse and focus your attention on your speech rather than on your nervousness.

   As an experiment, try the *Silent Reeelaaax* exercise. Break the word *relax* into two syllables: *re* and *lax*. Breathe in slowly through your nose while saying the sound "re" (ree) silently to yourself, holding the long *e* sound while inhaling for about three seconds. Then breathe out slowly, also for three seconds, thinking the sound "lax" (laks) silently to yourself, and hold the *a* sound while exhaling. Inhale and exhale, thinking "reee-laaax," four or five times. By the time you finish this thirty-second exercise, your pulse should be slower and you will feel calmer.

Focus on your audience   One of the best ways to build your confidence is to concentrate on your message and audience rather than on yourself. When you speak, try talking to individual listeners as though you are having a personal conversation with them. Look for positive responses—smiles, heads nodding in agreement, audience members sitting forward. Encourage more audience feedback.

   For example, as you talk, start nodding your head and watch as your listeners reciprocate. What you are doing is shifting your attention away from yourself and onto your audience. Giving less thought to yourself and more thought to reaching your audience with your message can reduce your level of anxiety and improve the quality of your performance and presentation.

KEY POINTS

Keys to Reducing Your Speech Anxiety

1. Keep your mind on your presentation rather than on yourself.
2. Don't talk about your nervousness during your presentation.
3. Don't memorize your speech; it's too easy to forget.
4. Approach the podium with the appearance of confidence.
5. Begin and end with a well-prepared introduction and conclusion.
6. Look directly at your audience while you are speaking.
7. Turn your nervous energy into a positive force.
8. Practice, practice, practice.

4 Listen to Others

Most speakers spend considerable time focused on what they want to *say*. The best speakers also spend time thinking about how their audiences listen. Effective **listening** involves the ability to understand, analyze, respect, and appropriately respond to the meaning of another person's spoken and nonverbal messages. Good listening is a critical communication skill regardless of whether you are a standing at a lectern or sitting in an audience.

At first, listening may appear to be as easy and as natural as breathing. After all, everyone listens. In fact, just the opposite may be closer to the truth. Although most of us can *hear*, we often fail to *listen* to what others have to say. Even though listening is what audiences are supposed to do when speakers talk, most audiences cannot accurately report 50 percent of what they hear immediately after listening to a short speech. Poor listeners rarely retain even 25 percent of what they hear, and much of that information can be distorted or inaccurate.

Highly effective speakers adjust to and compensate for the poor listening habits of their audiences. At the same time, learning to listen to your audience is just as important as learning to listen as an audience member.

4a Learn to listen

Fortunately, speakers and audience members can become better listeners by developing and practicing good listening habits.

 KEY POINTS

Effective Listening Habits

- Plan to listen.
- Overcome distractions.
- Listen for the big ideas.
- "Listen" to nonverbal behavior.
- Listen before you leap to conclusions.

Plan to listen Do some prior study—the more you know about a topic, the more you will get out of hearing a presentation about it. Ask yourself: What do I want to get out of listening to this presentation? If you can find a personal reason to listen, you will be a better listener. As a speaker, ask the same question about your audience and give them a good reason to listen.

Overcome distractions Regardless of whether distractions are loud noises, an uncomfortable room, or frequent interruptions, do what you can to reduce the problem. You are well within your rights as a speaker or audience member to shut a door, turn on more lights, or ask people who are talking to save their conversation for a time after the presentation.

Listen for the big ideas You will do your audience a favor if your presentation is clear and well organized. When faced with a disorganized speaker, most listeners lose track and drift off. Effective listeners try to identify a speaker's main ideas. Effective speakers make sure their big ideas are clear and memorable.

When people believe they have to report back on what they have heard, their comprehension increases significantly. As a listener, ask yourself the audience's side of the purpose questions: What does the speaker want me to know, think, believe, or do after hearing this presentation? Then try to list the key points or ideas the speaker used to achieve that purpose.

"Listen" to nonverbal behavior   Speakers don't always put everything they have to say into words. Very often, audiences can interpret a speaker's meaning by paying attention to nonverbal factors such as tone of voice, facial expression, eye contact, posture, and level of energy. Speakers and audience members should note how these nonverbal elements enhance or detract from a presentation. By "listening" to nonverbal behavior, you can learn a lot about a speaker and the audience.

Listen before you leap to conclusions   It's easy to reach a hasty judgment about a speaker. Good listeners, however, make sure that they accurately understand a speaker before reacting positively or negatively. Audience members who react before a speaker has finished may miss an important piece of information or a statement that might modify their initial reactions. Speakers who react to a yawn or frown in the audience may be responding to something that has nothing to do with their presentation. Whether you are presenting or listening to a speech, make sure that you understand what is being communicated before evaluating and reacting.

4b   Listen to your audience

One of the most important and valuable speaking skills to learn involves "listening" and adapting to your audience *during* a presentation.

All audience members react in some way. They may smile or frown, nod "yes" or "no," break into spontaneous applause, or refuse to applaud. As you speak, look at and listen to the ways in which audience members react to you. Do they look interested or bored, pleased or displeased? If you can't see or hear reactions, ask for feedback. There is nothing wrong with stopping in the middle of a presentation to ask audience members if they understand you. Not only does such feedback help you adapt to your audience; it also tells listeners that you are interested in their reactions.

Adjust to audience feedback Ask yourself the following questions as you speak: Do audience members appear to be listening? Do they seem to understand what I am saying, or do they seem confused? Depending on how you answer these questions, you may want to make mid-presentation corrections. For example, if an audience seems confused, you may want to slow down and re-explain a concept. If the audience looks bored, you may want to add an interesting story to rekindle their interest.

Adapt to listener differences Young and old, male and female, and national and international audience members bring different listening habits to any speaking situation. Adapting your presentation to the diverse listening styles and skills of audience members can be a complicated and challenging task. Understanding and adapting to different listening behavior can improve your ability to achieve the purpose of your presentation.

 KEY POINTS

Adapting to Your Listeners

1. Recognize that audience members are often poor listeners.
2. Speak clearly with adequate volume to accommodate all of your listeners.
3. Compensate for poor listening by overcoming distractions and emphasizing your main ideas.
4. Give audience members a good reason to listen.
5. Adjust your presentation to audience feedback as you speak.
6. Adapt to differences in audience members' listening abilities and styles, as well as to differences in their cultural backgrounds and personal orientations.

4c Listen to and evaluate other presenters

Learning how to listen to and evaluate a presentation is just as important as learning how to give one.

The seven basic principles of effective speaking (See **Part 1**: section **2**) can be turned into a set of evaluation guidelines that apply to almost any speaker, regardless of the topic, audience, or setting. By using these guidelines, you will be able to evaluate how well a speaker is achieving his or her purpose. The evaluation form that follows gives you a comprehensive list of evaluation criteria for assessing the effectiveness of a speaker.

 KEY POINTS

Criteria for Evaluating a Speaker

PURPOSE

Purpose: Is the speaker's purpose specific, achievable, and relevant?

Topic: Is the topic appropriate, focused, and appealing?

AUDIENCE

Audience: Does the speaker adapt to the demographic characteristics, motivations, interests, knowledge, and attitudes of the audience?

LOGISTICS

Setting: Does the presentation adjust to the audience size, facilities, equipment, and time?

Occasion: Is the presentation appropriate for the occasion?

CONTENT

Supporting Material: Does the presentation use sufficient, varied, and valid supporting material (facts, statistics, testimony, definitions, analogies, descriptions, examples, stories)?

Interest Factors: Does the speaker gain and hold audience attention by using expressive language, stories, humor, and audience involvement?

ORGANIZATION

Introduction: Is the introduction interesting, credible, topic related, and appropriate?

Organization: Are the key points clearly arranged and skillfully connected?

Conclusion: Is the conclusion clear, memorable, and brief?

CREDIBILITY

Credibility: Does the speaker appear to be competent, of good character, and/or charismatic?

PERFORMANCE

Vocal Delivery: Is the speaker's vocal delivery effective and appropriate?

Physical Delivery: Is the speaker's physical delivery effective and appropriate?

Presentation Aids: If the speaker uses presentation aids, are they well prepared and effectively employed?

5 Speak Ethically

Good speakers accept and practice ethical communication. They understand that their own credibility and the believability of their messages depend on audience members' seeing them as honest, ethical speakers.

5a Follow ethical principles

Questions of right and wrong arise whenever you communicate. Ethical communication is a fundamental responsibility of every speaker, regardless of the context or topic of a presentation. Unethical speaking threatens the quality of all communication and ultimately jeopardizes the personal success of a speaker.

5b Apply ethical standards to speechmaking

When audiences see you as an ethical speaker, they are more likely to believe what you have to say. Ethical decision making focuses on all seven basic principles of the speechmaking process.

Ethics and purpose Will you *and* your audience benefit if you achieve your purpose? Unfortunately, audiences are

KEY POINTS

Guiding Principles for Ethical Speakers

The following guidelines are based on the Credo for Ethical Communication developed and approved by the National Communication Association:[4]

- Speakers should be truthful, accurate, reasonable, and honest.
- Speakers should defend freedom of speech, diversity of perspectives, and tolerance of dissent.
- Speakers should be committed to the courageous expression of their personal convictions in pursuit of fairness and justice.
- Speakers should condemn the expression of intolerance and hatred.
- Speakers should respect the privacy and confidentiality of others.
- Speakers should accept full responsibility for the short- and long-term consequences of their presentations.

deceived sometimes by speakers who *appear* to be honest, but whose private purposes are selfish and even harmful to their audiences. If you would be ashamed or embarrassed to reveal your private purpose to an audience, you should question the honesty and ethics of your presentation. (See **Part 2**: section **6**.)

Ethics and audience   Have you used the information you gathered and analyzed about your audience to serve them or to deceive them? An ethical speaker has the responsibility to weigh what an audience wants to hear against what is truthful, fair, and beneficial. (See **Part 3**: section **8**.)

Ethics and logistics   Are you using the setting and facilities responsibly? Are you following your assigned time limits and honoring the protocol of the occasion? Make sure your adaptation to the place and occasion of your presentation will benefit your audience. (See **Part 3**: section **9**.)

Ethics and content   Have you used valid information to support your key points? Identify and qualify the sources of your information. Make sure your information is recent, complete, consistent, and relevant. Never plagiarize; ethical speakers do not represent someone else's words or ideas as their own. (See section **5c** and **Part 4**: sections **10** and **11**.)

Ethics and organization   Have you used a clear organizational pattern to highlight important topics? Does your supporting material truly support your key points? Unethical speakers may let poor organization obscure information they don't want their audiences to notice or understand. (See **Part 5**: section **13**.)

Ethics and credibility   Have you used your expertise or established a trustworthy image to deceive your audience in any way? Have you relied on a dynamic speaking style to mask poor arguments or weak information? Ethical speakers are well liked and respected by their audiences because they are honest, fair, caring, informed, and justifiably confident. (See **Part 6**: section **18**.)

Ethics and performance   Are you using an honest communication style, or are you acting out a false role? Ethical speakers do not use good delivery techniques to mask or avoid the truth. If, for example, an emotional response is inappropriate, it's unethical to fake emotions or to incite them in your audience. (See **Part 7**: section **21**.)

5c   Avoid plagiarism

Plagiarism occurs when a speaker passes off the original ideas or research of another person as his or her own. Although most speakers do not intend to commit plagiarism, it occurs more often than it should, usually with serious consequences.

The key to avoiding plagiarism and its consequences is to identify the sources of your information in your presentation. Also, understand that changing a few words of someone else's work is not enough to avoid plagiarism. If you aren't presenting original ideas, and most of the words are not yours, you are ethically obligated to tell your audience who wrote or said them and where they came from. The bottom line is this: Plagiarism is not just unethical; it is illegal. Plagiarism represents the theft of a person's hard work and good ideas.

KEY POINTS

How to Avoid Plagiarism

- If you include an identifiable phrase or an idea that appears in someone else's work, always acknowledge and document your source orally.

- Do not use exactly the same sequence of ideas and organization that your source did.

- Tell an audience exactly when and how you are citing someone else's exact words in your presentation.

- Never buy, find, or use someone else's speech as your own work.

Part 2

Determining Your Purpose and Topic

6 Establish Your Purpose

Students enrolled in public-speaking courses and training seminars often ask their instructors, "What should I talk about?" The question is a good one, but it may be unique to a speech communication class.

Public speakers outside the classroom rarely ask that question because what they should talk about is seldom a concern. They are usually invited to speak because they are experts on a subject, because events call for a particular topic, or because they are recognized celebrities. A noted scientist may present at an international conference; a mayoral candidate may speak at a political rally. In both cases, the speakers know their topic. Even more importantly, they know their purpose.

6a Identify your purpose

The first and most crucial step in developing a good speech is identifying your **purpose.** Ask: "What do I want my audience to know, think, feel, or do as a result of my presentation?"

Purpose focuses on *why.* Ask: "Why am I speaking, and what outcome do I want?" Having a clear purpose does not guarantee that you will achieve it. But without a purpose, you will find it difficult to decide what to say, what materials to include in your speech, and even how to deliver your presentation.

6b Differentiate public and private purposes

There can be more than one answer to the question "What is my purpose?" If you were asked to state the goal of your presentation to your audience, you would probably state

24

your **public purpose.** You may not need or even want to share your **private purpose,** the personal goal of your speech. Skilled speakers understand the absolute necessity of a public purpose, the advantages of a private purpose, and, most importantly, the difference between the two.

 KEY POINTS

Examples of Public and Private Purposes

PUBLIC PURPOSE	PRIVATE PURPOSES
I want to persuade my audience to visit the Public Gardens in June to see the display of late flowering azaleas.	1. I want to attract more visitors to the gardens in order to increase attendance. 2. I want to impress my boss by showing her how I can reach our new attendance goals.
I want to explain why all children must be immunized before starting kindergarten.	1. I can use this research when I prepare a booklet for the clinic where I work. 2. Given my instructor's comments about her young children, this topic should interest her and help me earn a good grade.

There is nothing wrong with having both a public and private purpose for speaking. However, there is something wrong if achieving your private purpose would hurt or deceive your audience. Don't miss the opportunity to get the most out of your presentation as long as your public and private purposes don't conflict or undermine each other.

7 Move from Purpose to Topic

Your purpose asks, "What do I want my audience to know, think, feel, or do as a result of my speech?" The topic completes the question by adding "about what?" Your **topic** is the subject matter of your presentation.

Speech topics can range from *rap music* to *repairing refrigerators* to *religion*. A topic is often a simple word or phrase: *rap music*. Yet two presentations that discuss the same topic can have very different purposes. Look at the differences between these two purpose statements dealing with the same topic:

- I want my audience to understand and appreciate rap music.

- I want my audience to boycott recording companies that promote rap music with violent and offensive lyrics.

7a Select a good topic

Four basic questions can be the keys to choosing a good topic for a presentation. The answers to these questions can help you find a topic that suits you, your audience, and your purpose.

 KEY POINTS

Questions for Choosing a Good Topic

1. What type of presentation are you supposed to give?
2. What topics interest you?
3. What do you know about these topics?
4. What topics will appeal to your audience?

What type of presentation are you supposed to give? Make sure you understand the type of presentation you have been asked to give or want to prepare and deliver. Is it an informative, a persuasive, or an entertainment speech? An **informative speech** instructs, explains, describes, enlightens, demonstrates, clarifies, corrects, or reminds. A **persuasive speech** seeks to change audience opinions and/or behavior. An **entertainment speech** tries to amuse, interest, divert, or "warm up" an audience. (See **Parts 8** and **9** for informative, persuasive, and special occasion speaking strategies.)

Some skilled speakers, regardless of their purpose, will try to do all three—inform, persuade, and entertain. For example, a professor may lecture to inform, but also try to persuade students that the information is important and interesting. She may also try to entertain students so that they will pay better attention to the information. You can make your presentation more interesting and compelling by considering ways in which you can include all three types of speaking.

What topics interest you? Many speakers have no trouble answering this question. They have a fascinating hobby, an area of special expertise, an intriguing or unusual job, or a subject they follow regularly. If, however, you have difficulty identifying a topic that interests you, ask yourself some leading questions.

 KEY POINTS

Leading Questions for Finding a Topic

Completing the following statements can help you find a topic worth considering for a speech:

- I've always wanted to know more about . . .
- If I had to read one book of nonfiction, it would be . . .
- If I had an unexpected week off, I would . . .
- If I could give away a million dollars, I would . . .
- If I could make one new law, I would . . .
- I've always wanted other people to understand . . .
- My favorite topic of conversation is . . .

If leading questions don't work, try creating a chart on which you list potential topics under broad headings—sports, food, hobbies, places and destinations, famous people, art and music, important events, personal goals, public and community issues, objects and things, theories and processes, natural and supernatural phenomena. By the time you have finished filling in your interests on such a chart, you may have dozens of good topics for a presentation.

What do you know about these topics? Everyone is good at something. Everyone knows more about a few things than most other people do. A fruitful source of topics is your work experience. So are your personal experiences and skills. Look at the following list of topics presented by speakers who were either topic experts or who had thoroughly researched a topic that interested them:

Interpretation of Dreams	Exercise and Long Life
Investment Strategies	Editing a Video
Vegetarian Diets	Playing the Cello
Closing a Sale	Genealogy and Your Family Tree
Wine Tasting	Becoming a Big Brother/Big Sister
Afro-Cuban Jazz	Restoring Cars
Therapeutic Massage	Duties of a Security Guard

Many of the best presentations are based on personal experiences. Don't underestimate your experiences and skills. Rely on your expertise and enlighten your audience.

What topics will appeal to your audience?   As you consider potential topics, think about ways to make your topic appealing to your audience. If you are interested in the interpretation of dreams, relate the theories to the kinds of dreams most people have experienced. If you are a Big Brother, tell stories that touch your listeners' hearts and feelings about their own families to demonstrate the importance of offering a helping hand. Find the links between your interests and those of your audience. (See **Part 3** for a detailed discussion of audience analysis.)

7b   Narrow your topic

At this point, you should make sure that you have appropriately narrowed or modified your topic in order to achieve your purpose and adapt to your listeners' needs and interests. Narrowing a topic involves selecting the most important and interesting ideas and information for inclusion in your presentation rather than trying to tell your audience everything you know or have learned about a topic.

Although you may be an expert on your topic, your audience may be hearing about it for the first time. Don't bury them with mounds of information. Ask yourself: "If I only have time to tell them one thing about my topic, what should it be?" Most likely, conveying a single important

idea will be enough to achieve your purpose. Focus on two
or three main points, not five or six. Consider the amount of
time you have to speak and narrow your topic to suit those
limits.

Look at how these speakers narrowed some broad, general topic ideas to produce more specific speech topics:

BROAD	**A Review of Greek Mythology**
BETTER	**The Origins of Aphrodite**

BROAD	**Advances in Semiconductor Technology**
BETTER	**What Is a Semiconductor Device?**

BROAD	**The New Employee Evaluation Plan**
BETTER	**How to Follow Deadlines in the New Employee Evaluation Plan**

7c Develop a purpose statement

Once you know *why* you are speaking (your purpose) and
what you are speaking about (your topic), you should develop
a clear **purpose statement** to guide your preparation.

A purpose statement asks the question "What is the
main idea that you want to communicate to your listeners?" Your reply to this question is your purpose statement. It identifies the main idea in your presentation or
the stand that you are going to take on an issue.

It is not enough to say, "My purpose is to tell my audience all about my job as a phone solicitor." This statement
is too general and probably an impossible goal to achieve
in a time-limited presentation. Instead, your purpose
statement must convey the specific focus of your speech,
such as "My purpose is to make my audience aware of two
common strategies used by effective phone solicitors to
overcome listener objections."

A purpose statement is similar to a writer's thesis
statement, which asks, "What is the main idea you want to
communicate to your reader in your writing?" Regardless
of whether you are speaking or writing, a purpose statement can guide the ways in which you research, organize,
and present your message. In most speaking situations,
effective purpose statements share the following three
characteristics.

KEY POINTS

Characteristics of a Good Purpose Statement

- Specificity
- Achievability
- Relevance

Specificity   A clear and specific purpose statement gives you both scope and direction while preparing a presentation.

"I want to talk about the benefits of staying healthy" is too general and vague to be an effective purpose statement. "I want my audience to understand how to use the government's new food group recommendations as a diet guide" is a more specific purpose statement. A specific purpose statement narrows your topic to the content appropriate for a specific audience and occasion within the assigned limitations of time and space.

Achievability   Inexperienced speakers often make the mistake of either trying to cover too much material in a presentation or asking too much of their audience. Since an audience can absorb only a limited amount of information during a single speech, present a few key points rather than an encyclopedia of ideas.

In general, a presentation should contain at least two key points and no more than five. Three are ideal. Because changing audience attitudes about a firmly held belief can take months rather than minutes, set goals that are achievable rather than unreasonable.

Relevance   If your topic is irrelevant to your audience's needs or interests, you will have trouble achieving your purpose. The characteristics of semiconductors or the different varieties of tree toads may fascinate you, but if you can't find a way to make the topic relevant or interesting to your listeners, you may find yourself talking to a bored or annoyed audience. Make sure your audience understands why your purpose and topic are important to them and their lives.

Part 3

Analyzing Your Audience and Adapting Your Presentation

8   Analyze and Adapt to Your Audience

Once you have identified the purpose and topic of your presentation, it is time to turn your attention to your audience. **Audience analysis,** the ability to understand and adapt to listeners, separates good speakers from great ones. The goals of audience analysis include finding out something about your audience, interpreting those findings, and, as a result, selecting appropriate strategies that will help you achieve your purpose.

A thorough understanding of your audience will help you focus your presentation and decide how to narrow your topic. An audience-focused approach will also simplify and shorten your preparation time by using the audience as a criterion for deciding what to include or exclude. The examples you include in your presentation, the words you choose, and even your delivery style should be adapted to your audience's interests and needs.

In order to anticipate the reactions of your listeners, you must know as much as possible about them and how they see the world, and you must understand the ways in which you and your listeners are alike as well as the ways in which you differ.

8a Analyze your audience

Get to know your audience by asking relevant questions about its members. The answers to four basic questions about audience characteristics can help you understand, respect, and adapt to your listeners.

KEY POINTS

Five Basic Audience Analysis Questions

1. Who are they?
2. Why are they here?
3. What do they know?
4. What are their interests?
5. What are their attitudes?

Who are they?   Gather as much **demographic information** as you can about the people who will be watching and listening to you. Consider the following demographic characteristics:

Age	Race	Gender
Religion	Marital status	Cultural background
Occupation	Income level	Place of residence
Education	Parental status	Disabilities

If you know that your audience will be composed of a particular group or will be meeting for a special reason, gather more specific information, such as:

Political affiliations	Professional memberships
Employment positions	Career goals
Military experience	Individual and group achievements

As you collect demographic information about your audience, use caution when drawing conclusions. Avoid "one-size-fits-all" conclusions about people based on visible or obvious demographic characteristics such as age, race, gender, occupation, nationality, or religion. These over-simplified conceptions, opinions, or images are called **stereotypes.** Stereotyping allows your beliefs and biases about a particular group to distort your perceptions about audience members.

Try to understand how similarities and differences in audience characteristics are relevant to your purpose and topic. Moreover, remember that *your* age, nationality, race, gender, educational level, and socioeconomic background may be just as critical in determining how well an audience listens to you.

Why are they here?   Audiences attend meetings and presentations for many different reasons.

REASONS FOR ATTENDING	EXAMPLES
They are required to attend	College classes, employee training sessions
They habitually attend	Monthly staff meetings, a popular social event, religious worship
They are interested in the topic	Topic related to personal and professional interests
They are interested in the speaker	Political candidates, celebrities, experts
They will be rewarded	Paid to attend, earn "points" with the boss
They are not sure why they are there	Accompanying a friend, representing a group, having nothing else to do

Audience members who are interested in your topic or who stand to benefit from attending a presentation will be quite different from those who don't know why they are there or who is required to attend. Each type of audience presents its own special challenges for a speaker. A highly interested and well-informed audience demands a compelling, knowledgeable, well-prepared speaker. An audience that is required or reluctant to attend may be pleasantly surprised and influenced by a dynamic speaker who has the ability to give audience members a reason to listen.

Entire audiences rarely fit into one type or group. You may find yourself speaking to an audience that includes several people representing each reason for attending.

What do they know?   Audience knowledge is based on factors such as educational level, demographic characteristics, and interest or expertise in a topic. The educational level can tell you about an audience's general knowledge and vocabulary. Demographic information can reveal something about their knowledge of religion, childcare, and firsthand experience with recent or past events. An audience being introduced to a new theory or concept—regardless of their educational levels, demographic characteristics, or interests—may need a carefully worded and basic-level introduction to a complex topic.

 KEY POINTS

Questions to Ask When Assessing Audience Knowledge

- How much do they know about the topic?
- How much background material should I cover?
- Will they understand my vocabulary and specific, topic-related terminology or jargon?
- Have they heard any of this information before?

Answering these questions is essential to matching your presentation to an audience's level of understanding and knowledge. Almost nothing is more boring to an audience than hearing a speaker talk about a subject they know very well, or listening to a speaker talk over their heads. In the following example, we see a speaker who failed to ask and answer the question "What do they know?"

A new, eager manager decided to use his time during a staff meeting to describe the principles and values of Emotional Intelligence (EI) in team decision making. He gave a highly informative presentation that included recent research on EI studies demonstrating its value in decision making, and recommendations for ways to incorporate EI into the business' planning process. What he failed to realize was that the audience had been through an extensive EI training seminar and probably knew more about the topic than he did. The result: The other managers, who had looked forward to welcoming a new member to their team, were disappointed with his presentation and disturbed by his arrogance in assuming he knew more than they did about EI.

What are their interests?   Find out whether or not audience members have interests that match your purpose and topic. Consider two types: self-centered interests and topic-centered interests.

Self-centered interests are aroused when a presentation can result in personal gain or loss. Some audience members will become enthralled by speeches that can teach them how to earn or save money. Others will be riveted by advice on career advancement strategies, or ways to improve their appearance or health.

Audiences also have **topic-centered interests**—subjects they enjoy hearing and learning about. Topic-centered interests can include hobbies, favorite sports or pastimes, or subjects loaded with intrigue and mystery.

What are their attitudes?   When you ask questions about **audience attitudes,** you are asking about audience opinions—whether they agree or disagree with you. There can be as many opinions in your audience as there are people. Some audience members will already agree with you, others will disagree no matter what you say, and still others will be undecided or have no opinion. (See sections **26a–26c** for ways to adapt your presentation to different audience attitudes and needs.)

At the same time, there can be many different reasons that people have the same opinion. For example, audience members who oppose longer jail sentences for convicted criminals may do so for a variety of reasons, including these:

- The jails are too crowded now, and there's no money to build new ones.

- Longer sentences do not prevent crime.

- Rehabilitation should be stressed instead of jail time.

- Rich people will get off; poor people will go to jail.

- Longer sentences don't work if criminals can be released on early parole.

Adapting to audience beliefs and attitudes can produce a winning combination for most speakers. Ignoring these factors can lead to failure, as illustrated in the following example:

A student speaker tried to convince her class to join her church and to become born-again Christians. She warned the audience that failure to embrace her religion would condemn their souls to hell. The result: Although the speaker was sincere in her beliefs, listeners of different religions and of other Christian denominations resented her talk and were offended by her warning.

8b Gather audience information

Now that you know why you should gather information about your audience, how do you go about doing it? The method that will work best for you depends on how much time, energy, and resources you can devote to the audience analysis process. In general, though, two very basic techniques can tell you a great deal about your audience: Learn to *look* and *listen.*

Look   The simplest method of gathering audience information is to observe your audience or to imagine what they look like and try to answer as many questions as you can on the basis of their appearance.

What percentage will be male or female?

Will there be a wide age range?

Will the audience be racially diverse?

Will they be dressed formally, professionally, or casually?

Before and during your presentation, observe their behavior. Are they restless, or do they appear to be eager to listen? Are they smiling or frowning? Depending on your conclusions about their behavior, you may want to shorten your presentation or add more examples. You may want to inject more or less energy into your delivery. Your ultimate success may depend on how well you observe and adapt to audience reactions.

Listen   Ask questions about the people in your audience and listen to the answers. Interview the person who invited you to speak or someone who has previously spoken to this group. (See section **10b** for interviewing guidelines.) If you can, arrange to talk to some audience members in advance. Listen for common characteristics and concerns. But be careful—one person's opinion may not represent those of most audience members.

In most speaking situations, you will only have time to look and listen to your audience. There is, however, another way to obtain valuable information about an audience: using an audience survey. A survey is a series of written questions designed to gather information about audience characteristics and attitudes. Several guidelines can help you write a useful audience survey.

KEY POINTS

Characteristics of a Good Survey

- A good survey tells you something you need to know, something you don't already know. Don't ask obvious questions: "Do you want to earn more money?" or "Should the United States oppose terrorism?"

- A good survey should give you specific and useful information. The question "Do you exercise regularly?" does not tell you whether *regularly* means twice a day, week, or month.

- A good survey should ask inclusive questions. If you don't word your questions carefully, you may miss some important answers. *Yes* or *No* questions often don't elicit responses from audience members who don't know the answer or who are undecided. Questions such as "Are you against gun control?" don't leave room for answers such as "It depends on the circumstances" or "I haven't made up my mind."

- A good survey should be confidential. People are less likely to give you information about themselves, their opinions, or their behavior if you also ask for their names.

- A good survey should be short. Most people won't fill out a long survey. A lengthy questionnaire also gives away too much about your presentation and can ruin the effect you are trying to achieve.

8c Adapt to your audience

Everything you learn about your audience tells you something about how to prepare and present your speech. Depending on the amount of audience research and analysis you do, you can adapt your presentation to your audience as you prepare it. In other cases, you may have to rely on audience reactions to modify your presentation as you speak.

Prepresentation adaptation   Once you have researched and analyzed information about your audience's characteristics and attitudes, go back to your purpose statement and apply what you have learned. Note how the answers to the five basic audience questions discussed in section **8a** affect the ways in which you can modify your preliminary purpose to create one that better suits your audience.

Preliminary purpose: To provide general information on ways to grow tomatoes.

> *Who are they?* They are twenty women and eight men who are long-term members of the local garden club. Most are over forty years old.
>
> *Why are they here?* They attend monthly club meetings at which they discuss group-selected topics.
>
> *What do they know?* They already know a lot about growing tomatoes but want to improve the health and output of their plants.
>
> *What are their interests?* They are very interested in plants of all kinds, but a few may be more interested in flowers. Fortunately, the group picked the topic.
>
> *What are their attitudes?* They are avid gardeners who may be a bit wary about *my* ability to tell them something new and interesting about tomatoes.

Revised purpose: To share my knowledge of the latest and best research on improving the health and output of a tomato plant in this growing region.

Midpresentation adaptation Sometimes, no matter how well you have prepared for an audience, you may get unexpected audience reactions. What if your presentation doesn't seem to be working? If your audience members seem restless, bored, or hostile, how can you adjust? What if your twenty-minute speech must be shorted to ten minutes in order to accommodate another speaker?

Adapting to your audience *during* a presentation requires you to do three things at once: deliver your speech, correctly interpret audience responses as you speak, and successfully modify your content.

Interpreting audience responses requires that you look at your audience members, read their body language, and sense their moods. If audience feedback suggests that you're not getting through, don't be afraid to stop and ask comprehension questions such as "Would you like more detail on this point before I go on to the next one?"

Think about adjusting your presentation in the same way that you would adjust your conversation with a friend. If your friend looked confused, you might ask what was wrong. If your friend interrupted with a question, you probably would answer it or ask if you could finish your thought before answering. If your friend told you that he had a pressing appointment, you would probably shorten what you had to say. The same adaptations can work just as well when you are speaking to an audience.

8d Adapt to cultural differences

The cultural diversity of audience members plays a critical role in audience analysis. Respecting and adapting to cultural diversity begins with understanding the nature and character-istics of different cultures. **Culture** can be viewed as the com-mon characteristics and collective perceptions that distinguish one group of people from another. Given this definition, a Georgia peanut farmer and a New York advertising executive can have different cultural perspectives as would a Nigerian, an Indonesian Moslem, and a Navaho tribal member.

Although there are many cultural dimensions to con-sider, three stand out as particularly relevant to the task of audience analysis and adaptation.[1]

High power distance and low power distance   **Power distance** refers to varying levels of equality and status among the members of a culture. In high power distance cultures such as those of Mexico, Malaysia, Arab countries, and India, there is great inequality between high- and low-status members. In low power distance cultures such as those of New Zealand, Denmark, and Israel, there is more equity and interdependence among all members.

The United States sits right in the middle range of this cultural dimension. Although the rich, famous, and power-ful enjoy many special perks and privileges in the United States, influential Americans often downplay power differ-ences. President George W. Bush is often photographed wearing casual clothes, corporate executive officers may promote an "open door" policy that makes them accessible to all employees, and college freshmen and full professors may interact on a first-name basis. If most audience members reflect a low power distance culture, you can ask them to chal-lenge authority and make independent decisions. If, however, most audience members embrace a high power distance per-spective *and* if you also command authority and influence, you can describe what you want them to do—and expect compliance. These audience members are accustomed to accepting and following directions from their "superiors."

Individualism and collectivism   In individualistic cultures such as those of the United States, Canada, and Australia, members value individual achievement, independence, and personal freedom. In collectivist cultures—those of most Asian and Latin American countries—members emphasize group identity and group goals. Whereas Australians may be eager to strike out on their own, Asians may be reluctant to leave their communities and families.

When speaking to individualistic audiences, you can appeal to their sense of adventure, their desire to achieve personal goals, and their defense of individual rights. When speaking to a collectivist audience, you may be more successful demonstrating how a particular course of action would benefit the family or community. A collectivistic audience is more willing to make personal sacrifices for others.

Masculinity and femininity   The masculine and feminine cultural dimension does not refer to how many men or women are in your audience. Instead, it focuses on the extent to which a culture embraces values considered masculine or feminine. Masculine cultures (those of Japan, Austria, Italy, and Mexico) are more assertive and task focused. Feminine cultures (those of the Scandinavian countries, Chile, and Thailand) focus on sharing and caring.

When speaking to members of a masculine culture, you might focus on competitive goals and the glory of winning. A presentation to audience members from feminine cultures would be more successful if you focused on ways in which the audience could achieve social and interpersonal harmony. In the United States, values tend to be more masculine than feminine.

9 Analyze and Adapt to Logistics

Whether you are preparing a presentation for a formal banquet, a family barbecue, a prayer meeting, or a retirement party, take time to analyze the logistics of the situation before you decide what you want to say. **Logistics** refers to planning, arranging, and adapting to the physical location of your presentations, to the amount of time you will be speaking, and to the nature of the occasion.

9a Analyze and adapt to the setting

Paying proper attention to the physical arrangements at the location of your presentation can help ensure its success. Whereas most audience members are unaware of or unconcerned about the audience size, facilities, or equipment when everything is going smoothly, logistical problems can distract their attention from you and your message.

KEY POINTS

Questions for Analyzing the Location

1. *Audience size:* How many people will be in the audience?
2. *Facilities:* What are the physical arrangements of the place where I will be speaking?
3. *Equipment:* What equipment will I need?

Audience size Audience size can and should affect the ways in which you prepare and deliver your presentation. If there are only fifteen people in your audience, you probably don't have to worry about whether they will be able to hear you. If there are several hundred or thousands of people in your audience, you should plan to use a microphone and to make sure it's supported by a good sound system.

Knowing the size of your audience also can help you figure out what kinds of visual aids to use. For example, if there were five hundred people in your audience, projecting images onto a large screen would be more effective than using a small chart or demonstrating a detailed procedure. (See sections **24a–24d** for a complete discussion of techniques for using presentation aids.)

The size of an audience also affects the amount of eye contact you can establish, the extent to which you can ask audience members to interact with you, and the amount of time it takes an audience to get settled before you begin speaking.

Facilities Make sure you know as much as you can about the facility in which you will be speaking.

Make sure you ask questions about the seating arrangements. Will audience members be seated in a theater-style auditorium, around a long conference table, or at round tables scattered throughout a seminar room? If you find

KEY POINTS

Questions to Ask About Presentation Facilities

- What are the size, shape, and décor of the room?
- Does the room have good ventilation, comfortable seating, or distracting sights or sounds?
- Will the audience sit or stand? If the audience is seated, what are the seating arrangements (rows, tables)?
- What kind of lighting will there be? Can it be adjusted for the presentation?
- Will I speak from a stage or platform? Will I have a lectern and a table for materials or equipment?
- Is there a good public-address system?

yourself in an auditorium that seats eight hundred people, and you only expect one hundred listeners to attend, consider closing off the balcony or side sections so that the audience will be seated in front of you.

Equipment   Today advanced communication technology offers speakers amazing resources. Computer-generated slide presentations have become the norm in many speaking situations. Wireless microphones and sophisticated sound systems enable speakers to address large audiences with ease. Make sure that you know in advance what is— and just as important, what isn't—available at the location where you will be speaking so you can consider those factors when preparing your presentation.

 KEY POINTS

Questions to Ask About Presentation Equipment

- What equipment, if any, do I need to be seen and/or heard?
- What equipment, if any, do I need for my presentation aids?
- Is there a lectern that is adjustable, with a built-in light or microphone and enough space to hold my notes?
- Are there any special arrangements that I need to make (requests for a timer, water, special lighting, wireless microphone, a media technician)?

Try to show up at least forty-five minutes before you have to speak. Make sure that everything you need is in the room, that the equipment works, and that you know how to dim or brighten the lights. Allow enough time to find equipment if something is missing or to make last-minute changes so that you can speak without your presentation aids.

9b Adapt to time

Asking questions about the time and duration of a speech is essential to planning a successful presentation.

KEY POINTS

Questions to Ask About Presentation Time and Duration

- At what hour will I be speaking?
- For how long am I scheduled to speak?
- What comes before or after my presentation (other speakers, lunch, entertainment, questions and answers)?
- Is there anything significant about the date or time of my presentation (birthday, holiday, anniversary)?

Of all the questions to consider when planning your speech, the most important one may be how long you are *scheduled* to speak. Most audiences will become impatient if you exceed your allotted time.

Plan your presentation so that it fits well within your time limit. Time yourself, keeping in mind that real presentations often take longer than the one you are practicing. Put a watch next to yourself when you speak or ask someone to give you a signal when it's time to begin your conclusion. And when that signal comes, don't ignore it, even if it means skipping major sections of your presentation. Audiences rarely like, appreciate, or return to hear a long-winded speaker.

9c Analyze and adapt to the occasion

What's the occasion of your presentation? Is it a staff briefing, an oral class assignment, a celebration, a memorial service, or testimony before a government agency? Make sure that you understand the reason for the event and what kind of presentation best suits the **occasion,** the reason that an audience has assembled at a particular place and time.

When you analyze the occasion of a presentation and adapt your speech for it, take into account the nature and significance of the event as well as the circumstances that motivated audience members to attend your speech. Ask yourself the following questions:

What is your relationship to the occasion?   When you are asked to make a presentation, ask yourself, "Why have *I* been invited to speak to *this* audience in *this* place on *this* occasion?" Speakers are not selected randomly. Each is chosen because she or he is the most knowledgeable, most able, most popular, most appropriate, or most available person to speak at a specific occasion. Make sure that you understand how you are personally connected to the occasion.

What does the audience expect?   The occasion raises audience expectations about the way in which a presentation will be prepared and delivered. Business audiences expect well-qualified speakers to pepper their presentations with sophisticated, computer-generated graphics. Audiences at political events have become accustomed to sound bites on television and expect to hear short, crisp phrases.

Think about what style of presentation you would expect to hear at a particular occasion. Then try to match your speaking style and content to those expectations.

What behavior is appropriate for the occasion? Special events often have specific rules of **protocol,** a term that refers to the expected format of a ceremony, or to the etiquette observed at a particular type of event. We expect a certain tone at a graduation ceremony and a very different tone at a pep rally. At a funeral, a eulogy may be touching or funny, but it's almost always very respectful and short.

Inquire about the protocol of an occasion. Ask what customs or rules may require special adaptation on your part. Understanding customs and rules of delivery style, timing, language, or appearance can help you plan what you want to say, organize your message, choose the most appropriate delivery style, and even select what to wear for your presentation.

9d Dress for the occasion

Deciding how to dress for a presentation requires an understanding of the occasion: why an audience is assembled, why you are the speaker, what the audience expects at the occasion, and what the "rules" of protocol are. In short, your clothes should fit the occasion.

Long before an audience hears what you say, they will see you, so wear something that matches the purpose and tone of your presentation. Your clothes don't have to be expensive or make a fashion statement. What matters most is that they are comfortable and appropriate for the situation.

Wear comfortable clothes Presentations are stressful enough without your having to worry about uncomfortable clothes. Brand-new clothes or shoes can become a source of irritation or embarrassment if they haven't been broken in. Make sure that your clothes don't wrinkle if you must sit in a chair before you speak. If you perspire, wear cool fabrics and colors that mask wet stains. If you're not comfortable moving about in constricting clothing or high heels, save them for less stressful public occasions.

Wear appropriate clothes and accessories If there is a rule of thumb for selecting appropriate clothes for a presentation, it is this: Be as conservatively dressed as the key members of your audience. If you know in advance that everyone will be wearing cowboy boots or tropical wear, use your best judgment and consider joining them. If, however, you've never worn cowboy boots or brightly colored clothing, stick with a comfortable and professional outfit. Generally, it's a good idea to wear standard business clothing for a presentation unless you have been told or know otherwise.

As important as appropriate clothing is to your appearance, so are your grooming and accessories. If you have long hair, wear it up or pull it away from your face so that your audience can see your facial expressions. An unshaven face, uncombed hair, and smeared makeup have no place in most speaking settings.

Nothing on or about your body (clothes, grooming, accessories) should draw attention to itself. Clanging bracelets or earrings and ties featuring big patterns or cartoon characters may not be appropriate. Take items out of your pockets, whether they are pens in your shirt pocket or the change and keys in your pants pockets. Women should leave their purses with a friend or colleague. Remember that your presentation should be the center of an audience's attention. If something about your appearance could distract your listeners, fix it or leave it at home.

Part 4

*Supporting
Your
Presentation*

10 Select Supporting Material

As soon as you know the purpose and topic of your presentation, you should begin collecting ideas and information to support it.

Expert speakers are information specialists. They know their subjects well and can recite names, dates, statistics, stories, and sayings about their topics. If you are not an expert or are not comfortable sorting through all the information you *do* know about a topic, you will need to search for and select strong supporting material. **Supporting material** consists of ideas, opinions, and information that help to explain and/or advance a presentation's main ideas and purpose.

10a Find the right types of supporting material

Supporting material comes in many different forms. The best presenters use a mix of supporting material; they don't rely on just one type. The types of supporting material you choose will depend on your purpose, the audience, the logistics and occasion of the presentation, and the key ideas you plan to cover.

Facts   A **fact** is a verifiable observation, experience, or event known to be true. Most presentations—regardless of their purpose—are supported to some extent by facts. Facts are most effective when the audience has no trouble

KEY POINTS

Types of Supporting Material

- *Facts:* Observations, experiences, or events accepted by the audience as true
- *Statistics:* Systematically collected and numerically classified information
- *Testimony:* Reported experiences or opinions of others
- *Definitions:* Explanations or clarifications of a word's or phrase's meaning
- *Analogies:* Comparisons of unfamiliar concepts or objects with familiar ones
- *Descriptions:* Detailed mental images of people, concepts, or things
- *Examples:* References to specific cases or illustrations
- *Stories:* Real or fictitious accounts about something that has happened

accepting them as true. For example, most audiences know that Americans spend a lot of time watching television, that AIDS can be transmitted through contaminated injection needles, and that only two sons of United States presidents have become presidents themselves.

Facts are used to remind, clarify, illustrate, demonstrate, and emphasize. For example, a speech on the racial barriers in American broadcasting could use the following historical fact to emphasize one of its key points:

> During the 1930s, millions of Americans tuned in
> *Amos 'n' Andy,* the nightly radio series in which a pair
> of white actors portrayed the adventures of two southern black men making a new life in a northern city.

Statistics **Statistics** organize, summarize, and analyze numerical information that has been collected and measured. Although audiences often equate statistics with facts, statistics are factual only if they have been collected and analyzed fairly.

In a presentation, using statistics is an efficient way to describe what a population is like, as well as what a population likes. Note how the speaker in the following excerpt uses statistics to bolster her point about the problem of geographical illiteracy:

> The *Los Angeles Times* reported on a survey in which college students were asked to name and locate the leading trading partners of the United States. Most students could not find Japan on a map. Only 29 percent were able to locate Canada.

Testimony   **Testimony** refers to statements or opinions that someone has said or written. You can support a presentation with testimony from books, speeches, plays, magazine articles, radio or television programs, courtroom statements, interviews, or web pages. The believability of testimony depends on the credentials and credibility of the speaker or writer. For example:

> In her book *Mommy, I'm Scared,* Professor Joanne Cantor writes: "From my 15 years of research on mass media and children's fear, I am convinced that TV programs and movies are the number-one preventable cause of nightmares and anxiety in children."

Use testimony from famous people, expert sources, respected public figures, and celebrities to add believability to a presentation and to enhance your credibility.

Definitions   **Definitions** explain or clarify the meaning of a word, phrase, or concept. A definition can be as simple as an explanation of what *you* mean by a word, or as detailed as an encyclopedia or unabridged dictionary meaning.

Use definitions when your speech includes words or ideas that your audience may not know or may misunderstand. For example, in a presentation attempting to explain the differences between jazz and the blues, a speaker uses two different types of definitions:

> The technical definition of the blues is a vocal and instrumental music style that uses a three-line stanza and, typically, a twelve-measure form in which expressive inflections—blues notes—are combined with uniquely African American tonal qualities. Or according to an old bluesman's definition: The blues ain't nothin' but the facts of life.

Descriptions   **Descriptions** create vivid mental images for your listeners. They provide more details than definitions by offering causes, effects, historical background information, and characteristics.

In the description that follows, a speaker expands the definition of the blues by quoting a description of the musical style's origins and essence from the *New Grove Dictionary of Music and Musicians:*

> From obscure and largely undocumented rural, (African) American origins, it became the most extensively recorded of all folk music types. . . . Since the early 1960s, blues has been the most important single influence on the development of Western popular music.

Analogies   **Analogies** identify similarities. Analogies can point out similarities in things or situations that are alike, as well as in those that are not really alike. Here are two examples of each kind of analogy:

ALIKE   If the traffic plan worked in San Diego, it should work in Seattle.

NOT ALIKE   If a copilot must be qualified to fly a plane, a U.S. vice president should be qualified to govern the country.

Use analogies to describe a complex process, or to relate a new concept to something the audience understands very well. Here's how Jesse Jackson used an analogy to describe the Rainbow Coalition, a political group committed to fostering diversity:

> America is not like a blanket—one piece of unbroken cloth, the same color, the same texture, the same size. America is more like a quilt—many patches, many pieces, many colors, many sizes, all woven and held together by a common thread.

Examples   An **example** provides a reference to a specific case or instance in order to make a large or abstract idea concrete and understandable. Examples can be facts, brief descriptions, or detailed stories. When, in everyday conversation, someone asks you to "give an example," you may reply with an illustration, a model, or an instance that helps explain your idea.

Good examples clarify complex concepts or illustrate important points. By listing several examples, you also reinforce an idea by repeating it in the form of well-selected illustrations. And, by choosing examples carefully, you can customize your presentation for a particular audience. Here are two such examples:

> Individualistic cultures—those more focused on independence, privacy, and self-centered needs—include the United States, Australia, Great Britain, and Canada.

> Today most of us associate the blues with male performers—Muddy Waters, Howlin' Wolf, B. B. King, and Buddy Guy. In the 1920s, the blues stars were women—Ma Rainey, Bessie Smith, Victoria Spivey, and Alberta Hunter.

Stories   Almost nothing else has the impact of real stories about real people in the real world. **Stories** are accounts or reports about things that have happened. Audiences often remember a good story even when they can't remember much else about a presentation.

Use stories to arouse attention, create a mood, or reinforce an important idea. In addition to gaining and holding an audience's interest, a story should also reinforce your message. (See section **20b** for storytelling techniques.)

In the following example, a successful attorney with a crippling disability uses her personal story to emphasize the importance of hope, hard work, and determination:

> I was in an automobile accident just after high school, which left me in a wheelchair for life. I was trying to deal with that, a new marriage, and other personal problems, not the least of which was uncertainty about what I could do—about the extent of my own potential.

10b   Search for supporting materials

Once you have a general idea about your content and the types of supporting material you want to include in your presentation, you may have to do some research to find what you need. The research process should begin with you. However, even if you are an expert on a topic or have a unique background or life experience related to your topic, you will still need to consult other sources to verify, support, and reinforce your views.

Librarians   Do not feel daunted by the vast amount of information in libraries and museums and on the Internet. Your best resource is the reference librarian, trained to know what materials are available and how to locate them. Librarians can put you on track and direct you to valuable sources like reference books, indexes, and databases as well as to specialized sources.

Keyword searching   The first decision you have to make as you approach a catalog or database is whether to search by author, title, subject, or keyword. Keyword searching is the type most widely used for finding materials on a specific topic.

1. Find out from the database's or search engine's instructions on screen how to conduct a search. Many searches operate on the Boolean principle; that is, they use the "operators" *AND, OR,* and *AND NOT* in combination with keywords to define what you want the search to include and exclude. Imagine that you want to find out how music can affect intelligence. A search for "music AND intelligence" would find sources in the database that include both the word *music* and the word *intelligence*. A search for "music AND (intelligence OR learning)" would expand the search. You would find sources, in the database, that included both the word *music* and the word *intelligence* or the word *learning*. Some search engines let you use terms such as NEAR and ADJ (adjacent to) to find phrases close to each other in the searched text.

2. Use wildcard abbreviations (commonly * or ?) to truncate a word or to provide optional spellings. For example, *lab?r* will search for *labor* or *labour*; the truncation *music** will find instances of *music, musical, musicale, musician(s),* and *musicology.*

3. Require or prohibit a term. Many search engines allow you to use a symbol like + and no space before a term that must be included in the indexed document; a

– symbol with no space following it prohibits a term: +"Civil War"–Gettysburg would direct the search engine to find *Civil War* but not *Gettysburg.*

4. Make terms into phrases. Generally you can use double quotation marks—"Martin Luther King Jr."—or parentheses—(Martin Luther King Jr.)—to surround a search term and group the words into a phrase. If you entered the search term *Martin Luther King Jr.* without quotation marks or parentheses that signal a phrase, the computer would search for all instances of each word and could produce references to, among others, Martin Luther, Steve Martin, Luther Vandross, Stephen King, and Roy Blount Jr.

5. Be flexible. If your search results in no hits, try again with a different term or terms. Try variant spellings, too: *Chaikovsky, Tchaikovsky, Tschaikovsky.*

6. Use the results to help tailor your search. If your search produces only one useful source, look at the terms used in that one source and its subject headings and search again, using those terms.

Web sources   Before you begin, check with your instructor about the role he or she wants Internet research to play in your presentation. In general, you should plan your research so that Web searching is a supplement to library research, not a replacement for it. Decide whether the time available to you will be spent more productively with traditional and online academic sources rather than with online discussion groups and individual promotional web pages. Stay focused; once you begin Internet surfing, it is easy to be sidetracked.

Search engines, reference works, indexes, databases, and web sites   To begin research in a subject area that is new to you, go first to general reference sources, indexes and databases, and, when appropriate, informational web sites. These will give you a sense of the field and the issues. Many reference works and indexes are available online, some accessible on the Internet, some available only by subscription.

• *Search engines for Internet searching*   Many search engines are available to help you find the material you need on the Internet. Good ones to try are *AltaVista,* <http://

www.altavista.digital.com>; *Excite*, <http://www.excite
.com>; *MetaCrawler*,<http://www.metacrawler.com>; and
Google, <http://www.google.com>. *Yahoo!*, <http://www.
yahoo.com>, and Google provide a subject directory.

- *Encyclopedias, both general and specialized by subject matter*
Use general encyclopedias, in print or online, to check
factual information and dates, consult the bibliographies
listed, and do initial exploration of a topic. However,
do not consider a general encyclopedia a major source
for your research. Go beyond it to more specialized
sources.

- *Dictionaries, general and specialized* General dictionaries
are useful for looking up word meanings, usage, etymol-
ogy, and spelling. Specialized subject dictionaries, especially in the sciences and computer field, include
explanations as well as definitions.

- *General reference works* In many fields, you will find survey works that present an overview of a field or collect
relevant reviews.

- *Bibliographies* Bibliographies list titles of books and
articles on a specific subject.

- *Geographical reference sources* Consult maps, atlases,
almanacs, and gazetteers when you need current
information about population, boundaries, climate,
products, and history.

- *Government documents* The Government Printing Office
(GPO) provides numerous documents containing
statistical information useful for business, economics,
and political science.

- *Indexes and databases* Indexes, often on CD-ROM or
online by library subscription, provide information
about books and articles published in periodicals. You
can find newspaper and journal articles published on a
specific topic. Indexes often contain abstracts of articles
and sometimes full texts. Online indexes and databases
are best accessed by keyword searching. Ask librarians
about specialized indexes, too.

- *Web sites for research in academic subject areas* Some
web sites contain vast amounts of information and useful
links to other sites. Bookmark any sites you find
useful.

Interviews   In addition to doing library and online research, you may want to conduct an interview with someone who is an expert or who holds a different point of view. Once you know the purpose and topic of your presentation, start looking for a good person to interview. Interviews are rich sources of facts, statistics, testimony, examples, and stories.

 KEY POINTS

Interviewing for Information
Careful planning is the key to successful interviews. Make sure that you can answer the following questions:

- Why am I conducting this interview? What do I hope to learn that I cannot find in some other way?
- Whom am I interviewing? How can I learn more about this person's background and areas of expertise?
- What do I want or need to know for my presentation?
- What questions should I ask, and in what order should I ask them?
- How can I get the interview off to a good start?
- How do I keep the interview running smoothly? What can I do to fully engage the person I'm interviewing?
- Do I need to follow up?

Interviewing is as much an art as a skill. One of the keys to conducting a successful interview is to listen well. Good listening will tell you if your questions have been answered before you ask them and will give you new insights that can lead to additional questions.

11   Evaluate Your Content

Before you take detailed notes from any source, make sure that it will provide suitable supporting information. If your topic involves a serious academic issue, your listeners will expect your sources to include more than popular magazines, newspapers, and Internet postings. Be sure to diversify your sources.

Books

- Check the date of publication, notes about the author, table of contents, and index.

- Skim the preface, introduction, chapter headings, and summaries to get an idea of the information contained in the book and of its theoretical basis and perspective.

- Do not waste time taking detailed notes from an out-of-date book (unless your purpose is to discuss and critique its perspective) or a book that deals only tangentially with your topic.

Articles

- Check the date of publication.

- Evaluate the type of periodical the article appears in (popular or scholarly?).

- Note any information given about the author or about the stated purpose of the publication: Is the article likely to contain an unbiased examination of any controversial issues?

Internet sources   The Internet is democratic. Anyone can "publish" anything on the Web. To distinguish between serious information and junk, do the following:

- Check the thoroughness of the document and the number of reliable print and web sources it cites.

- Check the date of the material and when the information was last updated (in *Netscape*, check "Document Information").

- Scrutinize the author's credentials, if any are listed.

- Evaluate the purpose and objectivity of the sponsor of the site: What appears to be an article may, in fact, be an advertisement or propaganda.

- Beware of slick web sites with no named author.

- Use the domain names in URLs to assess the quality of the information: *.edu* (education) and *.gov* (government) pages are more likely to include substantial information than a private individual's home page or a listserv posting.

11a   Test your content

Speakers rely on researched information to enhance their credibility and to demonstrate their depth of knowledge about a topic. Information that's not accurate and up-to-date can undermine an entire presentation. Make sure your information is **valid**—that the ideas, opinions, and material you want to include are well founded, justified, and true.

KEY POINTS

Questions to Test Your Content

1. Is the source identified and credible?
2. Is the source biased?
3. Is the information recent?
4. Is the information consistent?
5. Are the statistics valid?

Is the source identified and credible?   How credible are your sources of information? Are the author and publisher identified? Are they known to be reputable? Sources such as *The Information Please Almanac* and the *New York Times Almanac* have been in business for many years, and their continued success depends on their ability to collect and publish information that is correct and current.

Also check newspapers and online news and information services. Their reputations depend on their ability to publish accurate information. There are, however, big differences among such sources. The sensational and often bizarre *National Enquirer* may be fun to read, but the *Wall Street Journal* is more likely to contain reliable information. Ask yourself whether the source you are quoting is a recognized expert, a firsthand observer, or a respected journalist.

Is the source biased?   Make sure that you use objective sources of information. A source can be **biased,** meaning that it states an opinion so slanted in one direction that it may not be objective or fair. If the source has a strong opinion or will gain from your agreement, be cautious.

What biases do you think special interest groups such as the National Rifle Association, pro-choice or pro-life groups, or the American Association of Retired Persons may have?

The information they publish may be true, but the conclusions they draw from that information may be biased.

Is the information recent?   Always note the date of the information you want to use. When was the information collected? When was it published? In this rapidly changing information age, your material can become old news in a matter of hours. Although books can provide a wealth of background information and historical perspectives, you would probably be better off using magazines, journals, or newspaper articles and reliable web sources when researching current events and scientific breakthroughs.

Is the information consistent?   Check to ensure that the information you want to include reports facts and findings similar to other information on the same subject. Does the information make sense based on what you already know about the topic? For example, if most doctors and medical experts agree that penicillin will *not* cure a common viral cold, why believe an obscure source that recommends it as a treatment?

Remember that although information that is different can be interesting and worth noting, it may be wise to wait for more collaborating information before making a presentation based on one study.

Are the statistics valid?   Interpreting statistics is an art and a science. The average speaker and audience member may not know how to use the sophisticated research methods required to provide valid statistical results. Instead, we rely on the numbers reported by others.

 KEY POINTS

Questions for Determining the Validity of Statistics

- Who collected and analyzed the data?
- Is the researcher a well-respected expert?
- How was the information collected and analyzed?
- When was the information collected and analyzed?
- Who is reporting the statistics: the researcher or a reporter?
- Are the statistics believable?

Good statistics can be informative, dramatic, and convincing. They also can mislead, distort, and confuse. Use them carefully.

11b Keep track of your content

Once you find a good source—whether in the library, online, or through an interview—you need to record what you find, in a form that will be useful when you develop or write out your speech.

 KEY POINTS

Record Your Sources

1. Make a bibliography card (one for each source; use one side only) or fill out a bibliographical database on your computer. Record all the relevant information for each source you read and intend to use, including reference works. Record inclusive page numbers for all print sources.

2. Make copies of material you know you will use. Make sure to copy complete journal or magazine articles and the periodical's table of contents (which will provide date and volume number); with book chapters, copy the title page and copyright page of the book. You will need this information for your list of works cited.

3. Save material you find online by printing it out, e-mailing it to yourself, or saving it on a disk. Record complete document information (address, author, date posted or updated, if available), along with the date you access the material. Note a URL (Uniform Resource Locator) completely and exactly. Bookmark all the useful sites you visit so that you can easily find them again.

4. Read the copies you have made carefully. Annotate the copies with comments relating the source to your topic and thesis.

5. Take careful notes, relating what you read to your paper topic. Give each note a heading.

6. Distinguish exact quotations from summaries and paraphrases (**12b**), and record all exact page numbers, or paragraph numbers if given in electronic sources.

12 Cite Your Sources

All forms of supporting material used in a presentation should be documented in writing and/or orally cited in your speech. Even if an author, magazine, or web site grants you permission to use its material in a presentation or written report, you should give the source of that information credit.

12a Cite your sources in writing

The only difference between source citations in a presentation and in a paper is that you may not be citing a reference in full when you speak. You should, however, have a full, written citation for every reference you use in your presentation, particularly if someone in your audience wants more information or if someone challenges your sources.

When you refer to a source for a *written* work, you must systematically and thoroughly record the author, title, publisher, and date of your source. Be sure to document sources so that there will be no questions about which words and ideas are yours and which belong to other people.

 KEY POINTS

Cite Your Supporting Material

Cite your sources and provide full documentation for all of the following:

1. Cite all the facts, statistics, testimony, definitions, and other supporting materials unless the information is common knowledge and accessible in many sources.

2. Cite somebody else's ideas and opinions, even if you restate them in your own words in a summary or a paraphrase. (See section **12b** on paraphrasing.)

3. Cite each sentence in a long paraphrase if it is not clear that all the sentences paraphrase the same original source.

Citation is not necessary in a written work or speech for facts regarded as common knowledge, such as the dates of the Civil War; facts available in many sources, such as chronological events and authors' birth and death dates; or allusions to folktales that have been handed down for centuries. If you are not sure whether or not a fact is common knowledge, cite your sources.

12b Use paraphrases

A **paraphrase** is similar in length to the original material. It presents the details of the author's argument and logic, but *it does not use the author's exact words or sentence structure.* Note how the content changes in the following three examples:

Original Source:

> We cannot legislate the language of the home, the street, the bar, the club, unless we are willing to set up a cadre of language police who will ticket and arrest us if we speak something other than English.
>
> —James C. Stalker, "Official English or English Only," *English Journal,* 77 (Mar. 1988: 21)

Plagiarized Paraphrase:

Uses words and structures that are too close to those of the original source.	As Stalker points out, we cannot pass legislation about the language we speak at home, on the street, in bars, or in restaurants, unless we also want to have a group of special police who will take us off to jail if they hear us not speaking English (21).

Valid Paraphrase:

Summarizes the author's position without plagiarizing.	Stalker points out in that in a democracy like the United States, it is not feasible to have laws against the use of a language, and it certainly would not be possible to enforce such laws in homes and public places (21).

If you keep the sources out of sight as you write a paraphrase, you will not be tempted to use any of the sentence patterns or phrases of the original. Even if you are careful to cite your source, your writing will still be regarded as plagiarized if your paraphrase resembles the original too closely in wording or sentence structure. In a written work, you can use common words and expressions without quotation marks, but if you use longer and more unusual expressions from the source, always enclose them in quotation marks.

12c Cite your sources orally

Unlike writers, speakers cannot use punctuation marks and footnotes to cite their sources during a presentation. Nor should they recite every detail such as the publisher, publisher's city, and page number of a citation. In speaking situations, citations must be oral. Although it would sound foolish to recite complete citations following MLA or APA style guidelines, you should provide enough oral information to credit the sources of your material.

Your spoken citation should include just enough information to allow an interested listener to find the original source you are crediting. Generally, it's a good idea to provide the name of the person (or people) whose work you are using, saying a word or two about that person's credentials and mentioning the source of the information.

The first of the following examples quotes the author directly; the second paraphrases the author.

<u>*Citing a Quotation Orally:*</u>

In a 1988 article published by *English Journal,* Dr. James C. Stalker described the absurdity of adopting an official language for the United States. He wrote: "We cannot legislate the language of the home, the street, the bar, the club, unless we are willing to set up a cadre of language police who will ticket and arrest us if we speak something other than English." [quotation marks not mentioned orally]

<u>*Paraphrasing a Quotation Orally:*</u>

In a 1988 *English Journal* article, Dr. James C. Stalker noted that in a democracy like ours, we cannot pass laws against the use of other languages. If nothing else, it would be impossible—even foolish—to enforce such laws in our homes and public places.

Note that in these examples, the speaker does not recite the complete citation—that can be provided in writing for interested listeners.

To document electronic sources orally, you should identify key words that would enable listeners to find each source through a search engine. Here's an example:

> The National Communication Association's Credo for Ethical Communication can be found on the association's web site at <www.natcom.org>. [angled brackets not mentioned orally]

If you believe that your audience should have permanent access to the information you have used, you can provide a handout listing your references with complete citations.

Part 5

Organizing and Outlining Your Presentation

Part 5 Organizing and Outlining Your Presentation

13 Organize Your Content

Effective **organization** helps you stay focused on the purpose of your presentation while you're deciding what to include and how to put it all together in an effective way. Before you put all the pieces of a presentation into an organizational pattern, structure, or order, though, you should decide which ideas and information to use. Review your purpose, your audience, and the logistics of the situation when making these decisions.

- **Purpose.** Include ideas and information that will help you achieve your purpose. Leave out anything that's not relevant to your goal.

- **Audience.** Select ideas and information that will interest, serve, and involve audience members.

- **Logistics** and **Occasion.** Use what you know about where, when, and why you will be speaking to guide your selection and ideas and information.

Research confirms that audiences react positively to well-organized presentations and speakers, and negatively to poorly organized ones. The value and benefits of good organization should never be overlooked.

 KEY POINTS

Benefits of Speech Organization

Organization helps the audience:

1. understand the message,
2. remember the message,
3. decide how to react to the speech.

Organization helps the speaker:

1. gather and include appropriate ideas and information,
2. arrange those ideas strategically,
3. enhance his or her credibility.

13a Select your key points

The first step in organizing a presentation is answering a single question: *What are the key points that you want to cover in your speech?* **Key points** represent the most important issues or the main ideas that you want your audience to understand and remember.

The second step in organizing will help you look for a pattern or a natural grouping of key points. Two methods—applying the 4Rs of Organization and mind mapping—can help you in this process.

The 4Rs of Organization Begin your search for key points and organizational patterns by applying the **4Rs of Organization** to find an effective ordering method for your presentation.

1. **Review.** Find an uninterrupted block of time in which to reread and critique the material you have written or collected. Ask yourself:

    • Do the ideas and information you have collected support your purpose, or are they marginal or irrelevant?

- Is there enough or too little information?
- What *must* be included, and what can and should be left out?

By thinking critically about your material, you may find that certain information and ideas jump out as must-include "keepers," whereas others can be put aside.

2. **Reduce.** Once you have reviewed your material, try to boil the keepers down to their essential points. Ask yourself:
   - Can you combine your ideas and information into two to four essential points?
   - Which points will the audience notice and remember?

3. **Regroup.** Try regrouping the ideas and information you want to include in your presentation into different categories. Ask yourself:
   - Can you identify an organizational pattern that will accommodate your key points?
   - Are there any major headings that can bring related ideas together?

4. **Refine.** Once you have reviewed, reduced, and regrouped your material, it is time to refine—time for the finishing work. Very often, refining means rewording an idea in a creative or memorable way. Ask yourself:
   - Can you arrange your key points into an organizational form that will make your presentation more interesting and memorable?
   - Can you word your key points clearly, eloquently, and creatively?

Mind mapping   A second method for identifying and organizing key points is **mind mapping,** a technique that encourages the free flow of ideas and lets you define relationships among those ideas.

Start with a clean piece of paper and write down the major ideas you want to cover in your presentation. (Neatness does not count.) If possible, put related ideas near each other on the page and draw a circle around that group of ideas. If groups of ideas are related, let your circles overlap or draw lines between those circled.

The mind map in Figure 1 explores the topic "motivating groups at work" and contains many more concepts than should be included in a single speech. A mind map suggests the possibilities—but *you* must review, reduce, regroup, and refine the mapped ideas to identify the key points for your presentation.

FIGURE 5.1   Mind Mapping

Mind maps let you see all of your ideas without super-imposing an organizational pattern on them. They also let you postpone the need to arrange your ideas into a pattern until you have collected enough information to think about how you want to organize the content of your presentation.

Use mind mapping when you have many ideas and much information about a topic but are having trouble decid-ing how to select and arrange your material for a presentation.

13b Identify your central idea

Once you have discovered your key points, you must link them to your central idea. Your **central idea** (sometimes called a *thesis statement*) is a sentence that summarizes the key points of your presentation. The central idea can also provide a brief preview of the organizational pattern you will follow to achieve your purpose.

The following examples illustrate how topic area, purpose, and central idea are different but closely linked to one another:

TOPIC AREA:	Growing tomatoes
PURPOSE:	To teach the audience how to grow healthy tomatoes
CENTRAL IDEA:	Growing healthy tomatoes requires good soil, bright sun, plenty of water, and a watchful eye.

TOPIC AREA:	Refugee families
PURPOSE:	To increase donations to the church's refugee assistance program
CENTRAL IDEA:	Because the church's refugee families program has been a blessing for all of us—the families, our church, and you—please make a financial contribution to our ministry.

As you mind map and/or review, reduce, regroup, and refine your material, your central idea may change. But by the time you are ready to speak, the central idea should be clear, indicating what you are going to say and even the order in which you will present your material to achieve your purpose.

13c Select an organizational pattern

Several commonly used organizational patterns will help you clarify your central idea and find an effective format for your presentation.

Arrange by subtopics **Topical arrangement** involves dividing a large topic into smaller subtopics. Subtopics can describe reasons, characteristics, techniques, or procedures.

Use a topical arrangement if your ideas and information can be divided into discrete categories of relatively equal importance. For example:

TOPIC AREA:	Facial expressions in different cultures
PURPOSE:	To appreciate that some facial expressions don't always translate between cultures
CENTRAL IDEA:	Americans and Native Japanese often misinterpret facial expressions depicting fear, sadness, or disgust.

KEY POINTS: A. Fear
               B. Sadness
               C. Disgust

Use sequence in time   **Time arrangement** orders information according to time or calendar dates. Most step-by-step procedures begin with the first step and continue sequentially (or chronologically) through the last step.

Use a time arrangement when your key points occur in time relative to each other, as in recipes, assembly instructions, technical procedures, and historical events. For example:

TOPIC AREA: Saving a computer file
PURPOSE: To explain how to save a computer file
CENTRAL IDEA: In order to ensure that your work has been saved and is easily accessible, make sure that you name your file and place it in a convenient folder.
KEY POINTS: A. Click the Save button on the standard tool-bar.
                B. Click an icon on the Places bar to open a frequently used folder.
                C. Double-click the folder in which you want to save the file.
                D. Type a name for the file and click Save.

Use position in space   Use a **space arrangement** if your key points can be arranged in the order of their location to one another. For example:

TOPIC AREA: Brain structure
PURPOSE: To explain how different sections of the brain are responsible for different functions
CENTRAL IDEA: A guided tour of the brain begins in the hind-brain, moves through the midbrain, and ends in the forebrain, with side trips through the right and left hemispheres.
KEY POINTS: A. The hindbrain
                B. The midbrain
                C. The forebrain
                D. The right and left hemispheres

Present problems and solutions   Use a **problem-solution arrangement** to first describe a situation that is harmful or difficult (the problem) and then offer a plan to solve the problem (the solution). Problems can be as simple as a squeaky door or as significant as world famine.

In the following example, each key point presents guidelines for dealing with a specific people problem often found in group discussions:

TOPIC AREA:	People problems in groups
PURPOSE:	To provide suggestions for solving common people problems that occur in group discussions and meetings
CENTRAL IDEA:	Learning how to deal with a few common behavioral problems in groups will improve a group's performance.
KEY POINTS:	A. Dealing with nonparticipants B. Dealing with loudmouths C. Dealing with latecomers and early leavers

Show causes and effects   Use **cause-and-effect arrangement** either to present a cause and its resulting effects or to detail the effects that result from a specific cause.

The following example identifies how watching too much television adversely affects children:

TOPIC AREA:	Children and television
PURPOSE:	To describe the harmful effects that television has on children
CENTRAL IDEA:	Television has a negative influence on children and their families because it displaces time that could be spent on more important activities.
KEY POINTS:	A. Television has a negative effect on children's physical fitness. B. Television has a negative effect on children's school achievement. C. Television watching may become a serious addiction.

In cause-to-effect speeches, speakers may claim that eating red meat causes disease or that lower taxes stimulate the economy. In effect-to-cause presentations, speakers may claim that sleepiness or lack of energy can be caused by an iron deficiency or that a decrease in the population of lake fish is caused by acid rain.

Be careful when using cause-and-effect arrangements. Just because one situation follows another does not mean that the first causes the second. Lack of sleep, not lack of iron, can be a cause of sleepiness.

Tell stories   A series of well-told stories can be so compelling and interesting that they easily can become the organizational pattern for a speech. (For more on storytelling, see section **20b**.)

For example, dramatic stories about successful individuals who escaped from poverty and prejudice or who triumphed despite their disabilities can be the key points of a presentation

TOPIC AREA:	Leaders and adversity
PURPOSE:	To convince listeners that disabilities are not barriers to success
CENTRAL IDEA:	Many noteworthy leaders have lived with disabilities.
KEY POINTS:	A. Franklin D. Roosevelt, president of the United States who had polio
	B. Jan Scruggs, disabled soldier and Vietnam Memorial founder
	C. Helen Keller, deaf and blind advocate

Compare and contrast   Use a **comparison-contrast arrangement** to show your audience how two things are similar or different. This pattern works well when you can explain an unfamiliar concept more easily by comparing it to a familiar concept or when you are trying to demonstrate the advantages of one alternative over another.

Comparisons can be real (comparing products or contrasting medical treatments) or fanciful (comparing student success to racehorse success). For example:

TOPIC AREA:	Family sedans and SUVs
PURPOSE:	To recommend a way of evaluating medium-sized cars and SUVs
CENTRAL IDEA:	Comparing vehicle performance, comfort, fuel economy, and reliability can help you decide whether to purchase a new mid-sized car or an SUV for your family.
KEY POINTS:	A. Performance
	B. Comfort
	C. Overall fuel economy
	D. Predicted reliability

Use memory aids   Use **memory aids**—easy-to-remember phrases and combinations of letters—to help your audience remember important ideas or key points. Journalists use the "Who, What, Where, When, and Why" questions to remind them of the key parts of a news story. First-aid instructors teach the *ABCs* of first aid (*A*irways, *B*reathing, and *C*irculation) and the 4-H Club reminds members of its fourfold aim to improving *H*ead, *H*eart, *H*ands, and *H*ealth. You can use memory aids separately to organize a presentation or in combination with any of the other organizational patterns. Here's an example from this handbook:

TOPIC AREA: Organizing a presentation
PURPOSE: To provide a method for selecting and organizing the key points of a presentation
CENTRAL IDEA: The 4Rs represent a series of critical thinking steps that can help you develop an effective organizational pattern for your presentation.
KEY POINTS: A. Review
               B. Reduce
               C. Regroup
               D. Refine

13d Order your key points

Once you have identified the key points that will support your central idea and have chosen the organizational pattern that you want to use, you will need to determine which key points should go first, second, or last. In many cases, the organizational pattern you have chosen will dictate the order. (For example, if you use time arrangement, the first step in a procedure should come first.)

If your format does not dictate the order of key points, try to place your best ideas in strategic positions. Your choice of strategy depends on your purpose, audience, logistics, and occasion.

- **Strength and familiarity** Place your strongest points first and last and your weakest or least familiar idea in the middle position so that you start and end with strength.

- **Audience needs** If your audience requires current information, satisfy that need early. Background information can come later.

  If you anticipate that your audience may not be very interested in your topic, don't begin with your most technical, detailed point.

If you are speaking about a controversial topic, you may want to begin with a point that focuses on the background of the issue or on the reason that there is a need for a change.

- **Logistics** If you are one of a series of presenters, you may end up with less time to speak than was originally scheduled. Plan your presentation so that your most important key points come first in case you need to cut your speech short.

14 Outline Your Presentation

Outlining is an essential and valuable planning tool for speakers. A good outline will help you package your main ideas and information and can be used to reject irrelevant or uninteresting material.

14a Create a preliminary (working) outline

Begin with a **preliminary outline,** an initial planning outline that puts the major pieces of a presentation in a clear and logical order.

Preliminary Outline
  I. Introduction
    A. Purpose/Topic
    B. Central Idea
    C. Brief Preview of Key Points
       1. Key Point #1
       2. Key Point #2
       3. Key Point #3
 II. Body of the Speech
    A. Key Point #1
       1. Supporting Material
       2. Supporting Material
    B. Key Point #2
       1. Supporting Material
       2. Supporting Material
    C. Key Point #3
       1. Supporting Material
       2. Supporting Material
III. Conclusion

Use this model outline to organize almost any presentation, modifying it depending on the number of key points and the types and amount of information you use as supporting material. Aim for at least one piece of supporting material under each key point—a fact, statistics, testimony, definition, description, example, story, and so on.

14b Create a formal outline

Refining a preliminary outline to guide a complete presentation often requires the creation of a formal outline. A **formal outline** provides a comprehensive framework that follows established conventions concerning content and format. Whereas a preliminary outline helps you plan your presentation, a formal outline creates the first draft of your speech.

Three basic rules of formal outlining can help you develop a valuable planning tool for your presentation.

Use numbers, letters, and indentations All parts of a formal outline are systematically indented and numbered or lettered. Roman numerals (*I, II, III*) signify the largest major divisions such as the introduction, body, and conclusion. Indented capital letters (*A, B, C*) can be used for key points. Further intended Arabic numbers (*1, 2, 3*) are even more specific and can be used to list supporting material or any other subdivision of a key point. If you need a fourth level, indent again and use lowercase letters (*a, b, c*).

Divide your subpoints logically Each major point should include at least two subpoints indented under it—or none at all. If there is an *A*, there must be a *B*; for every *1*, there must be a *2*.

WRONG: I.
                   A.
               II.

RIGHT: I.
                   A.
                   B.
               II.

Keep the outline consistent Use either a topic, a phrase, or a full sentence for each key point in your outline rather than a mix of styles. Use a consistent grammatical form; if you begin each subpoint with a verb, don't switch to beginning with nouns halfway through the outline.

WRONG: I. Consistent style
          II. Use a consistent grammatical form.

RIGHT: I. Keep the outline consistent in style.
          II. Use a consistent grammatical form.

RIGHT: I. Consistent style
          II. Consistent grammatical form

 KEY POINTS

Additional Benefits of a Formal Outline

A formal outline:

- helps you select and order your supporting material,
- helps you focus on and choose appropriate and eloquent words,
- enables you to change and adapt your presentation,
- checks your structure to make sure every key point is clear and supported,
- reveals flaws, irrelevancies, digressions, and unnecessary repetitions.

14c **Create a presentation outline**

Formal outlines provide a great way to organize your material and to double-check the content of your message, but they are not the same as speaking notes.

The notes you use during a presentation should not be as long or as detailed as a formal outline. Instead, use a **presentation outline,** one that includes little more than a list of key points and reminders of supporting material.

The following example illustrates a presentation outline for a presentation on the importance of customer service. Note that the introduction, central idea, key points, and conclusions are written out whereas the reminders about the type and substance of support material are put in parentheses.

I. Introduction
   A. Question: What will be the most important factor for competitive business success in the first decade of the twenty-first century? (Gallup Poll of CEOs, business owners, and company presidents)
   B. Answer: 18% said operating efficiency; 25% said product/service quality; 27% said *customer service*
   C. Central Idea: Become a service-centered business if you want to succeed.

II. Body
   A. Your job security and business success depend on how valuable you are to your customers. (stories, statistics, and descriptions of successful employees and businesses)
   B. Customers will replace you with better service-providers. (When product and price are the same, service is the only area in which you can be different from the competition. Ask the audience for examples.)
   C. Develop a reputation for responsiveness. (Examples: Nordstrom, Saturn, Ritz Carlton Hotels, the local hospital)

III. Conclusion
   Customers are the lifeblood of your business. They are not dependent on you; you are dependent on them. So remember the secret of keeping good customers: Exceed their expectations! That's how you succeed in business!

15 Connect Your Key Points

An outline shows how you have structured and developed your key points, but it's missing the "glue" that attaches the key points to each other and makes your presentation a coherent whole. **Connectives** are this glue, and they include the internal previews and summaries as well as transitions and signposts.

15a Provide internal previews and summaries

An **internal preview** reveals or suggests your key points to the audience. It tells them what material you are going to cover and in what order.

In the body of a presentation, an internal preview describes how you are going to approach a key point. For example:

> How do researchers and doctors explain obesity? Some offer genetic explanations; others offer psychological ones. Either or both factors can be responsible for your never-ending battle with the bathroom scale.

If your topic is straightforward and uncomplicated, you may only need an internal preview in your introduction. However, regardless of where you include them , audiences like internal previews because they prepare listeners for hearing and remembering important ideas.

Internal summaries are a useful means for ending a major section and reinforcing important ideas. They also give you an opportunity to repeat critical ideas or pieces of information. Internal summaries usually come at the end of major sections or key points and serve as a way to help the audience review and remember what you have said. For example:

> So remember—before spending hundreds of dollars on diet books and exercise toys, make sure that your weight problem is not influenced by the number and size of your fat cells, your hormone level, your metabolism, or the amount of glucose in your bloodstream.

15b Include transitions and signposts

The most common type of connective is the **transition**—a word, number, brief phrase, or sentence that helps you move from one key point or section to another. Transitions act like lubricating oil to keep a presentation moving smoothly. In the following examples, the transitions are italicized:

> *Yet* it's important to remember . . .
>
> *In addition* to metabolism, there is …
>
> *On the other hand*, some people believe . . .
>
> *Finally,* a responsible parent should …

Transitions can also function as mini-previews and minisummaries that link the conclusion of one section to the beginning of another. For example:

Once you have eliminated these four genetic explanations for weight gain, it's time to consider several psychological factors.

A fourth type of connective is the **signpost,** one or more short phrases that, like signs on the highway, tell or remind listeners where you are in a presentation. For example, if you were providing four genetic explanations for weight gain, you could begin each explanation with numbers—*first, second, third,* and *fourth:* "Fourth and finally, make sure your glucose level has been tested and is within normal levels. . . ."

Signposts can also focus attention on an important idea or piece of information. They can even highlight an eloquent phrase or special insight. Here are two examples:

> Even if you can't remember his every accomplishment, please remember one thing: Alex Curry is the only candidate who has been endorsed by every newspaper and civic association in the county.

> As I read this section of Toni Morrison's novel, listen carefully to the way that she uses simple metaphors to describe the cemetery scene.

16 Begin Your Presentation with Flair

The best introductions capitalize on the power of first impressions. They create a positive, lasting impression and provide an opportunity for a highly successful presentation that achieves your purpose. A weak beginning gives audience members a reason to tune out, misunderstand, or remember you as a poor speaker.

16a Goals of the introduction

To create an effective introduction, you must understand what it can and should accomplish. Your introduction gives the audience time to adjust, to block out distractions, and to focus attention on you and your message. A good introduction establishes a relationship among three elements: you, your message, and your audience.

KEY POINTS

Goals of the Introduction

1. *Focus audience attention and interest.* Capture audience attention by relating your purpose and topic to your audience's characteristics, interests, needs, and attitudes.

2. *Put yourself in your presentation.* Link your own expertise, experiences, and enthusiasm to your topic or purpose. Personalize your message. Make a strong first impression.

3. *Preview the message.* Give your audience a sneak preview of the subject of your speech. Give them a clear sense of how you will develop your central idea. You can even state your central idea and briefly list the key points you will cover.

4. *Set the emotional tone.* Make sure that your introduction sets an appropriate emotional tone that matches its purpose. Use suitable language, delivery styles, and supporting material.

16b **Ways to begin**

There are almost as many ways to begin a presentation as there are speakers, topics, and audiences. The following methods represent only a few of the strategies you can use to begin a speech effectively. Any of these methods can be used separately or in combination with one another.

Use an interesting statistic or example Sometimes your research will turn up a statistic or example that is unusual or dramatic. If you anticipate a problem in gaining and keeping audience attention, using a striking statistic or example can do it for you. For example:

> The statistics are appalling: More than 5,000 juveniles and 35,000 adults die each year from gunshot wounds. Millions of latchkey kids come home to a house or apartment in which there is a gun. Since 1984, the homicide rate for males has tripled. This is an epidemic! An epidemic that is about ten times as big in

terms of lives lost as the great polio epidemic of the first half of the twentieth century.

Quote someone A dramatic statement or eloquent phrase written by someone else may be ideal for the beginning of a presentation. Rather than trying to write the perfect introduction, you may find that someone else has already done it for you.

A good quotation can help an audience overcome their doubts, especially when the writer or speaker is a highly respected or an expert source of information. But regardless of whom you quote, remember to give the writer or speaker full credit. In the following example, a speaker quotes a columnist who thinks we need much more than gun control to end gun violence:

> Syndicated columnist Don Feder began an article
> about an Arkansas murder with these words:
> "Blame the guns. Don't blame the wretched little
> monsters who murdered four children and a
> pregnant teacher because one of them had just been
> dumped by a girlfriend; blame the guns. Don't blame
> a culture where many parents spend more time
> watching televised sports than with their kids; blame
> the guns."

Tell a story Speakers can have great success by beginning a presentation with stories about their personal hardships, triumphs, or even embarrassments. Stories can be personal, well known, or fictional. All kinds of stories can be used to illustrate a concept or idea.

Audiences love to hear stories and will give you their undivided attention if you tell a good one and tell it well (see section **20b**). For example:

> When I was fifteen, I was operated on to remove the
> deadliest form of skin cancer, a melanoma carcinoma.
> My doctors injected ten shots of steroids into each scar
> every three weeks to stop the scars from spreading. I
> now know that it wasn't worth a couple of summers of
> being tan to go through all that pain and suffering.
> Take steps now to protect yourself from the harmful
> effects of the sun.

Ask a question   Asking a question can attract your audience's attention and interest because it challenges them to think about an answer. Asking a question works well when the question has a direct effect on the audience.

One of the best kinds of questions is one that elicits a response such as "I had no idea!" For example:

> Which of the following eight products are owned by American companies and made in America: Bic pens, Arrow shirts, Godiva chocolates, Vaseline petroleum jelly, Firestone tires, Holiday Inns, and Tropicana orange juice? All? Half? The answer is *one.* Godiva chocolate is made and sold by the Campbell Soup Company.

Refer to the place or occasion   A simple way to begin a presentation is to refer to the place in which you are speaking or the occasion for the gathering. Sometimes your audience's memories and feelings about a specific place or occasion can conjure up the emotions needed to capture their attention and interest.

When Dr. Martin Luther King Jr. made his famous "I Have a Dream" speech on the steps of the Lincoln Memorial, his first few words echoed Abraham Lincoln's renown Gettysburg Address ("Four score and seven years ago . . . "). Dr. King began:

> Five score years ago, a great American, in whose symbolic shadow we stand, signed the Emancipation Proclamation.

Refer to a well-known event   Citing events that have occurred shortly before your presentation or in the recent past can provide a means of gaining audience attention and interest. For example:

> Soon after the September 11 tragedy, I saw a proliferation of highway billboards that celebrated our country and citizen patriotism. One billboard stood out. It was both simple and eloquent. A stars-and-stripes ribbon sat on a plain white background. Three words declared its purpose: United we stand. The same three words are just as relevant at this college. Immediately

following the September 11 tragedy, we united to counsel our students. Today, we unite to recognize and celebrate the achievements of our colleagues at our annual convocation.

The "recent event" technique is a big part of political speechmaking. If you listen carefully to the news or watch the president's State of the Union address, you are bound to hear references to well-known recent events. Much like making references to a place or occasion, evoking memories and feelings about a recent event can create an appropriate mood for your introduction.

Address audience needs　When there is a crisis, you will need to address the problem at the outset. If budget cuts will require salary reductions, audience members will want to hear the details and will not be interested in clever questions or dramatic statistics. For example:

> As you know, the state has reduced our operating budget by 2.7 million dollars. It is also just as important that you know this: All of you will have a job here next year—and the year after. There will be no layoffs. Instead, there will be cutbacks on nonpersonnel budget lines, downsizing of programs, and possible, short furloughs.

 KEY POINTS

Tips for Starting Strong

1. *Plan the beginning at the end.*　Don't plan your introduction before you have determined and developed the content of your speech.

2. *Don't apologize.*　Don't use your introduction to offer excuses or apologize for poor preparation, weak delivery, or nervousness.

3. *Avoid beginning with "My speech is about . . ."*　Boring beginnings do not capture audience attention or enhance a speaker's credibility. Be original and creative.

17 Conclude Your Presentation with Flair

What is true of introductions is also true of conclusions. Your final remarks can determine how your audience thinks and feels about you and your presentation. In addition to remembering things that are presented first, audiences also recall items presented last. Final words can have a powerful and lasting effect on your audience.

17a Goals of the conclusion

The first step in deciding how to end your speech is to understand the goals of a conclusion. Like the introduction, a conclusion should establish a relationship among you, your topic, and your audience.

 KEY POINTS

Goals of the Conclusion

1. *Be memorable.* Give audience members a reason to remember you and your presentation. Show them how your message has affected you personally and how it can affect them as well.

2. *Be clear.* Make sure that your conclusion repeats the one thing you want your audience to remember at the end of your speech. Use your conclusion to reinforce your central idea and make your message sharp and clear.

3. *Be brief.* The announced ending of a presentation should never go beyond two or three minutes, no matter how long you have spoken. When you say you are about to end, end.

17b Ways to conclude

Some methods of concluding your presentation will reinforce your message; others can strengthen the audience's final impression of you. As with introductions, these methods can be used separately or in combination with one another.

Summarize   Reinforcing your key points in a succinct summary is the most direct way to conclude a presentation. This is also the best way to review and repeat the key points in your presentation. A summary should be memorable, clear, and brief.

In the following example, a speaker uses questions to emphasize her central idea and key points:

> Now, if you hear someone ask whether more women should serve in the U.S. Congress, ask and then answer the two questions I discussed today: Can women and their issues attract big donors? And are women too nice to be "tough" in politics? Now that you know how to answer these questions, don't let doubters stand in the way of making a woman's place in the House.

Quote someone   What is true about quoting someone in your introduction is just as true about concluding with a quotation. Because quotations can be memorable, explicit, and concise, speakers often use them to conclude their presentations.

Good research can provide a quotation that will give your presentation a dramatic and effective ending. When, for example, Rudolph Guiliani gave his farewell speech as mayor of New York City, he ended by reciting the conclusion of Abraham Lincoln's Gettysburg Address as a tribute to those who had died in the terrorist attack on the World Trade Center:

> " . . . that we here highly resolved that these dead shall not have died in vain—that this nation, under God, shall have a new birth of freedom—and that the government of the people, by the people, for the people shall not perish from the earth." God bless New York and God bless America.

Tell a story   End with a story when you want to help your audience visualize the outcome of your speech. A well-told story can also help an audience remember the central idea of your presentation. (See section **20b** on storytelling.)

Ending a presentation with a good story is often much more memorable than any other method for concluding.

Marge Anderson, chief executive of the Mille Lacs Band of Ojibwe Indians, concluded a speech with this story:

> Years ago, white settlers came to this area and built the first European-style homes. When Indian People walked by these homes and saw [windows], they looked through them to see what the strangers inside were doing. The settlers were shocked, but it made sense when you think about it: windows are made to be looked through from both sides. Since then, my People have spent many years looking at the world through your window. I hope today I've given you a reason to look at it through ours.

Use poetic language   Being poetic doesn't mean ending with a poem. Rather, it means using language in a way that inspires and creates memorable images. (See section **19** for ways to develop eloquent and memorable language.) A speech about respecting older people ended with the following short but poetic phrases:

> For old wood best to burn, old wine to drink, old authors to read, old friends to trust, and old people to love.

Call for action   One of the most challenging but effective ways to end a presentation is to call for action. Use a call for action when you want to tell your audience to do more than merely listen—when you want them to *do* something.

Even if you are just telling an audience to remember something important, to think about a story you have told, or to consider a question, you have asked them to become involved. The reverend Jesse Jackson began his conclusion to a speech at the 1984 Democratic Convention with a call to action:

> Young Americans, dream. Choose the human race over the nuclear race. Bury the weapons and don't burn the people. . . . Dream of lawyers more concerned with justice than a judgeship. Dream of doctors more concerned with public health than personal wealth. . . .

Refer to the beginning When you can't decide which concluding method to use, consider ending your presentation with the same technique you used to begin it. If you began your speech with a quotation, end with the same or a similar quotation. If you began with a story, refer back to that story.

Audiences like this concluding method because it returns to something familiar and "bookends" the content of your presentation. For example:

> Remember the story I told you about two-year-old Joey—a hole in his throat so he can breathe, a tube jutting out of his stomach so he can be fed. For Joey, an accidental poisoning was an excruciatingly painful and horrifying experience. For Joey's parents, it was a time of fear, panic, and helplessness. Thus, it is a time to be prepared for, and even better, a time to prevent.

KEY POINTS

Tips for a Strong Conclusion

1. *Make sure it matches.* Don't tack on an irrelevant or inappropriate ending. Match the mood and method of your conclusion to the mood and style of your speech.

2. *Have realistic expectations.* Most audience members will not act when called upon unless the request is carefully worded, reasonable, and possible. Don't end by demanding something from your audience unless you are reasonably sure you can get it.

Part 6

Generating Credibility and Interest

Part 6 Generating Credibility and Interest

18 Enhance Your Credibility

One of the key elements in developing an effective presentation is enhancing your credibility as a speaker.

An audience's perceptions of a speaker—good or bad—have a direct impact on the success of a speech. The more credible you are in the eyes of your audience, the more likely you will achieve your purpose. **Speaker credibility** represents the extent to which an audience believes you and the things you say.

18a Include the components of credibility

Three components of speaker credibility have an especially strong impact on the believability of a presenter: *character*, *competence*, and *charisma*.

As much as you may wish to possess all three components of speaker credibility, keep in mind that most successful speakers rely on one or two of these characteristics to ensure their believability. For example, if you are neither an expert nor charismatic, work on demonstrating your good character and your commitment to being as well prepared as possible.

Speaker credibility comes from your audience: Only the audience decides whether or not you are believable. Fortunately, you can foster or heighten your credibility by doing two things: developing a credible presentation and making ethical decisions at every step in the speechmaking process.

KEY POINTS

Components of Speaker Credibility

- *Character:* Character relates to a speaker's honesty and goodwill. Does the audience see you as a good person—truthful, sincere, and fair?
- *Competence:* Competence relates to a speaker's perceived expertise and abilities. Does the audience regard you as experienced, well prepared, qualified, up-to-date, and intelligent?
- *Charisma:* Charisma is reflected in your level of energy, intensity, vigor, and commitment. Does the audience view you as enthusiastic, confident, stimulating, and dynamic?

18b Develop a credible presentation

Although speaker credibility comes from your audience, there are things you can do to influence your audience's opinion of you and your presentation.

Know your strengths   In order to enhance your credibility, you must believe that you have something to offer an audience. Every speaker is unique, and therefore every speaker can claim unique skills, perspectives, or experiences. To identify your strengths, take a personal inventory. Find the answers to the following questions:

- What are your unique experiences? Have you lived or worked in a unique place? Have you had an unusual job? What experiences have had a major impact on your life?
- What are your achievements? What are your special skills? What awards or contests have you won? What are your special hobbies or interests?
- What are your skills and traits? What qualities have helped you succeed?

Be well prepared   A well-prepared presentation is more believable. Likewise, lack of preparation communicates that you don't care about your audience, that you didn't do enough research, or that you didn't take enough time to organize your content or to practice. If you didn't have time to prepare for your audience, why should they have time for you?

Put yourself in your speech   There is nothing wrong with using words such as *I*, *my*, and *me* in a speech if they are appropriate. A true and personal story about *you* can be much more compelling than a story about a stranger. Being open and honest about your feelings and opinions can enhance the audience's view of your character as long as you respect their feelings and opinions. Letting the audience know why or how you became an expert can help demonstrate your competence. Sharing your own enthusiasm and emotions can create a memorable and charismatic moment.

19 Use Effective Language

Although delivery is a significant part of any presentation, the words you use form the foundation of your presentation. When both experienced and novice speakers are asked about the most challenging tasks they face when speaking, "finding the right words" is often near the top of the list.

Finding the right words for a presentation and the right words for a written work have much in common. At the same time, there are special considerations about language choice that can help transform an effective speech into an exceptional presentation.

19a Follow the 5C's of style

Readers and listeners sometimes find themselves bored by language characterized by wordiness, flatness, inappropriate word choice, clichés, and sentences constructed without interesting variations. The **5Cs of Style** can help prevent you from losing audience attention and interest in both writing and speaking situations. (See **Part 11** for a discussion of written style.)

19b Choose effective oral language

Well-chosen words lie at the heart of effective and memorable presentation. How you use words can determine your ultimate success as a speaker. The best words can give presentations a unique flavor, emotional excitement, and brilliant clarity.

KEY POINTS

Build Your Oral Language Power

- Use an oral style.
- Use more personal pronouns.
- Spice up your speech.
- Strive for eloquence.

Use an oral style   The words you use for writing and for speaking differ. In a speech, you should say what you mean by speaking the way you talk, not the way you would write a report, essay, or memo. Oral style uses shorter words and shorter sentences. In most cases, oral style is also less formal than written style and can even include incomplete sentences and colloquial expressions.

Note how a speaker begins a presentation on *Cliffs Notes* by using an oral style that incorporates short words, short sentences, phrases, and colloquial expressions:

> Eight o'clock Wednesday night. I have an English exam bright and early tomorrow. It's on Homer's *Iliad*. And I haven't read page one. I forego tonight's beer drinking and try to read. Eight forty-five. I'm only on page 12. Only 282 more to go. Nine thirty, it hits me. Like a rock. I ain't gonna make it.

Use more personal pronouns   Personal pronouns put the word *you* in your presentation and help you establish a connection with your audience. Use the pronouns *you* and *your* frequently—and focus your attention on people in different parts of the room. As you do so, make each audience member feel singled out. Remember President John F. Kennedy's challenge: "Ask not what your country can do for you. Ask what you can do for your country."

Also use pronouns such as *I*, *me*, and *my*. By taking responsibility for your message, you can enhance your credibility. (See section **16**.) First person accounts engage an audience.

Using pronouns such as *we*, *us*, and *ours* intensifies the connection between you and your audience. "We shall overcome" has significantly more power than "You shall overcome" or "I shall overcome."

Spice up your speech Great speakers have long understood the power of using repetition (words and sounds) and resemblances (similes, metaphors, and analogies) to make their words memorable.

- *Repetition of words* You can repeat a word, phrase, clause, or entire sentence to heighten the impact of an idea. Dr. Martin Luther King Jr. used the statement "I have a dream" nine times in his famous 1963 speech in Washington, D. C. He used "let freedom ring" ten times.

- *Repetition of sounds* **Alliteration** refers to beginning words placed closely together with the same sound. For example, the first part of Lincoln's Gettysburg Address— "*F*our score and seven years ago our *f*athers brought *f*orth"—includes three words beginning with the letter *f*.

- *Resemblances* Similes, metaphors, and analogies are figures of speech that highlight resemblances.

 KEY POINTS

Similes, Metaphors, and Analogies

Similes and **metaphors** make a direct comparison between two things or ideas. Similes usually use the word *like* or *as*.

Chilean novelist Isabel Allende uses metaphors and a simile to describe the value of the arts: "Art is a rebellious child, a wild animal that will not be tamed. Like dreams, it obeys only its own rules."

Analogies can compare similar things or dissimilar things. (See section **10a**.) Muhammad Ali talked about his ability to "float like a butterfly, sting like a bee." Winston Churchill, Great Britain's wartime prime minister, coined a common phrase when he said, "An iron curtain has descended across the continent of Europe."

Strive for eloquence **Eloquence** is the ability to phrase thoughts or feelings in a way that makes them crystal clear and memorable. Eloquent language does not have to be flowery or grand; it can use an oral style, personal pronouns, and the power of repetition. Statements like Abraham Lincoln's "government of the people, by the people, for the people shall not perish from the earth" are memorable and inspiring because Lincoln searched for the best words to communicate his thoughts and feelings.

20 Generate Interest

Paying special attention to generating audience interest can improve your chances of preparing and delivering a successful presentation.

20a Overcome the boredom factor

Bored audiences are often victims of two bad habits: a short attention span and poor listening. Two other bad habits can be attributed to the presenters: speaking too long and poor delivery. Learning to compensate for these habits is the first step in ensuring an interesting presentation.

Limited attention span Even in the best of circumstances, audience members drift in and out of speeches, paying more attention to some sections than to others. Effective speakers understand this and adjust a presentation to an audience's attention span.

For example, when talking about factual, technical, or instructional material, ease into your topic to capture audience attention; put your strongest content in the middle of your speech and then ease out with a review or summary. If you are trying to motivate your audience, start out slowly but keep building and building; put the most electrifying and memorable material at the end. If your audience seems unwilling to listen from the beginning, try to gain their attention immediately. Then set a mood and pace that will keep them listening.

Poor listening habits Most audiences (and speakers) are not very good listeners. (See section **6**.) One way to counteract the effects of poor listening is to give your audience more than one opportunity to hear your ideas. For example, if you cite a statistic, also give an example or tell a relevant story. Use a presentation aid or provide a handout to reinforce your spoken message visually.

As you move from key point to key point, use connectives to reinforce your message. Internal previews and summaries give your audience additional opportunities to listen to each key point. (See section **16** on connectives.)

Length of presentation   One reason that some audiences dread listening to speeches is that many of them go on for too long. Make sure that you stick to your assigned time limit. Plan a presentation that runs slightly shorter than your allotted time in order to ensure that you won't go overtime.

 KEY POINTS

Shorten Your Speech

- If your audience can understand or reach a conclusion without your help, don't burden them with unnecessary explanations, stories, or visuals.

- Don't spend time on a point if the audience already shares your opinion or belief.

- Delete or shorten any section, statement, idea, or supporting material that isn't directly relevant to your purpose.

Poor delivery   Poor delivery can bore an audience and undermine even the best-prepared presentation. One performance component has a particularly strong impact on audience interest levels: expressiveness. **Expressiveness** is the vitality, variety, and sincerity that speakers put into their delivery. When you speak expressively, you feel good about yourself, are excited about your message, and are truly interested in sharing your ideas with an audience. If you care about your topic and audience, you are more likely to communicate enthusiasm and energy.

20b Tell stories

Audiences remember stories because they create lasting images. Stories are accounts of real or imagined events. They can be success stories, personal stories, stories about famous people, humorous stories, or historical stories. Regardless of the type of story you use, each story must have a point that relates to your purpose—a good reason for being told.

What makes a good story?   When you decide to tell a story, make sure that your story hangs together, makes sense, and seems believable. To test whether a story should be included in a presentation, ask yourself several important questions about the believability and structure of your story.

> ### KEY POINTS
>
> **Qualities of a Good Story**
>
> 1. Do the facts and incidents in the story ring true and seem believable?
> 2. Does the story address or support your purpose and key points?
> 3. Does the story omit, distort, or take out of context any key facts and events?
> 4. Does the story progress clearly, logically, and reasonably?
> 5. Does the story have the potential to create the impact that you want?

Storytelling techniques   Most people are good story-tellers in conversations. Crafting and telling a story for a presentation, however, is not the same as describing the day's events. It requires paying attention to several features of a good story:

- **Simple story line**   Long stories with complex themes are hard to follow and difficult to tell. If you can't summarize your story in less than twenty-five words, don't tell it.

- **Punch line**   Most good stories have a punch line in which a sentence or phrase communicates the climax or purpose of the story. You can determine which sentence is a punch line by leaving it out. Without the punch line, a story won't make sense.

- **Limited characters**   Unless you are an accomplished actor or storyteller, limit the number of characters in your story. If your story has more than three or four characters, look for another story.

- **Exaggeration**   You can exaggerate both content and delivery when telling a story. Exaggeration makes a story more vivid and helps you highlight its message. The tone of your voice, sweep of your gestures, and your facial expression add a layer of meaning and emphasis to your story.

- **Audience links** Stories won't work if the audience can't relate to the setting, characters, or topic. Make sure that your story is appropriate for your audience. (See section **8** for ways to analyze and adapt to your audience.)

- **Practice** Practice telling your story to others—your friends, colleagues, or family members. Practice until you can tell it without notes. Storytelling skills come from lots of practice.

20c Use humor

Injecting humor into a presentation can capture and hold audience attention and help listeners remember you and your message. Audience members tend to remember humorous speakers positively, even when they are not enthusiastic about the speaker's topic.

Types of humor Using humor in a presentation does not necessarily mean telling jokes. It means poking fun and having fun. Speakers who look up and memorize jokes from books may find their audience less than amused.

Presenting humor is difficult. Most listeners will give you the benefit of the doubt and forgive you if your joke or a humorous story doesn't end up being as funny as you intended. There are, however, some approaches to humor that an audience will not and should not forgive. Offensive humor tops the list because it insults your audience and seriously damages your credibility. Irrelevant humor is a close second because it wastes the audience's time and makes you appear poorly organized. Stale, prepackaged humor comes in third. It's often irrelevant *and* offensive—or just plain boring.

Self-effacing humor You are your own best source of humor. **Self-effacing humor**—your ability to direct humor at yourself—is usually much more effective than telling funny stories you have made up or borrowed from a book. But be careful that you don't poke too much fun at yourself. If you begin to look foolish or less than competent, you will damage your credibility and weaken the power of your message.

When looking for humorous material, remember situations in which you have said, "I can't believe this is happening to me" or "Someday we'll laugh about this." Such situations can later be retold as humor. President Ronald Reagan was well known for making fun of his age, an approach that also defused campaign controversy about his being the oldest president in U.S. history:

> There was a very prominent Democrat who reportedly told a large group, "Don't worry. I've seen Ronald Reagan, and he looks like a million." He was talking about my age.

 KEY POINTS

Guidelines for Humorous Speaking

- *Focus on one humorous idea.* Make sure that your humor supports the central idea of your presentation. All humorous stories, jokes, puns, and gags should relate to your topic.

- *Let the humor suit you.* Decide which types of humor you do well—jokes, stories, puns, imitations, and so on. Don't contort yourself to fit your material; adapt the material to fit your personality and style.

- *Practice; practice; practice.* Humorous speaking requires more than knowing the content of your speech. It requires comic timing—knowing when and how forcefully to say a line, when to pause, and when to look at the audience for their reactions.

20d Involve your audience

One of the most powerful ways to keep an audience alert and interested is to ask audience members to participate actively in your presentation. When audience members are encouraged to speak, raise their hands, write, or interact with other audience members, they become involved in the speechmaking process.

Ask questions One of the easiest ways to involve audience members is to ask questions, pose riddles, or ask for reactions before, during, or after your presentation. Even if your listeners do little more than nod their heads in response, they will have become involved in your speech. Also, when audience members know that they will be quizzed or questioned during or after a presentation, they will be more alert and interested in what you have to say.

Encourage interaction Something as simple as asking a general audience to shake hands with each other or to introduce themselves to the people sitting on either side of them can generate more audience attention and interest. Depending on the purpose of your presentation, you could add something beyond a handshake that relates directly to the content of your speech. For example, in a talk to a business audience, ask members to exchange business cards. If you are addressing young college students, ask them to identify their majors or career aspirations.

Do an exercise Both simple games and complex training exercises can involve audience members with your presentation and with each other. Most large bookstores contain shelves filled with training manuals describing ways to involve groups in games and exercises. Interrupting a presentation for a group exercise gives both the audience and the speaker a break during which they can interact in a different but effective way.

Ask for volunteers If you ask for volunteers from the audience, someone will usually offer to participate. Volunteers can help you demonstrate how to perform a skill or how to use a piece of equipment. Some can even be persuaded to participate in a funny exercise or game.

Most audiences love to watch a volunteer in action. If possible, find a way to reward volunteers—with a small prize or special thanks. As long as everyone is involved and feeling safe, most audiences will go along with what they are asked to do.

Invite feedback During or at the end of a presentation, you can invite questions and comments from your audience. Once audience members know that they can interrupt you with a question or comments, some will do just that. Of course, it takes a skillful presenter to allow this kind of interaction without losing track of a prepared presentation.

Encouraging audience participation requires skill and sensitivity. Respect any feedback you get from your audience. If audience members seem reluctant to participate, don't badger or embarrass them. If no one responds, go on and deliver your presentation without such involvement. In all likelihood, however, you will find most audiences will be willing to participate.

Part 7

Delivering Your Presentation

101

21   Achieve Effective Delivery

You know what you want to say; now it's time to decide
how to deliver your presentation. Whether you choose to
rely on a few note cards or to read from a manuscript, your
decision about delivery will affect whether your audience
responds positively or negatively to you and your message. Just as you made decisions about the purpose, audience, logistics, content, and organization of your speech,
you will have to make decisions affecting how you use
your voice, body, and presentation aids to achieve your
purpose.

21a   Choose your mode of delivery

Choose a delivery mode that suits your purpose. You will
need to decide which form of delivery to use: impromptu,
extemporaneous, manuscript, memorized, or a combination of forms.

Impromptu   **Impromptu speaking** occurs when you make a presentation without advanced preparation or practice. For example, you may be called upon in class or at work to answer a question or share an opinion. You may be inspired to get up and speak about an important issue at a public meeting, religious gathering, or celebration.

Even though you don't have enough time to stop and give much thought to all seven basic principles of effective speaking (see section **2**), you can very quickly think of a purpose and the ways in which you intend to organize and adapt your message to the audience. The more experience you have as a speaker, the more instinctive the "basics" become, even in impromptu speaking. (See section **30** for impromptu speaking strategies.)

 KEY POINTS

Advantages and Disadvantages of Impromptu Delivery

ADVANTAGES:

- Natural and conversational speaking style
- Maximum eye contact
- Freedom of movement
- Easier to adjust to audience feedback

DISADVANTAGES:

- Limited time for making basic decisions about purpose, audience adaptation, and organization
- Possible high speaking anxiety
- Potential for awkward and ineffective delivery
- Difficult to gauge speaking time

Extemporaneous   **Extemporaneous speaking**, the most common form of delivery, occurs when you use an outline or a set of notes to guide yourself through a prepared speech. Your notes can be a few words on a card or a detailed outline that reflects the decisions you have made during the preparation process. Classroom lectures, business briefings, and courtroom arguments are usually delivered extemporaneously. No other form of delivery gives you as much freedom and flexibility with preplanned material. With practice, extemporaneous speaking can become your most powerful form of delivery.

 KEY POINTS

Advantages and Disadvantages of Extemporaneous Delivery

ADVANTAGES:

- Allows more preparation time than impromptu delivery
- Seems spontaneous, but is actually well prepared
- Enhances speaker's ability to monitor and adapt to audience feedback
- Allows more eye contact and audience interaction than manuscript delivery
- Generates positive audience response

DISADVANTAGES:

- Increases speaker anxiety in sections of the speech that are not covered by notes
- May cause language to be poorly chosen or ineloquent
- Makes speaking time difficult to estimate

Manuscript **Manuscript speaking** involves writing your presentation in advance and reading it out loud. Using a manuscript allows you to choose each word carefully. You can plan and practice every detail. It also ensures that your presentation will fit within your allotted speaking time. For very nervous speakers, a manuscript can be a life-saving document. When the occasion is an important public event at which every word counts and time is strictly limited, you may have no choice but to use a manuscript.

Manuscript speeches are difficult for all but the most skilled and practiced speakers to deliver. The most significant disadvantages are inappropriate word choice, poor reading, and inflexibility. (If you must use a manuscript, follow the language tips in section **19**.)

KEY POINTS

Advantages and Disadvantages of Manuscript Delivery

ADVANTAGES:

- Allows the speaker to pay careful attention to all of the basic principles of effective speaking
- Facilitates choosing concise and eloquent language
- Eases speaker anxiety by having a "script"
- Allows the speaker to rehearse the same presentation over and over
- Ensures accurate reporting of speech content

DISADVANTAGES:

- Creates the potential for stilted and dull delivery
- Makes it difficult to maintain sufficient eye contact
- Allows limited gestures and movement
- May cause overly-formal language choices and may hinder oral style
- Makes it difficult to modify or adapt to the audience or situation

Memorized   A memorized presentation offers a speaker one major advantage and one major disadvantage when compared with the other three forms of delivery. The major advantage is physical freedom. You can gesture freely and look at your audience throughout your presentation. The disadvantage, however, outweighs any and all advantages. What if you forget a section or go totally blank? Rarely do speakers memorize an entire presentation. However, there's nothing wrong with trying to memorize your introduction or a few key sections, as long as you have your notes to fall back on.

 KEY POINTS

Advantages and Disadvantages of Memorized Delivery

ADVANTAGES:

- Incorporates the preparation advantages of manuscript delivery and the delivery advantages of impromptu speaking
- Maximizes eye contact and freedom of movement

(continued)

(continued)
DISADVANTAGES:

- Requires extensive time to memorize
- May cause disaster if memory fails
- May sound stilted and insincere
- Makes it difficult to modify or adapt to the audience or situation

Learning how to deliver presentations in impromptu, extemporaneous, manuscript, and memorized form allows you to mix and match styles within a single presentation. An impromptu speaker can recite a memorized statistic. An extemporaneous speaker may read a lengthy quotation or series of statistics and then delivery a memorized conclusion. A speaker may stop in the middle of a manuscript or memorized speech to repeat a key phrase or to ask the audience a question.

21b Use notes effectively

Regardless of what form of delivery you select, you should be ready to use notes and to use them effectively. Even when you are speaking impromptu, you may find yourself using a few quick words which you jot down just before you stand to speak. In a memorized presentation, you should keep your notes nearby in case your memory fails.

The following guidelines can help you use your notes effectively if you are giving a manuscript speech or speaking extemporaneously using notes on $8\frac{1}{2}''$ x 11'' paper:

- Use large type fonts (14–18 point) and double- or triple-spacing.
- Number your pages.
- Type only on the top two-thirds of the page so that you don't have to bend your head to see the bottom of each page.
- Make sure that none of your sentences run over to a new page.
- Consider underlining important words and phrases.

If you prefer to put your notes on index cards (which work especially well for extemporaneous speaking) follow these guidelines:

- Use key words rather than complete sentences.
- Use only a select number of cards—one for your introduction, one for each key point, and one for your conclusion.
- Use only one side of a note card.
- Number the cards.
- Make sure your cards are in the proper order before you begin speaking.

Regardless of which type of notes you select, be sure to practice with the notes you plan to use when you deliver your presentation.

If you are using a lectern, put your notes down and try to leave them there. If you don't have a lectern, put the notes on a table or hold them in one hand only. Slip each page or card behind the others when you have finished with it, so that you don't end up revisiting the same information by mistake.

21c Practice your presentation

Practice is your best guarantee that you will perform well. However, practice requires more than repeating your speech over and over again. Pay attention to the fine points—whether there are words you have trouble pronouncing or sentences that are too long to say in one breath.

Practice giving your presentation to make sure you know how to work any audio or visual equipment, and to stay within your time limit. Depending on how much time you have, the length and importance of your presentation, and your familiarity with your material, there are several different ways to practice. (See Key Points box in section **3c** for tips on practicing.)

KEY POINTS

Practice Methods

- *Practice in private* If you practice in private, speak at the volume and rate you intend to use, only glance at your notes occasionally, and use appropriate body movements.
- *Practice on tape* Using audio or video recordings gives you an opportunity to assess what you are saying, how you sound, and in the case of video, how you look.

(continued)

(continued)
- *Practice with others* In addition to telling you whether or not you can be heard and whether or not your message is clear and well organized, friendly listeners can also provide a dose of confidence.

22　Enhance Your Vocal Delivery

Only a few lucky speakers are born with beautiful voices. The vast majority of speakers must work at harnessing their vocal instrument for the task of producing clear and expressive speech. Fortunately, there are ways to control and improve the qualities of your voice.

22a　Vocal characteristics

Developing a more effective speaking voice requires the same kind of time and effort that you would devote to mastering any skill. Focus on improving five basic vocal characteristics—breathing, volume, rate, pitch, and fluency.

Breathing　All of the sounds in spoken English are made during exhalation. The key to effective breathing for speech is controlling your outgoing breath, not just inhaling and holding more air in your lungs. The first step in learning to breathe for speech is to note the difference between the shallow, unconscious breathing you do all the time and the deeper breathing that produces strong, sustained sound quality.

 KEY POINTS

Breathing for Speech

The following exercise can demonstrate how to breathe for speech.

1. Lie flat on your back.
2. Place a moderately heavy hardbound book on your stomach, right over your navel.
3. Begin breathing through your mouth. The book should move up when you breathe in and sink down when you breathe out.

4. Take the book away and replace it with a hand. Your abdomen should continue to move up when you breathe in and sink down when you breathe out.

5. Try breathing the same way while sitting or standing.

6. Add sound. Try sighing and sustaining the vowel *ahh* for five seconds with each exhalation. Then try counting or saying the alphabet.

Volume   Volume measures your voice's degree of loudness. When you practice your presentation, try to practice in a room about the same size as the one in which you will be speaking, or at least imagine yourself speaking in such a room. Ask a friend to sit in a far corner and report back on your volume and clarity. Also, note that a room full of people absorbs sound; you will have to turn up your volume another notch once an audience is present.

To reach all audience members, learn to project. **Projection** is controlled vocal energy that concentrates and focuses the sound of your voice. You can learn to project by focusing your attention on audience members in the back of the room. You can practice projecting by asking someone to sit at the back of the room in which you will be speaking and reading nonsense sentences to her or him. In order to make someone understand "Samuel Hornsbee threw a turkey at the dragon's striped Chevrolet," you will need to tackle the consonants and vowels in these words with force and energy.

KEY POINTS

Using a Microphone

- If possible, test the microphone ahead of time.

- Determine whether the microphone is sophisticated enough to capture your voice from several angles and distances or whether you will need to keep your mouth close to it.

- Place the microphone about five to ten inches from your mouth. If you are using a hand-held microphone, hold it below your mouth at chin level.

(continued)

(continued)

- Focus on your audience, not on the microphone. Stay near the mike, but don't tap it, lean over it, or keep readjusting it.
- If your microphone is well adjusted, speak in a natural, conversational voice.

Rate   Your rate of speech equals the number of words you say per minute (wpm). Generally, a rate below 125 wpm is too slow; 125–145 is acceptable; 145–180 is better; 180 or higher exceeds the speed limit. But do not carve these guidelines in stone. Your wpm depends on you, the nature and mood of your message, and your audience.

In most cases, it's better to speak a little too fast than too slowly. Listeners perceive speakers who speak quickly *and* clearly as competent and interesting. Too slow a rate can suggest that you are unsure of yourself or not well informed. Practice reading passages that contain 145–180 words to see if you can complete them with clarity and comfort in sixty seconds.

Pitch   Just like the notes on a musical scale, pitch refers to how high or low your voice sounds. Anatomy determines pitch—most men speak at a lower pitch than women and children. The key to an effective pitch is finding your natural or **optimum pitch,** the pitch at which you speak most easily and expressively.

   KEY POINTS

Benefits of Using Optimum Pitch

- Your voice will be stronger and less likely to fade at the end of sentences.
- Your voice will not tire easily.
- Your voice will be less likely to sound harsh, hoarse, or breathy.
- You will have a more expressive and energetic voice.

One way to find your optimum pitch is to sing up the scale from the lowest note you can sing. When you reach the fifth or sixth note, you should be at your optimum pitch. Test your optimum pitch to see if you can increase its volume with minimal effort and if your voice is clear at that pitch. Think of your optimum pitch as *neutral,* and use it as your base line for increasing the expressiveness of your voice.

Fluency   **Fluency** is the ability to speak smoothly without tripping over words or pausing at awkward moments. The more you practice your presentation, the more fluent you will become. Practice will alert you to words, phrases, and sentences that look good in your notes, but sound awkward or choppy when spoken. Practice will reveal whether or not you have included any words that you have trouble pronouncing.

Too many filler phrases can impede a speaker's fluency. Annoying filler phrases such as *you know, and, uh, um, okay,* and *like* break up your fluency and can annoy your audience.

Please understand that there is nothing wrong with using an occasional filler phrase, particularly when you are speaking informally or impromptu. What you want to avoid is excessive and unconscious use of these phrases. Try tape-recording your practice sessions and listen for filler phrases as you play the tape back. In order to break the filler phrase habit, you must slow down and listen to yourself as you practice and as you speak. Do the same when you're not giving a speech. As in breaking any habit, you must work on it all the time, not just when you are speaking in front of an audience.

22b   Clarity and correctness

Having a strong, well-paced, optimally pitched voice that is also fluent and expressive may not be enough to ensure the successful delivery of a presentation. Proper articulation and pronunciation are just as important as your volume, rate, pitch, and fluency.

Articulation   **Articulation** is a term that describes how clearly you make the sounds in the words of a language. Poor articulation is often described as "sloppy speech," poor diction, or just plain mumbling. Fortunately, you can improve and practice your articulation by speaking more slowly, speaking with a bit more volume, and opening your mouth wider when you speak

Certain sounds account for most articulation problems. The culprits are combined words, *-ing* endings, and final consonants. Many speakers combine words—"what's the matter" becomes "watsumata." Some speakers shorten the "ing" sound to an "in" sound: "sayin" instead of "saying." The final consonants that are omitted most often are the ones that pop out of your mouth. Because these consonants—*p, b, t, d, k, g*—cannot be hummed like an "m" or hissed like an "s," it's easy to lose them at the end of a word. Although you can usually hear the difference between "Rome," and "rose," poor pronunciation can make it difficult to hear the difference between "hit" and "hid" or "tap" and "tab."

Pronunciation **Pronunciation** refers to whether or not you say a word correctly—whether or not you put all the correct sounds in the correct order with the correct stress. Pronunciation errors fall into five categories. Speakers add sounds, subtract sounds, substitute sounds, reverse sounds, and misplace stress.

KEY POINTS

Common Mispronunciations

CORRECT SPELLING	CORRECT PRONUNCIATION	INCORRECT PRONUNCIATION	TYPE OF ERROR
Nuclear	Nooklear	Nookyooler	Added sound
Pronounce	Pronouns	Pronaunseate	Added sound
Picture	Pikcher	Picher	Subtracted sound
Shouldn't	Should'nt	Shunt	Subtracted sound
Deaf	Def	Deef	Substituted sound
Both	Both	Bof	Substituted sound
Theater	*Thea*ter	The*a*ter	Misplaced stress
Police	Pol*ees*	*Pol*ees	Misplaced stress
Larynx	Larinks	Larniks	Reversed sound
Ask	Ask	Aks	Reversed sound

Accents and dialects   An **accent** is the sound of one language imposed on another. Some Asian speakers have difficulty pronouncing the "r" and "v" sounds in English. Spanish speakers often make the "i" sound in a word like *sister* sound like a long "e" sound as in *see*. Eastern Europeans may substitute a "v" for the "w" sound and say, for example, "I am vorried about Villiam."

Dialects differ from accents because they represent regional and cultural differences within the *same* language. What people call a southern *accent* is really a southern *dialect*. You can often tell what area of the United States people live in or come from by listening to their dialects.

Without years of study and work, most speakers cannot change or eradicate their accents or dialects, nor should they. An accent or dialect won't hinder your ability to communicate. Sometimes it can add charm and interest to your speech. In other cases, however, a heavy accent or an uncommon dialect can distract an audience and reduce your effectiveness. Many American speakers have learned to switch from a regional or ethnic dialect to Standard American English when it suits their purpose, audience, and message. If you're not sure whether using a dialect is appropriate, monitor your speech for phrases and words that could confuse your audience.

If American English is not your first language, and you believe that audiences will have trouble understanding you, work on your articulation and keep checking your pronunciation.

 KEY POINTS

Vocal Delivery Tips for English as a Second Language Speakers

- *Study and practice*   Identify and work on American English sounds that are difficult for you to make. Consult a good pronunciation dictionary or a voice and diction textbook as a reference.

- *Slow down*   Slow down during your introduction so that audience members have time to become accustomed to your accent. Slow down when you state a key point or share a significant piece of supporting material.

(continued)

(continued)

- *Substitute* If a particular word is very difficult for you to pronounce, try to find an equally good word as a substitute.

- *Listen to good speakers* Use good speakers as models. Listen to them in person, on television and radio, or on tape. Try repeating short phrases and sentences using the same articulation, pronunciation, and style.

- *Ask for feedback* Depending on the size and characteristics of your audience as well as the formality of the occasion, you can ask audience members for feedback. Ask if they understand a problematic word or phrase. In most cases, you will be perfectly understood.

- *Practice, practice, practice* Practice in private, practice on tape, and practice in front of someone who speaks Standard American English. (See section **21c**.)

23 Enhance Your Physical Delivery

Using a natural delivery style is the key to effective physical delivery. A natural delivery style tells your audience a great deal about who you are and how much you care about reaching them. Being natural, however, doesn't mean "letting it all hang out." Rather, it means being so well prepared and well practiced that your presentation is an authentic reflection of you. Effective physical delivery will support and highlight your presentation's most important words and ideas.

Audiences feel comfortable when you seem comfortable. When you appear competent and confident, they can relax and listen.

23a Components of physical delivery

Audience members jump to conclusions about speakers based on first impressions of their appearance and behavior. The way you stand, move, gesture, and make eye contact will have a significant impact on your presentation.

Eye contact Eye contact may be the single most important component of effective physical delivery. Quite simply, **eye contact** is establishing and maintaining direct visual links with individual members of your audience.

KEY POINTS

Benefits of Eye Contact

- *Initiates and controls communication* Eye contact lets you "catch the eye" of your audience and "gives the eye" to inattentive listeners.
- *Enhances speaker credibility* Eye contact communicates that you are competent, confident, and caring.
- *Provides feedback* Eye contact is the best way to gauge audience feedback during a speech.

When you speak to an audience, talk to them and look at them in the same way that you would talk and look at a friend, coworker, or customer. Move your gaze around the room, settle on someone, and establish direct eye contact. Then switch to someone else—someone sitting near the person at whom you just looked or someone all the way across the room. Don't move your eyes in a rigid pattern; try to establish eye contact with as many individual people as you can.

Generally, the more eye contact you have with your audience, the better. Ideally, you should maintain eye contact with your audience during most of your presentation. If you are using detailed notes or a manuscript, use a technique called eye scan. **Eye scan** involves training your eyes to glance at a specific section of your notes or manuscript, to focus on a phrase or sentence, to look back up at your audience, and to speak. Begin by placing your thumb and index finger on one side of the page to frame the section of your notes that you are using. Then, as you approach the end of a phrase or sentence within that section, glance down again and visually grasp the next phrase to be spoken. This way, you will be able to maintain maximum eye contact without losing your place.

Facial expression Audiences direct their eyes to a speaker's face. Unless your topic is very solemn or serious, try to smile. A smile shows your listeners that you are comfortable and eager to share your ideas and information. Audience members are more likely to smile if you smile. If, however, you do not feel comfortable smiling, don't force it. Try to let your face communicate your feelings. Let your face do what comes naturally. If you speak honestly and sincerely, your facial expression will be appropriate and effective.

Gestures   A gesture is a body movement that conveys or reinforces a thought, an intention, or an emotion. Most gestures are made with the hands and arms, but shrugging a shoulder, bending a knee, and tapping a foot are gestures, too. Gestures can clarify and support your words, help you relieve nervous tension, and arouse audience attention.

Many speakers complain that they don't know what to do with their hands. The answer to the problem is this: Do what you normally do with your hands. If you gesture a lot, keep doing what comes naturally. If you rarely gesture, don't try to invent new and unnatural hand movements. Effective gestures are a natural outgrowth of what you feel and what you have to say. If you start thinking about your gestures, you are likely to appear awkward, unnatural, and forced. Rather than thinking about your hands, think about your audience and your message. In all likelihood, your gestures will coordinate with your emotions in a spontaneous mixture of verbal and nonverbal communication.

As difficult as planned gestures are to develop, eliminating distracting gestures can be even harder. Repetitive movements such as constantly pushing upon your eyeglasses, tapping on a lectern, and jingling change or keys in your pocket can detract and eventually annoy an audience. One of the easiest ways to eliminate these unwanted gestures is to videotape and then watch your practice session. Once you see how often you fidget, you'll work even harder to correct your behavior.

Posture and movement   Posture and movement involve how you stand and move and whether your movements add to or detract from your presentation. If you stand comfortably and confidently, you will radiate alertness and control. If you stoop or look unsure on your feet, you will communicate anxiety or disinterest. Try to stand straight, but not rigidly. Your feet should be about twelve inches apart. If you stand tall, lean forward, and keep your chin up, you will open your airways and help make your voice both clear and loud.

Generally, a certain amount of movement can attract attention, channel nervous energy, or support and empha- size a point you are making. Movement provides you with short pauses during which you can collect your thoughts or give the audience a moment to ponder what you have said. Nevertheless, there are outstanding speakers who can all but glue their feet to the floor and their manuscripts to a lectern and still proceed to captivate and delight their listeners.

23b Delivering mediated presentations

The rise of community radio stations, public access cable television, video presentations, teleconferencing, and dis- tance learning means that you may find yourself speaking in mediated presentations. Despite the fact that radio, tele- vision, and video productions can reach huge audiences, they are still very personal and even intimate forms of com- munication. Consequently, mediated speeches can be relaxed and conversational.

Speaking on the radio   Speaking on the radio is, in a sense, easier than speaking on television because you don't have to worry about your appearance and physical deliv- ery. You should, however, think about your voice and its ability to communicate enthusiasm, sincerity, and vitality. If you are asked to speak on the radio, rely on the radio staff to show you how to use a microphone and then let them worry about the sound levels.

Speaking on television   Television adds the elements of physical delivery to your speech. When you're on camera, your face is the main focus of attention—not your gestures, your hands, or even your voice. Pay careful attention to how you look and how you dress in order to create a strong impression.

When confronted with a camera, do you look at it or at the other people in the studio? The only time when you should look at the camera is when you are the only person on the set, or when you are addressing the viewing audience directly.

If you are being interviewed, act as though you are hav- ing a conversation with the interviewer and no one else. If you are speaking on a panel, talk to the panel members, not to the camera. When other panelists are speaking, look at them. The camera may be shooting a reaction shot of the entire panel. Try to keep your delivery natural and sincere.

24 Use Presentation Aids

Presentation aids are the many supplementary resources available to speakers for emphasizing key ideas and providing supporting material. They give audiences an additional sensory contact with your presentation.

24a Functions of presentation aids

When used effectively, presentation aids will attract the audience attention and clarify, reinforce, supplement, compare, and illustrate information. They help an audience understand, learn, and remember. Presentation aids will also save you time, particularly when you use a graph, drawing, or chart to summarize a complex process or a set of statistics.

When deciding whether or not to use presentation aids, keep in mind the most basic principle of all: *Presentation aids are aids.* You and your presentation come first; the aid helps you achieve your purpose. Don't let your aids and their technical razzle-dazzle steal the show. Don't become one of those speakers who prepares a speech by preparing a series of slide images. Begin with your ideas, not with computer software. Outstanding speakers thoroughly prepare their presentations *before* creating their presentation aids. Only after carefully considering what they want to say and what they want their audience members to understand and remember do they prepare visuals.

24b Types of presentation aids

Preparing effective presentation aids requires strategic thinking. Which type of aid will best achieve your purpose? Which type will be best for gaining and maintaining audience attention, clarifying and reinforcing your message, and saving time? The first step in selecting appropriate graphics is to understand that certain types of aids work best for specific purposes.

KEY POINTS

Choosing Effective Presentation Aids

Pie charts show *how much*. They are best for showing percentages and proportions. When using a pie chart, try not to use more than six slices, and make those slices different in color or pattern from each other.

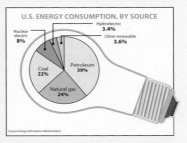

Graphs also show how much, but they are primarily used to demonstrate *comparisons* such as increases and decreases. Graphs, which can be displayed using bars or lines, usually represent countable things. Try to use contrasting colors or shading to emphasize the most important items on a graph.

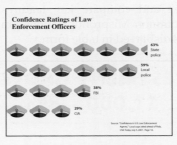

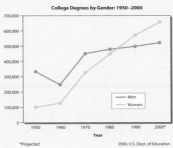

(continued)

(continued)

Text charts *list* ideas or key points, often under a title or headline. The Key Points features in this handbook are often displayed as text charts depicting goals, functions, types, recommendations, and guidelines.

Presentation Aids

- **Gain audience attention**
- **Clarify and reinforce ideas**
- **Improve speaker efficiency**
- **Enhance speaker credibility**

Tables *summarize and compare* data. Tables can also summarize and compare key features. (The Key Points: Common Mispronunciations graphic in section **22b** is displayed in table form.)

INVESTMENT GROWTH
$1,000 – 8%

5 years	$1,469
10 years	$2,159
15 years	$3,172
20 years	$4,666

Berger, *Feathering Your Nest*, 1995.

Other types of presentation aids include drawings, maps, photographs, models, audio and television recordings, objects, handouts, and physical demonstrations. Regardless of the form or type that you use, the key to selecting effective presentation aids is to make sure that each aid you select is relevant to your purpose and topic and that it has the potential to save time, gain attention, and clarify or reinforce your presentation's content.

24c Select appropriate media

Once you decide which type of presentation aid would best support your presentation, you can begin to consider which media to use. Apply these three criteria when choosing the best medium for your presentation aids: ease of use, audience expectations, and availability.

 KEY POINTS

Criteria for Media Selection

- *Ease of use*   Are you comfortable and experienced with media such as computer-generated slides or television equipment? If not, stick to overheads and flip charts.

- *Audience expectations*   Does your audience expect to see a computer-assisted multimedia presentation, or are they accustomed to and expecting simple handouts?

- *Availability*   Is the equipment that you will need available at the place where you will be speaking? If not, can you bring the equipment that you will need?

24d Design effective presentation aids

Even with the best intentions, equipment, and cutting-edge software, presentation aids can fail to have impact. They can be unattractive, distracting, and difficult to follow. Regardless of the type of supporting materials you use or the medium you choose to display them in, you can apply basic visual design principles to creating your presentation aids.

Preview and highlight   Presentation aids should preview what you want to say and highlight the most important facts and features in your presentation. They should not include every fact, statistic, and quotation you cover. Consider using an outline slide at the beginning of a presentation and repeating it at transition points during your speech. When the slide reappears, it will reinforce the basic structure and content of your presentation in a way that can increase the audience's ability to understand and remember your message.

Exercise restraint   Presentation software has made it possible for speakers to use a dazzling array of graphics, fonts, colors, and other visual elements and effects. At first, it's tempting to use them all. Resist that temptation. More often than not, a simple slide will be much more effective and memorable than a complex one. Three basic recommendations apply to almost all types of presentation aids:

- Place only one point on each chart or slide, and make sure the title of the slide states that point.
- Follow the *six-by-six rule.* Aim for no more than six lines of text with no more than six words per line.
- Limit your number of presentation aids. Fifty slides do not necessarily hold more information than ten carefully selected and explained ones.

Choose readable typefaces and suitable colors
Exercise restraint when selecting typefaces and colors. As a general rule, never use more than two different fonts on a single slide. When using computer-generated slides, try to avoid choosing a font size that is smaller than 24 points. Choose text colors with an eye to legibility. If you use a light background, use dark text, and vice versa. If your visuals are going to be projected onto a screen, it is often better to use a dark background with light text.

Also, consider whether the color scheme will be appropriate for the situation and your purpose. If you're not sure about the color, stick to proven color schemes. Most graphic software packages recommend colors that will sharply and effectively contrast with a background.

Use appropriate graphics   Make sure your audience really needs to see the graphics or pictures you've chosen. Artwork that doesn't have a specific purpose can get in the way of your presentation. Resist the temptation to use graphic elements just because you can. More often than not, a clip-art graphic can get in the way of your message if the clip-art image doesn't reinforce the slide's meaning.

24e   Handle presentation aids successfully

Using presentation aids well can make a dull topic interesting, a complex idea understandable, or a long presentation endurable. On the other hand, using presentation aids poorly can bore, confuse, and annoy your audience. Having spent the time and effort to plan and prepare presentation aids to enhance your speech, make sure that you handle your aids smoothly and professionally.

Focus on your audience, not on your aids   Don't turn your back to the audience or stand in front of your screen or flip chart while speaking. Remember this memory aid: *Touch; turn; talk.* Touch your aid (or refer to it with your hand or a pointer). Turn to your audience. Then talk.

Pick the right time to display your aids   Decide when to introduce your aids, how long to leave them up, and when to remove them. Here is a rule of thumb: An aid needs to be displayed for at least the length of time it would take an average reader to read it twice. When you have finished talking about a presentation aid, get rid of it.

Begin with yourself, not your visual   Establish rapport with your audience before you start using presentation aids. Even if you have numerous presentation aids to display, always start and end your presentation by making direct and personal contact with your audience.

Be prepared to do without No matter how well you plan and practice, something can always go wrong. One way to avoid presentation aid disasters is to do a dry run— a special practice session just to check your aids. Also, have a Plan B. Can you deliver your presentation without your presentation aids? In many cases, you can. Remember that presentation aids are not the presentation; they are only there to help and assist you. You and your message should always come first.

Part 8

Speaking to Inform and Persuade

25 Speak to Inform

The primary purpose of an **informative presentation** is to instruct, explain, describe, enlighten, demonstrate, clarify, correct, or remind. An informative presentation can provide new information, explain complex concepts and processes, or clarify and correct misunderstood information.

The best informative speakers consider multiple ways of gaining and keeping the audience's attention and interest.

- **Address audience needs** Begin by asking yourself what your audience members may already know about your topic and what they need to know. The information you share should be directly related to your purpose, and your purpose should likewise be developed with your audience's needs in mind. Otherwise, you may make a well-organized and perfectly delivered presentation that doesn't engage the audience.

- **Include a value step** A **value step** in your presentation's introduction tells audience members *why* the information should matter to them and *how* it can affect their success or well-being.

  If there's a good reason for you to make a presentation, there should also be a good reason for your audience to listen. Tell them how the information in your presentation can make them happier, richer, safer, more successful, healthier, and so on. Don't expect your audience members to figure out why they should listen. Tell them. A value step may not be necessary in all informative presentations, but it can motivate a disinterested audience to listen to you.

- **Enhance your credibility** Sometimes audience disinterest is really audience distrust in disguise. (See section **18** for factors that determine whether an audience regards you as competent, charismatic, and of good character.) Think about ways to enhance your credibility. For example, let your audience know that you are an expert on the topic or that you have done considerable research on it. Show them that you care about them. Audiences are much more likely to listen and learn from a speaker whom they respect, trust, and like.

25a Informative speaking strategies

Informative speaking goals are best achieved when you understand the basic nature of your informative purpose. Ask yourself: Are you reporting new information, explaining a difficult concept or complex process, or seeking to overcome confusion and misunderstanding? Depending on your answer, you will need to use different informative strategies to achieve your purpose.[1]

Reporting new information Reporting new information is what most news reporters do when they answer basic *who, what, where, when, how,* and *why* questions. You face two challenges when reporting new information. First, if your information is very new, an audience may have trouble grasping your central idea. Second, you may need to give an audience a reason to listen, learn, and remember such information.

 KEY POINTS

Strategies for Reporting New Information

1. Include a value step in the introduction.
2. Use a clear organizational pattern.
3. Use various types of supporting material.
4. Relate the information to audience interests, needs, and values.

The following examples provide the topic area, purpose, central idea, value step, organizational pattern, and key points for two informative presentations that present new information.

Topic area:	Fire ants
Purpose:	To familiarize audience members with the external anatomy of a fire ant
Central idea:	A tour of the fire ant's external anatomy will help you understand why these ants are so hard to exterminate.
Value step:	Besides inflicting painful, and sometimes deadly stings, fire ants can eat up *your* garden, damage *your* home, and harm *your* pets and local wildlife.
Organization:	Space arrangement—a visual tour of the fire ant's external anatomy
Key points:	A. Integument (exoskeleton)
	B. Head and its components
	C. Thorax
	D. Abdomen

Topic:	Early female blues singers
Purpose:	To demonstrate the influence of three female blues singers of the 1920s on musicians in later eras
Central idea:	In the 1920s, Sippie Wallace, Edith Wilson, and Victoria Spivey paved the way for other female blues singers.
Value step:	To be able to call yourself an honest-to-goodness blues fan, you should know more about the major contributions made by the early *female* blues singers.
Organization:	Stories and examples—brief biographies of three female blues singers
Key points:	A. Sippie Wallace
	B. Edith Wilson
	C. Victoria Spivey

Explaining difficult concepts Explaining a difficult concept is challenging because you cannot touch it, demonstrate it, or easily define it in simple terms. Concepts like quantum mechanics, the basic tenets of Islam, or the distinguishing characteristics of Karl Marx's theories are demanding topics for any speaker. Explaining a difficult concept requires more than reporting. It requires special strategies to address the essential characteristics of an abstract concept.

KEY POINTS

Strategies for Explaining Difficult Concepts

1. Define or list the concept's essential features. Explain how it differs from other related concepts.

2. Use typical examples.

3. Contrast examples and nonexamples. (For example: The opposite of communism is capitalism, not democracy. Antibiotics treat *bacterial* infections, not the *viral* infections responsible for the common cold and flu.)

4. Quiz the audience. Pose questions and be sure to give audience members time to think about their responses. Then make sure you provide the right answers to your questions.

In the following example, a speaker tries to explain the meaning of the terms *diversity* and *disparity* as they are used in studying animal species. By using typical examples (rats, horses, mice, insects), contrasting examples (the minor body differences in "three blind mice," compared with the major differences in the body plans of insect species), and quizzing the audience, the speaker may succeed in explaining a difficult concept.

TOPIC AREA: Biological diversity and disparity

PURPOSE: To explain how the differences between the diversity and disparity of species account for a central principle in life's evolutionary history

CENTRAL IDEA: A realistic picture of evolution requires an understanding of the distinction between biological diversity and disparity.

VALUE STEP: What you learned in high school biology may have distorted your understanding of the true nature of life's history.

KEY POINTS: A. Diversity
(High density: 1,500 species of rats versus low diversity: 10 species of horses.)

B. Disparity
(Minor differences in body plans of "three blind mice" versus major differences in body plans of insect species.)

C. Quiz about diversity and disparity

Explaining complex processes   When you explain a complex process, you are asking audience members to unravel something that is complicated and multidimensional. You are trying to explain how something works or functions. Before you begin, make sure that *you* understand the "big picture" and can break that picture down into its component parts.

   KEY POINTS

Strategies for Explaining Complex Processes

1. Provide clear key points. Make sure that you are very well organized.

2. Use analogies. Compare the unfamiliar process with one that the audience already understands.

3. Use presentation aids. Models and drawings can help your audience visualize the process.

4. Use connectives frequently—transitions, previews, summaries, and signposts—to help your audience understand the relationships among key components.

In the following example, the process of breathing for speech is outlined for a presentation designed to teach audience members how to improve the quality of their voices. By comparing something well known (breathing for life) with something less well known (breathing for speech), the speaker helps the audience understand the process. Within the presentation, the speaker explains the importance of breathing for speech by comparing it to playing a wind or brass instrument.

Topic area: Breathing for speech

Purpose: To explain how to breathe for speech in order to be a more effective and audible speaker

CENTRAL IDEA:	The ability to produce a strong and expressive voice requires an understanding of and control of the inhalation/exhalation process.
VALUE STEP:	Learning to breathe for speech will make you a more effective, expressive, and confident speaker.
ORGANIZATION:	Compare or contrast the three components of the breathing process
KEY POINTS:	A. Active versus passive exhalation
	B. Deep diaphragmatic versus shallow clavicular breathing
	C. Quick versus equal time for inhalation

Overcoming   confusion   and   misunderstanding
Audience members often cling to strong beliefs, even when those beliefs have been proven wrong. Informative speakers frequently face the challenge of replacing old, erroneous beliefs with new, more accurate ones. A special organizational strategy can help speakers meet this challenge.

 KEY POINTS

Strategies for Overcoming Confusion and Misinformation

1. State the misconception.
2. Acknowledge its believability and the reason(s) that it is believable.
3. Reject the misconception by providing contrary evidence.
4. State and explain the more acceptable or accurate belief.

In the following example, the speaker tries to dispel some misconceptions about the fat content in our diets.

TOPIC AREA:	Fat in food
PURPOSE:	To explain that fat is an important element in everyone's diet
CENTRAL IDEA:	Our health-conscious society has all but declared an unwinnable and unwise war on any and all food containing fat.
VALUE STEP:	Eliminating all fat from your diet can hurt you, rather than help you lose weight.

ORGANIZATION: Problem (misinformation)-Solution (accurate information)

KEY POINTS: A. Many people believe that eliminating all fat from their diet will make them thinner and healthier.

B. This belief is understandable since fat is the very thing people are trying to reduce in their bodies.

C. Fat is an essential nutrient.

D. Fats are naturally occurring components in all foods that, in appropriate quantities, make food tastier and bodies stronger.

25b Informative speaking tips

In addition to strategies that directly address different types of informative speeches, two general tips can help you make your informative presentations more effective and memorable.

KISS   Keep It Simple, Speaker. Most audience members cannot absorb and retain complex information, no matter how important or valuable it may be.

Keep your topic focused if you want the audience to remember you and your message. Concentrate on one or two important details, not ten. Explain two key concepts, not five. The following examples demonstrate how narrowing a topic can help focus your speech on just one aspect of a broader topic.

BROAD TOPIC AREA	NARROW TOPIC AREA
Herbal Medicines	Chamomile
The Vatican	The Vatican's Swiss Guard
Auto Maintenance	Changing the Oil in Your Car
Insects	Fire Ants

One sensory image   You can make an informative presentation more interesting and memorable by focusing on one sensory image. Choose a topic that taps one of the five senses. For example, a presentation about garlic could focus on methods for getting rid of garlic's strong odor on your hands and breath. An informative speech about chocolate chip cookies could describe how to bake a soft and chewy cookie. A presentation about vocal delivery could focus on breathing techniques.

25c Sample informative presentation outline

Most informative presentations are prepared for extemporaneous delivery. The language is usually informal, with a focus on clarity rather than on eloquence. In this section, an address on marketing to women over age fifty on the Internet by Candace Corlett is presented in outline form.[2] Interestingly, the content of Ms. Corlett's speech reinforces the importance of audience research, analysis, and adaptation as a key to developing strategic messages. (See sections **8a–8d**.)

Because Ms. Corlett was speaking to an audience of marketing professionals interested in her topic, she did not have to spend time addressing audience needs. Nor did she need a value step or a section devoted to establishing her credibility. She did, however, have to prepare a very well-organized presentation in order to cover the wealth of information she wanted to share with her audience. Given her credibility as president of 50+ Marketing Directions, a division of WSL Strategic Retail, she did not need to identify the sources of her information.

The presentation is *very* well organized. Her introduction uses a song lyric as an attention-getter, helps her listeners visualize a foot-stamping group of demanding consumers, and identifies why it's important for the audience to understand the consumer over age fifty. Two major key points are well supported. Ms. Corlett uses facts, statistics, testimony, definitions, analogies, descriptions, examples, and stories to support her conclusions and recommendations.

The subpoints under each key point are also well structured. Clear statistics and an audience involvement quiz are used in the first key point to help the audience understand the demographic characteristics of the over-fifty consumer market. The second key point is divided into three subsections. The first describes three separate target markets in the over-fifty population. The second subpoint describes seven market indicators for "getting to know" the over-fifty market. The final subpoint offers three guidelines for speaking to the over-fifty consumers.

Although the presentation is well organized, the supporting material and subpoints do not always address the speech's purpose and central idea. Very often, Ms. Corlett's supporting material applies to *all* consumers over fifty (not just to women) and to their buying habits in general (not just on the Internet). However, to the extent that women belong to this group and share these buying habits, the speaker implies that the research and advice can be applied to the needs and interests of women over age fifty who use the Internet.

The informal style and clever use of terms give the speech vigor and a sense of humor. Key words or phrases in parentheses provide the speaker with reminders of how to explain or describe each point.

Notice how the presentation incorporates many informative speaking strategies: having a clear organizational pattern and key points, using various types of supporting material, defining essential features, employing typical and contrasting examples, quizzing the audience, using appropriate transitional phrases, and providing information to counter misinformation.

The conclusion is short but nevertheless invites listeners to take on the challenge of advertising to an older generation of consumers.

Marketing to Women 50+ on the Internet: Promote the Upside of Aging

Address by Candace Corlett, President,
50+ Marketing Division
Delivered to the World Research Group Conference,
Orlando, Florida
May 27, 1999

I. Introduction
   Baby boomers are not a generation to be ignored. What's that song—"I know what I want and I want it now"? You can almost see them stamping their feet and demanding new products and services: skin creams to erase lines, medications to manage menopause, biotechnology to replace damaged body parts. That is why we are all here today, because the fifty-plus population, even before the onslaught of the baby boomers, is a significant target audience that is getting attention. Why?

II. Central idea and preview
   A. There are several strategies that can help you approach women over fifty with products and services on the Internet.
   B. Key points
      1. Understand over-fifty consumer demographics.
      2. Three steps to successful Internet marketing to women over fifty
         a. Define your target audience.
         b. Get to know them.
         c. Speak to them in a voice they will hear.
III. Demographics are too compelling to ignore any longer.
   A. Characteristics of over-fifty consumers
      1. They represent 38 percent of the total U.S. adult population.
      2. They are 70 million people strong.
      3. They control 55 percent of the discretionary spending in the American economy.
      4. Seventy-seven percent of all U.S. assets are in their names.
      5. Eighty percent of U.S. savings dollars are in their names.
      6. Because women live longer than men, the over-fifty population is skewed—52 percent women versus 48 percent men.
      7. The over-fifty consumers have money to spend, but they demand service, information, and value.
      8. Sixty-eight percent of online buyers are over forty, and they spend thirty-eight hours a month online, more time than any other demographic group does.
   B. "Test Your Assumptions" quiz about consumers over fifty
      1. What percentage of baby boomers expect to work at least part-time during their retirement? (Answer: 80 percent)

2. What percentage of people over age fifty use a computer at home? (Answer: 40 percent)

3. What percentage of computer owners over age fifty access the Internet? (Answer: 25 percent)

4. What percentage of people over age fifty feel these years are the best years of their lives? (Answer: 54 percent)

IV Three steps to successful internet marketing to women over fifty

  A. Define your target audience.

    1. The G. I. generation of women

      a. Age 74 and older

      b. Housekeepers, dependent on husband-providers, have traditional roles and values.

      c. Most do not use computers.

    2. The Anything But Silent generation

      a. From 54 to 73 years old (22 million women)

      b. Caught between the homemaker era and the liberation of women

      c. Many use computers and the Internet.

    3. The Boomers—the demanding, demanding, demanding generation

      a. From 40 to 53 years old (26 million women)

      b. Businesses are adjusting to this large market.

      c. The majority use computers and the Internet.

  B. Get to know them (women consumers between the ages of 40 and 73).

    1. Characteristics

      a. Affected by the liberation of women

      b. Have identities apart from family and children

      c. Have the freedom to make choices

2. Seven indicators of the mature market consumer
   a. They experience lifestyle changes (after children leave home and during retirement).
   b. The self regains position of importance ("Now it's time for me").
   c. Spirits are renewed ("Take time for yourself—live a richer life").
   d. New time needs to be filled (they need ideas on how to fill the time).
   e. Money has new dimensions (no mortgage and no tuition = more spending).
   f. Their bodies send new messages (consumers want products to help compensate for an aging body).
   g. Purchases are viewed with new perspective (consumers have been released from peer pressure and have more time to comparison shop).
C. Speak to them in a voice they will hear.
   1. Talk about what is of interest to them.
      a. You can talk about "hush-hush" topics (such as menopause) on the Internet.
      b. Offer information about how to make the most of aging.
   2. Promote the upside of aging.
      (Transition: People are all too familiar with the downside of aging. You don't need to remind them of it. Sell your message to them with the promise of the second stage of life!)
      a. Vitality (Explain how to live a long, fulfilling life. Example: Going to Club Med)
      b. Glow (Everything good will glow: the glow of good health, glow of skin.)

    c. Growth (personal, financial muscle, and hair growth—but not weight gain)

    d. Advertising copy

       i. *First* will replace *new* (people want to experience firsts).

      ii Use call-to-action words—*begin, start, fast, instantly.*

    e. Graphics (Small, tightly spaced type is illegible—LARGE BOLD TYPE IS OFFENSIVE.)

    f. Models (Use "ageless," age forty-five and older models.)

    g. Active symbols (Replace golf carts with sailboats, bicycles, hiking boots, walking sticks, carpentry tools, and exercise equipment.)

  3. Avoid ageism in advertising—insensitivity to aging will replace racism and sexism as fatal offenses.

V. Conclusion

Will it be much fun to grow old? Of course not. But if advertising can make being a teenager or starting out young and single in one's twenties appear to be fun, then why can't it present the fifties, sixties, or seventies as enjoyable ages?

26 Speak to Persuade

Persuasive speaking encourages audience members to change their opinions (what they think) or their behavior (what they do). Whereas an informative presentation might explain why Brand X is better than Brand Y, a persuasive presentation may urge you to buy Brand X instead of Brand Y.

    In informative presentations, you *tell* an audience something by *providing* directions, advice, explanations, or insights. In persuasive presentations, you *ask* for something *from* your audience—their agreement or a change in their opinions or behavior.

26a   Adapting to audience attitudes

Persuading audience members to change their opinions or behavior requires an understanding of why they may resist your efforts. As noted in section **8a**, the more you know about your audience members, the more effective you can be in adapting your message to their attitudes.

Begin this process by classifying expected audience attitudes along a continuum such as this one:

| Strongly agree with me | Agree | Neutral | Disagree | Strongly disagree with me |

An audience of homeowners, for example, may strongly agree that their property taxes are too high, whereas a group of local college students may support more taxes for higher education. If you are scheduled to talk to a group of gun collectors, you can probably assume that they strongly disagree with calls for stricter gun control legislation.

Review what you do know about your audience's characteristics and presumed attitudes. Then do your best to place your audience along a continuum that measures the extent to which *most* members will agree or disagree with you. Once you understand where audience members stand, you can select persuasive strategies that you can adapt to the people you're trying to persuade.

When audience members agree with you   Although you don't have to sway audience members to your way of thinking, you can strengthen existing attitudes and encourage behavioral change among those listeners who do share your opinions. Several strategies can help you achieve your purpose with an audience that already agrees with you.

KEY POINTS

Persuasive Strategies for Audiences That Agree with You

- *Present new information*   New information reminds them of why they agree with you, and reinforces their agreement.

(continued)

(continued)

- *Strengthen audience resistance to opposing arguments* Prepare those who agree to answer questions asked by those who disagree.

- *Excite the audience's emotions* Use examples and stories that show them why they should feel pride, anger, happiness, or excitement about your topic.

- *Provide a personal role model and course of action* Tell them what *you* have seen or done. Explain why and how they should do the same.

When audience members disagree with you Disagreement does not mean that audience members will be hostile or rude. It *does* mean, however, that changing their opinions will be more challenging. In the face of disagreement, attempt to change only what can be changed.

KEY POINTS

Persuasive Strategies for Audiences That Disagree with You

- *Set reasonable goals* Do not expect audiences to radically change their opinions or behavior. Every small step taken in your direction can eventually be part of a big change.

- *Find common ground* Find a belief, value, attitude, or opinion that you and your audience have in common. Identify with your audience by beginning on common ground before moving into areas of disagreement.

- *Accept and adapt to differences of opinion* Acknowledge the legitimacy of their opinions and give them credit for defending their principles. Demonstrate respect for their viewpoint before asking them to respect yours.

- *Use fair and respected evidence* Your supporting material must be flawless. Choose evidence from respected, unbiased sources.

- *Build your personal credibility* Positive feelings about you may rub off on your arguments and help you achieve your persuasive purpose.

Finding common ground with your audience may be the key to persuading an audience that disagrees with you. Even pro-life and pro-choice opponents often agree that abortions should be allowed in order to save the life of the mother. Smokers and nonsmokers may agree that smoking should be prohibited in and around schools. If you can find areas of agreement, your audience will be more likely to listen to you when you move into less friendly territory.

When audience members are neutral   Some audience members may not have an opinion about your topic, or they may not be able to decide whether they agree or disagree with you. Some listeners may be uninformed, some unconcerned, and others adamantly undecided.

 KEY POINTS

Persuasive Strategies for a Neutral Audience

- *Persuade the uninformed* by (1) gaining their attention and interest and (2) providing information.
- *Persuade the unconcerned* by (1) gaining their attention and interest, (2) giving them a reason to care, and (3) presenting relevant information and evidence.
- *Persuade the adamantly undecided* by (1) acknowledging both sides of the argument, (2) providing new information, and (3) emphasizing or reinforcing the strength of arguments on one side of the issue.

In the following example, a college student addressed a group of "neutral" students by opening her presentation on the importance of voting with a strategy designed to get their attention and give them a reason to care.

More than half of the class raised their hands.

How many of you applied for some form of financial aid for college?

Less than one-fourth of the class raised their hands.

How many of you got the full amount you applied for or needed? I have some bad news for you. Financial aid may be even more difficult to get in the future. But the good news is that there's something you can do about it.

In the real world, audience opinions will rarely be perfectly homogeneous. You are more likely to face audiences with some members who agree, others who don't, and still others who are neutral. In such a case, you have several options. You can focus your persuasive efforts on just one group—the largest, most influential, or easiest to persuade. Or you can seek common ground among all three types of audience members by providing new information from highly respected sources.

All audiences deserve a clear and consistent persuasive speech. A well-prepared and well-delivered presentation by a credible speaker can be persuasive in and of itself.

26b Persuasive speaking methods

Researchers have devoted significant attention to developing theories and methods that explain why persuasion works. Two methods can help you increase your chances of persuading an audience.

Use different types of persuasive proof Like lawyers arguing before a court, persuasive speakers must prove their cases. **Proof** consists of the arguments you select and use to persuade an audience. In the early fourth century B.C., the philosopher Aristotle identified three major types of proof— **logical proof, emotional proof,** and **personal proof.** In the latter part of the twentieth century, communication scholars added a fourth type—narrative proof—to the list.

KEY POINTS

Four Forms of Persuasive Proof

- *Logical Proof* Are your arguments reasonable? Does your presentation make sense? Reasonable people agree with reasonable arguments.

- *Emotional Proof* Can you tap into audience emotions—joy, fear, sadness, anger, love, disgust, grief? Persuasion can also be aimed at deep-seated feelings and values about concepts such as justice, courage, and forgiveness.

- *Personal Proof* Can you establish and rely on your personal credibility? Does the audience see you as competent, of good character, and/or charismatic?

- *Narrative Proof*   Are there stories, sayings, and symbols that address audience values? Appeal to the ingrained values, beliefs, and myths that audience members have about themselves, their society, and their world.

In the following examples, both speakers address the issue of health care coverage. The first speaker relies primarily on logical proof. The second relies on emotional, personal, and narrative proof. Depending on the audience and the credibility of the speaker, either method could prove highly persuasive.

Speaker 1: Many hard-working Americans cannot afford the most basic forms of health care and health insurance. Some 41 million Americans, most of them low-income workers or their families, live without health insurance. In New Mexico and Texas, 25 percent of the population is not covered by any form of health insurance. And contrary to popular belief, most of the uninsured are jobholders.

Relies primarily on logical proof

Speaker 2: When I was 27 years old and only two weeks into a new job, I began losing weight and feeling ill. After days of testing and then finally undergoing surgery, I was diagnosed with colon cancer. The bills were more than $100,000. Then I learned that my new health insurance policy would not cover my expenses because I had a "pre-existing condition." Five weeks into exhausting chemotherapy, my doctor sat me down and told me that his practice was not being paid for my care. I hit bottom. Between having cancer and being told I had no insurance, I thought about committing suicide.

Relies primarily on emotional, personal, and narrative proof

Select a direct or indirect method of persuasion
Which forms of proof are more effective—logical, emotional, personal, or narrative? The answer is . . . it depends. Knowing more about your audience's thinking abilities and

motivations can help you decide whether to take a direct or an indirect route to persuasion.[3]

If your audience members are capable of thinking critically and if they are highly interested and motivated to listen to you (even if they disagree), take a direct route to persuasion. The best form of proof to use is a logical one in which your claims are backed up by strong and believable evidence. Research demonstrates that when audiences are highly involved critical thinkers, direct persuasion is more effective and more enduring.

If your audience is less involved, not inclined to think critically, and/or not interested in the issue, you are better off taking an indirect route to persuasion. These listeners are highly influenced by whether or not they like the speaker and by whether or not they think the speaker is credible. Rather than using logical arguments, rely on interest factors—relevant humor, dramatic stories, catchy phrases, good examples. Rely on expert or celebrity sources to strengthen your key points. Although the indirect route may not produce enduring attitude changes, it may be the only route available for you to deal with uninvolved audiences.

26c Persuasive speaking tips

Regardless of your audience's levels of involvement and/or agreement, several persuasive speaking tips can help you strengthen your presentation. Whereas some of these tips work well when taking a direct route to persuasion, others are more effective when you embark on an indirect route to persuasion. The key to choosing the best persuasive strategies and methods is fully understanding audience characteristics and attitudes. (See section **8.**)

Use persuasive evidence The quantity and quality of evidence you use to support your arguments have a direct bearing on your success as a persuasive speaker. If you claim that millions of Americans cannot afford health insurance, statistics from a highly reputable, unbiased source can help justify your claim.

Select your evidence according to the type of argument that you are trying to prove, the attitudes and needs of your audience, and whether you are seeking a direct or an indirect route to persuasion.

> ### KEY POINTS
>
> **Characteristics of Persuasive Evidence**
>
> - *Novel* Look for new and interesting evidence to support your presentation. New evidence can strengthen a friendly audience's resolve as well as persuade those who disagree.
>
> - *Believable* Take the time to explain why your evidence is true and why the sources of your evidence are reputable and worth believing.
>
> - *Dramatic* Find ways to make your evidence memorable. Use attention-getting comparisons, dramatic stories, and examples that appeal to emotions.

In speaking about the increasing disparity between the rich and poor in the United States, a speaker quoted the U.S. secretary of the treasury, who had noted that Bill Gates's net worth roughly equals the combined net worth of the poorest 40 percent of American households. This kind of novel, believable, and dramatic evidence drives home the point far better than a series of complex graphs illustrating the poverty level.

Create memorable slogans You probably associate many products with their slogans: "Breakfast of Champions" (Wheaties) or "Be all that you can be" (U.S. Army). Slogans briefly summarize a message in a short, easy-to-remember phrase.

Effective persuaders create and use memorable slogans, too. When Dr. Martin Luther King Jr. proclaimed, "I have a dream," and when his supporters sang, "We shall overcome," both statements became battle cries for the civil rights movement. A memorable phrase or statement can become a form of narrative proof—a way of tapping an audience's ingrained values and beliefs.

Address audience needs and benefits Effective speakers understand that if they satisfy audience needs, they are more likely to persuade. Psychologists have identified several types of human needs. Abraham Maslow maintained that people strive to satisfy physiological, safety, social, esteem, and self-actualization needs—in that order.[4]

William Schutz contends that our interpersonal needs for social inclusion, control, and affection are vital to understanding human behavior.[5]

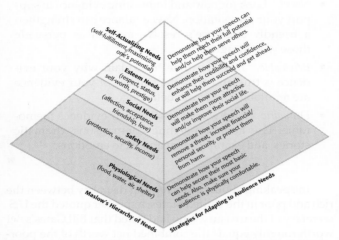

Motivation and Personality 3/e by Maslow, ©. Reprinted by permission of Pearson Education, Inc., Upper Saddle River, NJ.

When engaged in persuasion, try to address some of these needs in your presentation. Something as simple as using plural pronouns such as *we, our,* and *us* can help satisfy a need for social inclusion. A persuasive speech about the need for regular exercise could note its benefits for good health (physiological need), for the pleasant company of others (social need), and for building confidence (esteem need).

Enlist celebrities　Celebrity endorsements work in advertising. They also work in persuasive speeches, particularly when taking an indirect route to persuasion.

Use testimony from famous people who, at the very least, can attract listener attention. Finding a respected celebrity who agrees with your position can enhance your own credibility. When, for example, President Clinton was urging Congress to pass NAFTA (the North Atlantic Free Trade Agreement), he called on every living former president—both Republicans and Democrats—to publicly support the proposed trade agreement.

26d Persuasive organizational patterns

In addition to the organizational formats described in section **14c**, some other organizational formats are particularly well suited to persuasive presentations.

 KEY POINTS

Persuasive Organizational Patterns

- Problem/Cause/Solution
- Better Plan
- Overcoming Objections
- Monroe's Motivated Sequence
- Persuasive Stories

Problem/cause/solution As its name implies, the **problem/cause/solution organizational pattern** describes a serious problem, explains why the problem continues to exist (the cause), and offers a solution. This organizational pattern works best when you are proposing a specific course of action.

The basic outline for a problem/cause/solution presentation looks like this:

A. There is a serious and/or widespread problem.

B. The problem is caused by . . .

C. There is a solution to the problem.

In the following presentation outline, the speaker uses a problem/cause/solution organizational pattern to propose a national health care system for all U.S. citizens.

A. Americans are not getting needed medical care.

   1. Serious diseases such as cancer, heart disease, and diabetes go undetected and untreated.

   2. Millions of Americans do not get regular checkups.

B. The high costs of health care and health insurance prevent a solution.

C. A national health care system can guarantee medical care by providing free care for those in need without eliminating private care for those who want it.

   1. This plan works well in other modern countries.

   2. This plan will not result in low-quality care or long waiting lines.

Better plan   If a problem is complex and difficult to solve, a **better plan organizational pattern** may be a better way to structure a persuasive speech. In this pattern, you present a plan that will improve a situation and help to solve a problem while acknowledging that a total solution may not be possible.

The following is a basic outline for a better plan.

A. There is a good, workable plan.

B. This plan will be better than current plans.

In the following speech outline, the speaker contends that increased deer hunting is a better plan for alleviating the serious problems caused by the growing deer population.

A. There is a plan that will help reduce the deer population.

   1. The deer hunting season should be extended.

   2. States should allow hunters to kill more female deer than male deer.

B. This plan will reduce the severity of the problem.

   1. It will reduce the number of deer deaths from starvation and disease.

   2. It will save millions of dollars now lost due to crop, garden, and forest seedling damage.

   3. It will reduce the number of deer ticks carrying Lyme disease.

Overcoming objections   Sometimes audience members may agree that there is a problem and may even know what should be done to solve it. Yet they may not act because the solution is frightening, expensive, or difficult to implement. In other situations, an audience may disagree with a speaker and come prepared to reject the message even before hearing it. With both types of audiences, you must try to overcome these objections by selecting appropriate forms of proof and persuasive evidence.

The basic outline for an **overcoming objections organizational pattern** has three sections:

A. People should do *X*.

B. There are several reasons why people don't do *X*.

C. These reasons can and should be overcome.

This organizational pattern takes a very central route to persuasion by addressing audience reservations head-on.

In the following example, the speaker uses the overcoming objections organizational pattern to encourage listeners to donate blood.

A. People should give blood but often don't.
   1. Most people think that giving blood is a good idea.
   2. Nevertheless, most people don't give blood.

B. There are several reasons that people don't give blood.
   1. They are afraid of pain and needles.
   2. They fear that they could *get* a disease from giving blood.
   3. They claim that they don't have time or don't know where to donate blood.

C. These reasons can and should be refuted.
   1. There is little or no pain involved in giving blood.
   2. You can't *get* a disease by *giving* blood.
   3. The Red Cross makes it easy and convenient to give the gift of life.

Monroe's Motivated Sequence   In the mid 1930s, communication scholar and teacher Alan Monroe took the basic functions of a sales presentation (attention, interest, desire, and action) and transformed them into a step-by-step method of organization that can be used for all kinds of presentations. Many persuasive speakers have used the five basic steps in **Monroe's Motivated Sequence** quite successfully.[6]

 KEY POINTS

Monroe's Motivated Sequence

1. *The Attention Step:* Capture the audience's attention.

2. *The Need Step:* Show the audience that there is a problem related to the individual interests and needs that should be solved.

(continued)

(continued)

3. *The Satisfaction Step:* Propose a plan of action that will solve the problem and satisfy audience needs.

4. *The Visualization Step:* Describe what audience member's lives and/or the lives of others will be like once the plan of action is implemented.

5. *The Action Step:* Ask audience members to act in a way that demonstrates their personal commitment to the solution.

In the following example, a speaker uses Monroe's Motivated Sequence to focus on the problem of geographic illiteracy and to urge listeners to support the teaching of geography in public schools.

1. The Attention Step: Half of all Americans don't know where Columbus landed.

2. The Need Step:
   A. Americans need to know more about geography for environmental, economic, and political reasons.
   B. Citizens in other countries are much more literate about the world than Americans are.

3. The Satisfaction Step:
   A. Integrate geography into the curriculum.
   B. Reinstate geography as a separate school subject.

4. The Visualization Step:
   A. Heather Hill Elementary School's successful geography classes
   B. U.S. students would know as much about geography as foreign students now do.

5. The Action Step:
   A. Increase parent involvement in reinstating geography instruction.
   B. Put more pressure on local and national education agencies for such instruction.

The unique visualization step (4) in Monroe's Motivated Sequence makes this organizational pattern particularly useful when addressing audience members who are uninformed, unconcerned, or unmotivated to listen or for listeners who are skeptical of or opposed to the proposed course of actions. By encouraging audience members to "see" the results of taking or failing to take action, you can strengthen the impact of your message.

Persuasive stories   Stories can capture and hold audience interests and serve as a persuasive form of proof. (See sections **10a, 14c,** and **20b.**) Stories can also be used as the key points in a persuasive presentation.

When using a persuasive stories organizational pattern, rely on narrative and emotional proof to show how people, events, and objects are or could be affected by the change you are seeking.

A. The following stories show why people should change their opinions and/or behavior about *X*.

1. Story #1

2. Story #2

3. Story #3

B. Unless people change their opinions and/or behavior about *X*, there will be more (or fewer) stories like #1, #2, and #3.

Note how in the following outline a speaker uses a series of stories to convince an audience to support programs designed to help political refugees.

A. The stories of three refugee families demonstrate the need for and the value of migration ministries.

1. Story of Letai Teku and her family (Cambodia)

2. Story of Peter Musooli and his sister (Ethiopia)

3. Story of Nasir Rugova and his family (Kosovo)

B. More support for migration ministries can save even more families who are fleeing foreign tyranny and persecution.

The persuasive stories organizational pattern can be a very effective way of presenting a persuasive speech to neutral audience members who are uninformed or are unable or unwilling to listen critically.

26e Sample persuasive presentation

In this section, the full manuscript of a persuasive presentation is provided for review and analysis. The address "Looking Through Our Window: The Value of Indian Culture" was delivered by Marge Anderson, chief executive of the Mille Lacs Band of Ojibwe Indians.[7] Ms. Anderson's persuasive presentation includes many strategies for generating audience interest (see sections **19–20**) as well as persuasive strategies that use different types of proof and an indirect route to persuasion (see section **26b**). As you read Ms. Anderson's words, notice how she does the following:

- Accommodates the audience's attention span by limiting the length of her presentation;
- Adapts to the audience's level of motivation and listening habits;
- Enlists the power of language;
- Tells two stories—one real, one mythic.

Ms. Anderson delivers a highly informative presentation designed to persuade. By explaining "what it means to be Indian," "how my people experience the world," and "the ways in which our culture differs from yours," she uses interesting information to take an indirect route to persuasion. Thus, she informs her audience about her culture and helps them understand why they "should care about all this." For example, note how she does the following:

- Relies on her competence, character, and charisma to enhance her credibility;
- Uses Saint Thomas Aquinas and the story of Jacob wrestling the angel as a theme and a form of narrative proof;
- Avoids alienating her audience with a "laundry list" of Indian problems and complaints;
- Lists examples of the ways in which Indians have "given back";
- Uses logical, emotional, personal, and narrative persuasive proof;
- Acknowledges and respects differences between Indians and non-Indians.

Comments about the speech are included to highlight important speechmaking techniques and strategies.

Looking Through Our Window:
The Value of Indian Culture

Address by Marge Anderson, Chief Executive,
Mille Lacs Band of Ojibwe
Delivered to the First Friday Club of the Twin Cities
Sponsored by St. Thomas Aquinas Alumni Association,
St. Paul, Minnesota
March 5, 1999

Indian greeting, thank-you, and acknowledgment of audience interest introduce the speech. Chief Anderson acknowledges the audience's interest in Indian casino income and claims pride in the band's achievements.

She explains that she will pursue a different topic. She then identifies her **central idea:** Non-Indians should care about what it means to be Indian. She effectively uses oral styles—simple words, short sentences, active voice, personal pronouns, and repetition of *about.*

She uses *they* to refer to people who don't understand Indians instead of using *you,* and accusing the

Aaniin. Thank you for inviting me here today. When I was asked to speak to you, I was told you are interested in hearing about the improvements we are making on the Mille Lacs Reservation, and about our investment of casino dollars back into our community through schools, health care facilities, and other services. And I do want to talk to you about these things because they are tremendously important, and I am very proud of them.

But before I do, I want to take a few minutes to talk to you about something else, something I'm not asked about very often. I want to talk to you about what it means to be Indian. About how my People experience the world. About the fundamental way in which our culture differs from yours. And about why you should care about all this.

The differences between Indians and non-Indians have created a lot of controversy lately. Casinos, treaty rights, tribal sovereignty—these issues have stirred such anger and bitterness.

I believe the accusations against us are made out of ignorance. The vast majority of non-Indians do not understand how my People view the world, what we value, what motivates us.

audience of ignorance. She explains why *they* have given *you* (this audience) a distorted picture of Indians.

They do not know these things for one simple reason: [T]hey've never heard us talk about them. For many years the only stories that non-Indians heard about my People came from other non-Indians. As a result, the picture you got of us was fanciful, or distorted, or so shadowy it hardly existed at all.

It's time for *Indian* voices to tell *Indian* stories.

She acknowledges audience members' reluctance to listen to a talk about Indians. She attempts to overcome this resistance by identifying with St. Thomas Aquinas, a European and the namesake of the association that she is addressing.

Now, I'm sure at least a few of you are wondering, "Why do I need to hear these stories? Why should I care about what Indian People think, and feel, and believe?"

I think the most eloquent answer I can give you comes from the namesake for this university, St. Thomas Aquinas. St. Thomas wrote that dialogue is the struggle to learn from each other. This struggle, he said, is like Jacob wrestling the angel—it leaves one wounded and blessed at the same time.

To counter negative expectations, Anderson assures the audience that her speech will not be a long list of complaints. She also seeks common ground by describing Indian efforts to take the best of American culture into their own.

Indian People know this struggle very well. The wounds we've suffered in our dialogue with non-Indians are well documented; I don't need to give you a laundry list of complaints.

We also know some of the blessings of this struggle. As *American* Indians, we live in two worlds—ours, and yours. In the 500 years since you first came to our lands, we have struggled to learn how to take the best of what your culture has to offer in arts, science, technology and more, and then weave them into the fabric of our traditional ways.

This transition links Indian struggles with the audience's attempt to understand that struggle. Anderson repeats her **central**

But for non-Indians, the struggle is new. Now that our People have begun to achieve success, now that we are in business and in the headlines, you are starting to wrestle with understanding us.

Your wounds from this struggle are fresh, and the pain might make it hard for you to see

idea: audience members will benefit from understanding what it means to be Indian.

This section compares and contrasts perspectives by using a quotation from Genesis (a non-Indian source) and a quotation from Chief Seattle (an Indian source). The respectful nature of Seattle's quotation should not offend Anderson's non-Indian listeners. The quotations provide a basis for contrasting the difference between a European emphasis on mastery and an Indian focus on nature.

Anderson begins to link the Indian worldview with Indian struggles for treaty rights. Listeners may not believe in Mother Earth and Father Sun, but they may share a respect for and

beyond them. But if you try, you'll begin to see the blessings as well—the blessings of what a deepened knowledge of Indian culture can bring you. I'd like to share a few of those blessings with you today.

Earlier I mentioned that there is a fundamental difference between the way Indians and non-Indians experience the world. This difference goes all the way back to the Bible and Genesis.

In Genesis, the first book of the Old Testament, God creates man in his own image. Then God says, "Be fruitful, multiply, fill the earth and conquer it. Be masters of the fish and the sea, the birds of the heaven, and all living animals on the earth."

Masters. Conquer. Nothing, *nothing* could be further from the way Indian People view the world and our place in it. Here are the words of the great nineteenth-century Chief Seattle:

"You are a part of the earth, and the earth is a part of you. You did not weave the web of life, you are merely a strand in it. *Whatever you do to the web, you do to yourself.*"

In our tradition, there is no mastery. There is no conquering. Instead, there is kinship among all creation—humans, animals, birds, plants, even rocks. We are all part of the sacred hoop of the world, and we must all live in harmony with each other if that hoop is to remain unbroken.

When you begin to see the world this way—through Indian eyes—you will begin to understand our view of land, and treaties, very differently. You will begin to understand that when we speak of Father Sun and Mother Earth, these are not New Age catchwords—they are very real terms of respect for very real beings.

concern about the environment. By understanding that Indians are intertwined in the web of life, non-Indians may understand their worldview and their actions.

And when you understand this, then you will understand that our fight for treaty rights is not just about hunting deer or catching fish. It is about teaching our children to honor Mother Earth and Father Sun. It is about teaching them to respectfully receive the gifts these loving parents offer us in return for the care we give them. And it is about teaching this generation and the generations yet to come about their place in the web of life. Our culture and the fish, our values and the deer, the lessons we learn and the rice we harvest—everything is tied together. You can no more separate one from the other than you can divide a person's spirit from his body.

Here, she links casinos to a better understanding of the Indian worldview.

When you understand how we view the world and our place in it, it's easy to appreciate why our casinos are so important to us. The reason we defend our businesses so fiercely isn't because we want to have something that others don't. The reason is because these businesses allow us to give back to others—to our People, our communities, and the Creator.

I'd like to take a minute and mention just a few of the ways we've already given back:

In this section, Anderson provides multiple examples (factual and statistical) of the ways in which casino income has allowed Indians to "give back" to Indians and non-Indians. This is not a "laundry list" of complaints but rather a list of benefits. Note how all of the examples begin with the word *we*, a stylistic device that helps Anderson focus on Indian contributions.

- We've opened new schools, new health care facilities, and new community centers where our children get a better education, where our elders get better medical care, and where our families can gather to socialize and keep our traditions alive.

- We've built new ceremonial buildings, and new powwow and celebration grounds.

- We've renovated an elderly center, and plan to build three culturally sensitive assisted living facilities for our elders.

- We've created programs to teach and preserve our language and cultural traditions.

- We've created a small Business Development Program to help band members start their own businesses.

- We've created more than twenty-eight hundred jobs for band members, People from other tribes, and non-Indians.

- We've spurred the development of more than one thousand jobs in other local businesses.

- We've generated more than fifty million dollars in federal taxes, and more than fifteen million dollars in state taxes through wages paid to employees.

- And we've given back more than two million dollars in charitable donations.

Anderson concludes her list with a factual story (narrative proof) that describes how the Mille Lacs Band forgave a city's mortgage—a decision that reflects Indian values such as caring for others and the environment in which they live.

The list goes on and on. But rather than flood you with more numbers, I'll tell you a story that sums up how my People view business through the lens of our traditional values.

Last year, the Woodlands National Bank, which is owned and operated by the Mille Lacs Band, was approached by the city of Onamia and asked to forgive a mortgage on a building in the downtown area. The building had been abandoned and was an eyesore on Main Street. The city planned to renovate and sell the building and return it to the tax rolls.

Although the band would lose money by forgiving the mortgage, our business leaders could see the wisdom in improving the community. The opportunity to help our neighbors was an opportunity to strengthen the web of life. So we forgave the mortgage.

Now, I know this is not a decision everyone would agree with. Some people feel that in business, you have to look out for number one. But my People feel that in business—and in life—you have to look out for *every* one.

Anderson concludes by showing how non-Indians will "lose" if Indian ways are absorbed by American culture. She uses words from the Aquinas quotation—*struggle, dialogue, wounds, blessing* and repeats *no, not,* and *all.*

And this, I believe, is one of the blessings that Indian culture has to offer you and other non-Indians. We have a different perspective on so many things, from caring for the environment to healing the body, mind, and soul.

But if our culture disappears, if the Indian ways are swallowed up by the dominant American culture, no one will be able to learn from them. Not Indian children. Not your children. No one. All that knowledge, all that wisdom, will be lost forever.

The struggle of dialogue will be over. Yes, there will be no more wounds. But there will also be no more blessings.

Here her message is urgent. She talks about the risk that Indian culture will vanish.

There is still so much we have to learn from each other, and we have already wasted so much time. Our world grows smaller every day. And every day, more of our unsettling, surprising, wonderful differences vanish. And when that happens, part of each of us vanishes too.

This is more mythic than factual. She previews the story's moral: You can see something differently if you are willing to learn. This lets her return to the central idea that non-Indians will benefit by learning from Indians. She gently asks the audience to look at Indians in new ways.

I'd like to end with one of my favorite stories. It's a funny little story about Indians and non-Indians, but its message is serious: You can see something differently if you are willing to learn from those around you.

This is the story: Years ago, white settlers came to this area and built the first European-style homes. When Indian People walked by these homes and saw see-through things in the walls, they looked through them to see what the strangers inside were doing. The settlers were shocked, but it makes sense when you think about it: Windows are made to be looked through from both sides.

Since then, my People have spent many years looking at the world through your window. I hope today I've given you a reason to look at it through ours.

Mii gwetch.

Part 9

Speaking in Special Contexts

159

27   Adapt to Special Occasions

Although most presentations inform and/or persuade, a common group of presentations resists such classification. Sometimes called ceremonial speaking, **special occasion presentations** address people in a special setting in order to create social unity, build goodwill, memorialize, or celebrate. There are many types of special occasion presentations:

Words of welcome	Nominations
Award presentations	Dedications
Award acceptances	Toasts
Eulogies	Commencement addresses
Introducing a speaker	Tributes

Special occasion presentations often come with their own set of rules that a speaker is expected to follow. More often than not, the purpose, topic, audience, and logistics are predetermined. In these cases, you must decide how to achieve your purpose by choosing and using strong supporting material, effective organization, and an appropriate delivery style.

27a   Introducing a speaker

When asked to **introduce a speaker,** you are being asked to make brief remarks about the speaker and the upcoming presentation in order to motivate the audience to listen.

Your introduction should achieve goals similar to those in the introduction of a presentation: (1) gain audience attention and interest, (2) enhance the speaker's credibility, (3) refer to the speaker's topic, and (4) set an appropriate mood. (See section **17** on introductions.)

Apply the seven basic principles of effective speaking to your introductory comments, making a few adjustments for this type of special presentation.

PURPOSE: Introduce a particular speaker to a specific audience in order to make the listeners respect and want to hear the person being introduced.

AUDIENCE: Research the characteristics, opinions, and needs of your audience. Find out what the listeners already know or need to know about the speaker.

LOGISTICS: A speech that calls for an introduction will already have had many of its logistical decisions made. It's up to you to find out what they are and to adapt your introduction appropriately. How formal is the occasion, and how formal should the introduction be?

CONTENT: Your content should include details about the person you are introducing. Research background information such as the speaker's accomplishments, experiences, education, titles, and relevant personal information.

ORGANIZATION: Even though an introduction should be brief, it still needs to be well organized. Review, regroup, reduce, and refine the key points you want to make in the introduction. Begin and end with strong material.

CREDIBILITY: Focus the audience's attention on the speaker, not on yourself. Bolster the speaker's credibility. Try to impress the audience with information about the presenter's competence and character.

PERFORMANCE: Depending on the occasion, choose an appropriate mode of delivery—extemporaneous, manuscript, or memorized. Then practice. Make sure that you can pronounce the speaker's name correctly. Try to maximize eye contact with the audience.

KEY POINTS

Guidelines for Introducing a Speaker

- When making an introduction, look at your audience, not at the speaker whom you are introducing.

- Keep the introduction short. Don't share the speaker's entire life history. Keep your purpose in mind.

- Don't speak at length on the speaker's subject; that's the speaker's job.

- Don't steal the show or embarrass the speaker with extravagant compliments.

- Avoid using clichés such as "Tonight's speaker needs no introduction" or "So without further ado. . . ."

If you are not sure what to say in this type of presentation, ask the person you will be introducing. Consider asking questions such as "What do you hope to accomplish with your presentation?" "What are the two or three things that the audience should know about you and your topic?" or "Is there anything that you specifically want me to mention or not to mention?" In some cases, a professional speaker may have a ready-to-use introduction that you can adapt or read as-is.

27b Sample presentation: Introducing a speaker

In the following example, a speaker introduces a colleague to an assembled group of college professors attending a major humanities conference. Note how the presenter establishes the purpose of the speech and the presenter's relationship to the keynote speaker at the very beginning and then proceeds to build the credibility and stature of the speaker. Comments about the speech are noted in the margins next to the speech.

Introduction of Dr. Alicia Juarrero

Mentioning carefully selected courses provides a shorthand way of demonstrating the speaker's scholarly credentials. The

It is an honor to introduce our distinguished keynote speaker. And it is a delight to introduce my good friend and colleague, Dr. Alicia Juarrero.

Dr. Juarrero is a professor of philosophy at Prince George's Community College where smiley-face graphic ☺ reminds the speaker to say the second sentence in jest.

References to Plato and his Academy link the speaker to a revered philosopher as a way of enhancing her credibility. A quotation from the speaker demonstrates her commitment to teaching.

Two additional comparisons reinforce the speaker's talents. The presenter returns to the speaker's belief in the importance of teaching. Including a list of journals in which the speaker has published helps demonstrate her reputation.

The audience already knows about the appointment and award, but they must be

she teaches Introduction to Philosophy Ethics, Symbolic Logic, Philosophy and Literature, Business Ethics, Contemporary Moral Values, an honors course in Political Philosophy, and a colloquium she designed titled "Minds, Brains, and Machines." And that's just on Tuesdays and Thursdays. ☺

If Alicia had lived in the Golden Age of Greece and had been a male citizen of Athens, I have no doubt she would have founded the Academy before Plato got around to doing it. That's because first and foremost, Dr. Juarrero is a teacher. At the beginning of each semester, Dr. Juarrero shares a quotation from Plato with her students: "Thinking is the talking of the soul with itself." To that Alicia adds, "I welcome only thinkers to my classes." And rest assured, if they don't come *into* her classes as thinkers, they will have had plenty to think about by the time they leave.

If Alicia had been an Olympic athlete rather than an academic, I have no doubt that she would have won the decathalon. If she were male rather than female, I could call her a Renaissance man. Instead, I think she would be honored with the title of teacher-scholar.

Time does not permit me to read even a small portion of her scholarly publications to you. But in the last two years, her writing has been published in *Philosophy and Phenomenological Research,* the *Texas Law Review, Diogenes, Modern Language Notes,* and *World Futures.* Her book, *Dyanamics in Action,* is the first by a community college professor to be published by MIT press.

And, as you know, she was nominated by President Bush and has just been confirmed by the United States Senate to serve a six-year term on the Council of the National Endowment for the Humanities.

mentioned as important honors. The conclusion brings the audience back to the speaker's lifelong dedication to teaching in the humanities.

Dr. Alicia Juarrero, who demurely refers to herself as "just a teacher," has done and will do a great service to humanities education. In 2002, she was honored as one of only four "U.S. Professors of the Year" by the Council for the Advancement and Support of Education and the Carnegie Foundation for the Advancement of Teaching. Please join me in welcoming her as our keynote speaker.

27c Welcoming an audience

Welcoming remarks are one of the most common and most underappreciated types of special occasion presentations. What makes this type of presentation difficult is that there isn't much to say if you aren't well prepared. Once you say, "We are delighted to welcome you to [insert the name or the group or event]," then what?

Effective decisions about welcoming an audience are based on the material you know or have collected about a group, or on the reason that an audience has assembled. Paying careful attention to a series of basic questions can make your remarks memorable.

PURPOSE: How can you link your welcoming remarks to the goals of the organization you represent?

AUDIENCE: What are the audience's expectations and interests? What is the organization's goal or history? Who will be in the audience?

LOGISTICS: How formal is the occasion, and how formal and long should your welcome be?

CONTENT: What specific content should you include that relates to the assembled group, its purpose, and/or the occasion?

ORGANIZATION: How can you use a simple organizational pattern to accomplish your purpose? How can you gain the audience's attention at the beginning and leave them with a positive, memorable thought at the end?

CREDIBILITY: What can you say to demonstrate that you share the audience's interests, beliefs, and/or values?

PERFORMANCE: What form of delivery is best for this occasion? Can you deliver your remarks naturally and with maximum eye contact?

The key to presenting an effective welcome is to learn as much as you can about your audience and/or the occasion and then to link your purpose to audience characteristics, attitudes, and needs.

KEY POINTS

Guidelines for Effective Welcoming Remarks

- Link your goals or your organization's goals to those of the audience.
- Acknowledge the group's leader(s) by name during the speech.
- Make sure that you correctly pronounce the name of the group you are welcoming.
- Don't rush out when you have finished your welcome; your continued presence extends the goodwill created by your welcome.

27d   Sample welcoming remarks

The following welcome remarks were written for delivery at the opening of a large, annual public blues festival scheduled just two weeks after the September eleventh tragedy. The speaker faced the task of welcoming an audience under unusual and somber circumstances. Rather than ignoring the tragedy, the welcome remarks linked the two events in a way that gave the audience permission to celebrate and enjoy the festival.

Welcome to the Bluebird Blues Festival

I welcome you to the ninth annual Bluebird Blues Festival. Please, let us take a moment to pause in honor of the victims and victim families in New York and at the Pentagon. [pause]

Since the terrible tragedy on September eleventh, we have been searching for comfort to ease our anxiety and grief. I believe that you'll find a healing power at the Bluebird Blues Festival. When we began our Blues

Project back in 1993, we turned to the country's great blues musicians and scholars to help us understand the power of the blues. Barry Lee Pearson, a folklorist and blues scholar at the University of Maryland, describes the healing power of the blues. He wrote that some people think of the blues as sad and depressing music, the historical result of oppression, racism, and economic subjugation. Blues musicians see it otherwise. They see the blues as a cure for being down, a healing ritual that refreshes the spirit.

Legendary blueswoman Koko Taylor set the record straight when she said: "My blues is not depressing. My blues is designed to make people look up, to look forward." Roosevelt Sykes, a gifted piano player and blues composer, spoke of the curative power of the blues. The blues, he said, "provide invisible medicine for the soul. It is a healing force that the good blues doctor uses to cure those in need."

Phil Wiggins, who has performed at many Bluebird Blues Festivals, said, "The blues was a cure, an escape from hard times. The blues is nourishment for the human spirit. The blues is good for you because at the time it was created, the human spirit was under attack."

Today, as our great nation is under attack and in need of a good doctor to heal our souls, we can put our hands together for the musicians who bring a joyful spirit to our lives. Let me conclude by asking you for a round of applause for four groups of people:

- The great blues musicians who are performing today,
- The generous sponsors who have supported this festival year after year,
- The dedicated staff who make all of this possible,
- And a special thanks to all of you who become a joyous blues family on this festive day.

27e Making a toast

A **toast** consists of remarks that accompany an act of drinking to honor a person, a couple, a group, or a recent or future achievement. Even though many toasts appear impromptu in form, you can still prepare and practice delivering them. Answers to seven basic questions can help you prepare and present a successful toast.

PURPOSE: How can you help the audience join in and celebrate the reason that they have assembled?

AUDIENCE: What do the listeners already know and feel about the person or object being honored?

LOGISTICS: How formal is the occasion, and how formal should your toast be?

CONTENT: What can you discover or share in your toast that will help everyone celebrate (special stories, accomplishments, personal experiences)?

ORGANIZATION: How can you use a series of stories or experiences to support the key points in your toast?

CREDIBILITY: What can you say to show the audience how wonderful this person or cause is?

PERFORMANCE: What style of delivery would best suit the occasion?

A toast can be as solemn as a prayer or as risqué as a wedding-night joke. Because toasts are supposed to make everyone feel good, they can be more emotional, inspiring, and joyful than some other types of presentations.

 KEY POINTS

Guidelines for Great Toasts

- Carefully prepare your toast. Don't make it impromptu if you know in advance that you will be expected to speak.

- Avoid over-the-top or schmaltzy emotions that are inappropriate for you, the honoree, or the occasion.

- Avoid reading a toast unless you are reading a special poem or quotation. A toast should look and sound spontaneous and natural.

- Look at the audience *and* at the person or group whom you are toasting.

- Keep it short and simple.

- Make sure your dress and delivery style are appropriate for the occasion.

27f Sample toast

The following example of a brief toast was delivered by a college faculty member honoring Dr. Bernard M. W. Knox, a preeminent classics scholar who had spent part of a summer working with faculty engaged in the study of ancient Greek mythology and literature. The audience was accustomed to Dr. Knox's frequent references to Shakespeare and quotations from Shakespearean plays and poetry. Not only would Dr. Knox immediately recognize the quotations, most of the seminar participants would also. The use of "We few, we happy few" from *Henry V* provides a simple but inclusive celebratory phrase to make audience members feel as through they belong to a very special group.

A Toast to Honor Dr. Bernard M. W. Knox

> As the end of our summer seminar approached, I searched for stirring words to describe what this experience has meant to all of us. My search was fruitless until I remembered words written by one of Dr. Knox's cherished authors—Shakespeare, from his play *Henry V.* "And gentlemen in England, now abed, Shall think themselves accursed they were not here." We have become, as Henry V declared, "We few, we happy few" who shared this grand experience. That is how we think about this seminar. It has been a special honor and privilege for all of us to study here with you, Dr. Knox. [Raise glass.] A toast to Dr. Knox.

27g Delivering a eulogy

Eulogies are tributes that praise the dead. Most people think of a eulogy as a speech delivered shortly after a person's death. Some eulogies, however, may be delivered years later to commemorate the anniversary of a death or to celebrate an important person's historical achievements.

A eulogy can honor a person's life, offer comfort to those who mourn, awaken personal remembrances, celebrate a person's accomplishments, and/or urge others to embrace the deceased person's values and goals. Given the emotional circumstances of a eulogy, speakers face the difficult task of dealing with their own emotions as well as those of their audience.

Use the following guidelines to help you prepare and present an appropriate and meaningful eulogy.

PURPOSE: Make sure that your purpose is specific, appropriate, and achievable. Do you want to comfort those who grieve and/or focus your presentation on paying tribute to the deceased person? Do you need to familiarize audience members with the person's background and accomplishments, or do you want to celebrate the values the person held? Eulogies are most effective when they set out to accomplish a limited number of goals.

AUDIENCE: Understand the relationship of the audience to the person being eulogized. Is the audience composed of family members, close friends, colleagues, or acquaintances? What do the listeners already know and feel about the deceased person? In some cases, you may need to give the audience biographical information about the person. In other cases, you can assume that everyone knew the person well.

LOGISTICS: Eulogies often take place in formal settings—at memorials, funerals, and religious services. The speaker and audience are usually dressed conservatively. Eulogies rarely require special logistical arrangements other than a microphone for addressing large audiences. In some cases, a set of photographs, honors, or personal effects may be displayed and can be used to reference personal attributes or achievements.

CONTENT: Eulogies are usually delivered by someone who knows a great deal about the deceased person. However, there are occasions—such as the dedication of a memorial at a work site—when the speaker has limited information about the person beyond the work environment. In such cases, doing a bit of research can help you speak with authority. Most eulogies are personal and reflect the speaker's most cherished memories and experiences with the deceased person.

ORGANIZATION: Most eulogies employ simple organizational patterns. Use a series of stories to highlight the deceased individual's achievements, values, or personal qualities. Select some meaningful quotations to describe someone when your own words seem inadequate. Relate experiences in chronological order to document the length and depth of your relationship.

CREDIBILITY: When preparing a eulogy, you may face the daunting task of maintaining your composure throughout the speech. No one in the audience will think less of you if you cannot finish a eulogy or falter in its delivery. They will think a great deal more of you if you handle your difficult speaking task with serenity and skill.

PERFORMANCE: Given the emotional nature of a eulogy, many speakers decide to read their remarks from a well-prepared manuscript. In other cases, a short list reminding the speaker of a few personal stories may be all that is needed to deliver a meaningful eulogy. When giving a eulogy, concentrate on keeping your voice steady and loud enough to be heard.

Much like a toast, a eulogy can be as solemn as a prayer or can be amusing. Grieving audiences often appreciate a speaker who can inject a little humor into a solemn occasion. Depending on your purpose, your eulogy can be highly emotional, inspiring, or even joyful.

 KEY POINTS

Guidelines for Meaningful Eulogies

- Carefully prepare your eulogy. Maintaining your composure can be difficult during the presentation.

- Focus on one or two key points. Keep the eulogy short and simple, particularly if there are other speakers.

- Pay careful attention to the words that you choose. Family members often ask speakers for copies of their eulogies, so make sure that you want your words preserved.

- If appropriate, acknowledge and offer sympathy to the family and close friends of the deceased person during the eulogy.

- Personalize the speech. Anyone can read a list of a person's accomplishments—only *you* can talk about your relationship with the deceased person.

- Practice a eulogy many times so that you feel confident about its delivery under highly emotional conditions.

- Make sure that your clothing and delivery style are appropriate for the occasion.

27h Sample eulogy

On September 22, 2001, Senator John McCain delivered a eulogy honoring Mark Bingham, one of the brave passengers on United Flight 93 on September 11, who "grasped the gravity of the moment, understood the threat, and decided to fight back at the cost of their lives."

The eulogy begins with a reference to Bingham's personal support for McCain during the 2000 presidential campaign. Although this reference may seem self-serving, it allows McCain to establish his personal connection to Bingham. McCain also admits that his preoccupation with winning or losing distracted him from giving more attention to those who put their trust in his candidacy.

McCain organizes the eulogy by moving from his personal connection to Mark Bingham to praising the courageous passengers on United Flight 93 who gave their lives to prevent greater injury to others—including McCain, who at the time was working in the plane's designated target, the U.S. Capitol. Again, McCain links himself directly to the hero he is eulogizing.

In keeping with his plain-spoken style, McCain's language is clear, simple, and appropriate. Most sentences are short and direct. He frequently repeats brief phrases to emphasize an idea or communicate an emotion. (e.g., "I wish I had." "We will prevail.") The pronoun *we* helps McCain communicate shared emotions while *I* emphasizes his connections—particularly as a Vietnam War hero—to the brave passengers on Flight 93 and to the sacrifices made by New York's emergency personnel. McCain frequently uses words such as *honor, God,* and *love* to pay tribute to a fallen hero and to invoke God's love as a source of strength and comfort to the family and friends of Mark Bingham.

Eulogy in Honor of Mark Bingham
Senator John McCain
San Francisco, California
September 22, 2001

I didn't know Mark Bingham. We met briefly during my presidential campaign, yet I cannot say that I knew him well. But I wish I had. I wish I had. You meet a lot of people when you run for president. I was fortunate to have had the support of many Americans who were, until then, strangers to me. And I regret to say, that like most candidates, I was preoccupied with winning or losing. I had not thought as much as I should have about what an honor, what an extraordinary honor it was to have so many citizens of the greatest nation on earth place their trust in me, and use our campaign as an expression of their own patriotism. They were the best thing about our campaign, not me. Had I been successful, my greatest challenge would have been to prove myself worthy of the faith of so many good people.

I love my country, and I take pride in serving her. But I cannot say that I love her more or as well as Mark Bingham did, or the other heroes on United Flight 93 who gave their lives to prevent our enemies from inflicting an even greater injury on our country. It has been my fate to witness great courage and sacrifice for America's sake, but none greater than the selfless sacrifice of Mark Bingham and those good men who grasped the gravity of the moment, understood the threat, and decided to fight back at the cost of their lives.

In the Gospel of John it is written, "Greater love hath no man than this, that a man lay down his life for his friends." Such was the love that Mark and his comrades possessed, as they laid down their lives for others. A love so sublime that only God's love surpasses it.

It is now belived that the terrorists on Flight 93 intended to crash the airplane into the United States Capitol where I work, the great house of democracy where I was that day. It is very possible that I would have been in the building, with a great many other people, when that fateful, terrible moment occurred, and a beautiful symbol of our freedom was destroyed along with hundreds if not thousands of lives. I may very well owe my life to Mark and the others who summoned the enormous courage and love necessary to deny those depraved, hateful men their terrible triumph. Such a debt you incur for life.

I will try very hard, very hard, to discharge my public duties in a manner that honors their memory. All public servants are now solemnly obliged to do all we can to help this great nation remain worthy of the sacrifice of New York City firefighters, police officers, emergency medical people, and worthy of the sacrifice of the brave passengers on Flight 93.

No American living today will ever forget what happened on September 11, 2001. That day was the moment when the hinge of history swung toward a new era not only in the affairs of this nation, but in the affairs of all humanity. The opening chapter of this new history is tinged with great sadness and uncertainty. But as we begin, please take strength from the example of the American we honor today, and those who perished to save others in New York, Washington, and Pennsylvania. The days ahead will be difficult, and we will know more loss and sorrow. But we will prevail. We will prevail.

Pay no heed to the voices of the poor, misguided souls, in this country and overseas, who claim that America brought these atrocities on herself. They are deluded, and their hearts are cramped by hatred and fear. Our respect for Man's God-given rights to life, liberty, and the pursuit of happiness assures us of victory even as it made us a target for the enemies of freedom who mistake hate and depravity for power.

The losses we have suffered are grave, and must not be forgotten. But we should all take pride and unyielding resolve from the knowledge that we were attacked because we were good, and good we will remain as we vanquish the evil that preys upon us.

I never knew Mark Bingham. But I wish I had. I know he was a good son and friend, a good rugby player, a good American, and an extraordinary human being. He supported me, and his support now ranks among the greatest honors of my life. I wish I had known before September 11 just how great an honor his trust in me was. I wish I could have thanked him for it more profusely than time and circumstances allowed. But I know it now. And I thank him with the only means I possess, by being as good an American as he was.

America will overcome these atrocities. We will prevail over our enemies. We will right this terrible injustice. And when we do, let us claim it as a tribute to our liberty, and to Mark Bingham and all those who died to defend it.

To all of you who loved Mark, and were loved by him, he will never be so far from you that you cannot feel his love. As our faith informs us, you will see him again, when our loving God reunites us with all the loved ones who preceded us. Take care of each other until then, as he would want you to. May God bless Mark. And may God bless us all.

Thank you.

28 Learn How to Speak Impromptu

Impromptu speaking calls on you to make a presentation without advance practice and with little or no preparation time.

Impromptu speaking occurs everywhere, every day. You may be called upon to share your opinion in class, be asked by your boss or by a colleague to summarize a report with no advance warning, be moved to speak at a public forum, or be asked during a job interview to describe your accomplishments. In each of these cases, try to predict the topic you may be called upon to discuss. Then practice speaking on that topic. Know as much as you can about the topic and have a few ready-made remarks handy.

28a Impromptu speaking strategies

Speakers who sound as fluent during an impromptu speech as they do during a well-prepared presentation have mastered two important strategies. They have come equipped with ready-to-use organizational patterns, and they know how to make the best use of their time in front of the audience.

Ready-to-use organizational patterns Successful impromptu speakers always have a handful of standard organizational patterns that they feel comfortable using at a moment's notice. Since you will have little or no time to think about which pattern is best suited to your topic, try fitting your response into a simple pattern, one that clearly separates your key points.

Suppose someone has asked you to talk about the value of a college education. How would you structure your ideas and opinions with one of the following ready-to-use organizational patterns?

- **Past, present, future** This pattern is a variation of the time arrangement pattern. (See section **13c**.) You could begin by explaining that in the 1950s, a college education was not necessary for getting or keeping many jobs. Today, most good jobs require at least an A.A. or B.A. degree. Within a few years, many job applicants may also need a master's degree. Time arrangement can be as focused as yesterday, today, and tomorrow or as far-reaching as from the Stone Age to the dot-com era.

- **Me, my friend, and you** In this pattern, you begin by explaining how the topic affects or has affected you, then tell how it affects another person, and conclude with how it can affect audience members. In advocating a college education, you could start with your own story—why you went to college and what you have gained from the experience. Then tell a story about someone else who did or didn't go to college. Finally, draw conclusions about the importance of a college education for everyone in the audience. Move from your personal experience to establishing common ground with your audience.

- **Yes/no: Here's why** In this pattern, state your position and then preview the reasons why you have taken that position. For example, a college education can prepare you for a career, can inspire you to become a lifelong learner, and can help you meet people who will be your good friends for the rest of your life.

Time Management Time is precious to an impromptu speaker. If you're lucky, you may have a minute to collect your thoughts and jot down a few ideas before speaking. In most cases, though, you will only have a few seconds to prepare. Manage the brief amount of time you have to your advantage.

- **Use your thought speed** Most people can think much faster than they can speak. If you speak at 150 words per minute, your brain can race ahead of what you are saying because you can think as fast as 600 words per minute.

    The best impromptu speakers think ahead. As they get up to speak, they are choosing their two or three key points. When they reach the podium or lectern, they are formulating an attention-getting beginning. As they start talking, they are thinking ahead to their first key point. They trust that the words will come out right. The more you practice impromptu speaking, the better you will become at thinking ahead as you speak.

- **Buy time** In the few seconds between the time you are asked to make impromptu remarks and the moment when you start speaking, you have to plan and organize your entire presentation. Learn to stretch those seconds in a variety of ways.

 KEY POINTS

Buy Time to Think in Impromptu Speaking

- *Pause* Give yourself a few seconds to think before you begin speaking. Audience members are often impressed by a speaker poised enough to take a few moments for thought.

- *Paraphrase* If you have been asked a question or told to report on a specific issue, repeat or rephrase the question or topic. Not only does this give you time to think, but it also ensures that you will be addressing the right issue.

- *Use all-purpose quotations* Most speakers know a few quotations by heart—from a religious book, poem, song lyric, or famous person. Using a quotation makes you sound intelligent; it also gives you a little extra time to think.

28b Question-and-answer sessions

The question-and-answer session (often called "Q-and-A") is a special type of impromptu speaking that is directed by questions from members of the audience. Many speaking situations are followed by planned or spur-of-the-moment Q-and-A sessions. The key to making a question-and-answer session successful is to be prepared, to answer the questions that you are asked, and to respect your questioners.

Be well prepared Advanced preparation is the best way to ensure that you can and will answer questions effectively. Try to predict which issues will be most important to your audience, the questions they might ask about those issues, and the answers to those questions.

Answer the question Be direct, specific, and brief. Unless a question is technical and demands a lengthy response, your answer shouldn't be longer than three sentences. Don't ramble or change the subject. Audiences can tell if you are dodging an issue or fudging an answer; they won't like you any better if you evade their answers. And if you don't know the answer, be honest and tell them, "I don't know."

Respect your questioners Most questioners are good people seeking answers to honest questions. Even if they don't word their questions well, you will sense what they want or need to know. A few questioners, however, fall into a different category. They can be highly opinionated, incomprehensible, and even hostile. Nevertheless, you should treat all your questioners with respect.

KEY POINTS

Handling Difficult and Hostile Questions

- Take your time before answering a difficult question. Listen carefully. Don't strike back at a hostile question. Be diplomatic and keep your cool.

- Assist nervous questioners. Encourage, praise, and thank them for their questions.

- Don't let an audience member's question become a speech. After a reasonable period of time, ask what the question is. If the person keeps going, you may find audience members asking the questioner, "What's your question?"

- Never embarrass or insult a questioner. If a questioner is being abusive, offensive, or threatening, suggest that the person talk to you after the presentation. Then move on to another person who has a question.

- If possible, recognize questioners by name. Saying a person's name when you answer personalizes the exchange.

- Control your body language. Looking bored, annoyed, impatient, or angry sends a negative message and can damage your credibility. Instead, make full eye contact, smile, and lean toward the questioner.

29 Learn How to Speak in Business Settings

Every principle, guideline, tip, and recommendation in this handbook also applies to speaking in business settings. At the same time, special strategies can improve the success of this type of presentation.

29a Business briefings

A business **briefing** is a type of informative presentation in which a speaker *briefly* reports on the status of an upcoming event, past event, or current project in a business or organizational setting. For example, you might be asked to present a short report to your colleagues or managers on what you learned at a recent conference or meeting. In a government setting, you might be asked to provide a brief update to staff members on the public response to an elected official's actions or speech.

Although briefings are—by their very definition—short, they may be the only means to inform an audience about a very important issue. Applying the seven principles of effective speaking to every decision you make about a briefing can assure that it achieves its purpose.

29b Sales presentations

Sales presentations are a unique form of speechmaking that combines the strategies and skills of informative and persuasive speaking. Successful sales professionals excel as strategic speakers and listeners. They know how and when to apply effective speaking principles to achieve their business goals.

The purpose of your sales presentation Expert sales professionals have a clear vision of their task. Every time they communicate with a customer, they look for a match between their product and the needs and interests of the buyer. A purpose statement for a sales transaction must be specific. "I want to sell cars" is not specific. "I want to demonstrate why our dealership is best equipped to understand and meet this customer's personal and financial needs" is much more specific and offers a wide variety of sales strategies.

When establishing your purpose for a sales presentation, remember and apply some of the key points for persuading an audience that disagrees with you. (See section **26a**.) Set reasonable and appropriate goals. Cultivate a relationship, find common ground, respect their concerns and objections, and begin the process of building your personal credibility. Even if all you accomplish is getting a potential customer to return your business call or make a small purchase, you may have taken the first step in creating a long and lucrative sales relationship.

The sales audience Regardless of the size of an audience (a single customer, a family, a business, or millions of TV viewers), successful sales professionals are audience focused. They focus on customer needs and try to figure out

WIIFT—What's In It For Them?—as opposed to WIIFM—What's In It For Me? Like other effective speakers, sales professionals ask relevant questions about potential customers: What are their demographic characteristics (age, race, gender, income, occupation), their attitudes, and most importantly, their needs.

One of the most important questions to ask about your audience is this: What connections do I have with this person or group? Sales connections come in many different varieties.

KEY POINTS

Types of Customer Connections

- *Prospects* People who can afford and can benefit from buying the product
- *Leads* People who have the potential to become prospects
- *Past customers* People who have benefited from the product and may be inclined or persuaded to buy again
- *Existing customers* People who buy the product on a regular or contractual basis
- *Competitors' customers* People who have the potential to be wooed away from another product
- *Referrals* People who have been recommended by business associates, marketing research groups, existing customers, or past customers

---

Each type of customer is different and requires different adaptations in a sales presentation. Promising and providing responsive and high-quality service may be the key to keeping an existing customer whereas improving a product or offering a better financial package may interest a past customer. Investigating customer complaints about a competitor's product may give you the arguments you need to attract that customer to your product. Telephoning leads and referrals with a well-prepared sales pitch can "hook" a few new customers from the large sea of potential buyers. Three additional questions can help you adapt to customers:

- **Who will make the decision?** Will it be an individual or a group decision? For example, people in auto sales have learned that even though a husband may ask more questions about a car, the wife may be the final decision maker.

- **When will the decision be made?** In retail sales, most decisions are made in the store and on the spot. Major buying decisions or business purchases may take weeks of work responding to buyer specifications and financial parameters.

- **What criteria will be used to decide?** In personal shopping, variables such as price, color, availability, and style may be the criteria for a purchase. In corporate and public purchasing agreements, potential sellers submit comprehensive proposals that address a wide variety of technical and pricing specifications. Understanding a customer's criteria for deciding should influence the content of a sales presentation.

Sales logistics How will the sales transaction occur— face to face, before a group, on the phone, or via e-mail? Each medium requires different tactics. In a face-to-face meeting, you can zero in on the particular needs of a buyer. In a presentation to a large group, you have to consider differences and similarities in audience interests, needs, and financial resources. In mediated transactions, your writing and graphic displays must effectively compete against the information from competitors.

Sales content The content of your sales message must adapt to your purpose, your audience, and the logistics of the situation. All salespeople must be content experts. They must know their product inside and out, be able to describe the product using different forms of supporting material (facts; statistics; and examples of, testimony from, and stories about satisfied customers). If your listeners sense that you don't know your product and can't answer their questions, you won't make a sale.

Sales organization Organizing a sales presentation is very similar to organizing a persuasive speech.

Persuasive organizational patterns are particularly well suited to sales. (See section **26d**.) For example, the problem/cause/solution pattern works well with prospective customers who are looking for a product to solve a problem. The better plan pattern can be used to demonstrate why your product is better than the competition's. The overcoming objections pattern can dispel concerns and fears about making a major purchase. The persuasive stories pattern can influence potential buyers who have the time and are interested in hearing well-told tales about satisfied customers. The most applicable persuasive pattern, though, may be Monroe's Motivated Sequence because it is based on sales techniques.

 KEY POINTS

Applying Monroe's Motivated Sequence to Sales

1. *The Attention Step*   Capture attention, establish your credibility, clarify your purpose, and draw attention to the customer's need.

2. *The Need Step*   Ask questions about or discuss individual or group needs. Relate your product to the needs and interests of your customers.

3. *The Satisfaction Step*   Provide a compelling description of your product or service. Describe its benefits. WIIFT—What's In It For Them?

4. *The Visualization Step*   Vividly describe what their lives will be like if they make the purchase. Show how the benefits will be realized. Try to intensify their willingness to buy. Help them visualize a better or less problematic future.

5. *The Action Step*   Close the sale. Summarize the benefits. Arouse their determination. Ask if they have any questions.

Sales and personal credibility   No matter how well you have analyzed your audience and constructed a well-prepared sales presentation, you have no hope of achieving your purpose if you lack credibility. Many people have seen or experienced sleazy, dishonest, high-pressure salespeople. First impressions can make or break a sale.

You can improve your chances of succeeding in sales if you keep in mind the three components of speaker credibility: *competence, character,* and *charisma.* (See section **18a**.) Make sure that you are a product expert. Demonstrate your competence in customer service: Return your phone calls promptly; take time to get to know your customers; handle complaints without becoming defensive. Buyers also want salespeople of good character—professionals who are honest, friendly, and fair. Are you willing to tell customers that a product won't work for them, that they don't need an expensive repair, or that the outfit doesn't flatter them? If you are willing to lose a sale, you may have gained a loyal customer. Finally, consider ways to demonstrate enthusiasm about your product. If you don't like what you're selling, why should the buyer?

Sales delivery Using your voice, body, and presentation aids effectively is critical to successful sales. Make sure that you dress appropriately and that your conversational style matches that of your prospective buyers. If someone is using rather formal language with you, be careful of projecting a "good ol' boy" or "good ol' gal" personality. Don't try to be anyone but yourself—it's too hard to keep up false appearances for long.

Generally, it's a good idea to speak extemporaneously during a sale. That means being well prepared but also able to adapt to customer feedback. If you use presentation aids, don't overuse them, and make sure that they are as accurate and professional looking as possible. Don't talk your customers to death. Know when to stop and listen.

In addition to following the seven basic principles of effective speaking, sales professionals also follow effective listening guidelines. The most successful sales professionals are good listeners.

The more that a customer talks, the more you can learn about the person's needs, concerns, tastes, and financial resources. Listening also gives you time to think about what you want to say and how you want to say it. Learn to listen to your customers. (See section **4a**.) In addition to listening to what they say, "listen" to their nonverbal behavior. Even when they tell you that they're not interested, their nonverbal behavior may say the opposite.

Listen *comprehensively* when customers seem confused. If potential buyers believe that you are trying to learn about their needs and concerns, they are more likely to trust you.

Listen *analytically* when customers are skeptical or critical. Then try to answer their objections without belittling their concerns. Listen *empathically* when customers are describing problems or concerns. Listen *appreciatively* when customers seem enthused and interested in your product. Effective listening helps you understand and adapt to your customers and their needs.

29c Speaking in groups

Groups have become the American way of doing business. If you are employed, you probably belong to several work groups. You may be a member of a production team or work crew. You may be part of a sales staff, service department, management group, or research team. In almost every case, the work group to which you belong is responsible for achieving specific, business-related tasks. All work groups engage in **small group communication**—the interaction of three or more interdependent people working toward achieving a common goal.[1]

Ask group-focused questions about the basic principles of effective speaking to ensure that your group is productive and offers a positive experience for all members.

PURPOSE: What is the group's goal? Why are you meeting? If everyone agrees with and understands the group's goal, the group is more likely to achieve it.

AUDIENCE: Who will benefit from the discussion? Like audiences, group members have demographic characteristics, opinions, and needs. You are part of the "audience" when other group members speak. They become your "audience" when you speak. Effective group members understand, respect, and adapt to their fellow group members.

LOGISTICS: Where and when does the group do its work? Is the room large enough, clean, comfortable, and/or free of distractions? Does the group have the resources that it needs to achieve its goal? Group logistics require attention and maintenance if a group expects to achieve its purpose.

CONTENT: What does the group need to know and cover? If you want your group to succeed, make sure that everyone has access to quality information relevant to the group's task.

ORGANIZATION: How should the group organize its tasks and meetings? Groups that use and follow well-prepared agendas or work schedules are more likely to achieve their goal. If you don't have an agenda to guide and monitor your progress, your group may become sidetracked and discouraged.

CREDIBILITY: How can members enhance their believability? When group members interact with one another, their comments and behavior determine how credible they are in the eyes of other members. Member competence, character, and charisma are powerful predictors of individual and group success.

PERFORMANCE: What delivery skills will enhance the group's performance? Performing in a group means knowing how to speak well and how to deal with the inevitable interpersonal communication conflicts that can prevent a group from achieving its goals.

29d Team presentations

A **team presentation** is a well-coordinated presentation by a cohesive group of speakers who are trying to inform or influence an audience of key decision makers. Team presentations are common in nonprofit agencies and international corporations. They are seen in marketing presentations, contract competitions, and organizational requests for funding. For example, companies that make the "short list" of businesses considered for a lucrative government contract may be asked to give a team presentation to the officials who will award the final contract. In a presentation to the state legislature's appropriations committee, a state college's board chairperson, college president, academic vice president, and student representative may be given a half hour to justify their request for more state funding.

A team presentation is not a collection of individual speeches; it is a team product. Team presentations require efficient and effective decision making as well as coordinated performance. Much like a single speaker would, a team should consider every step in the speechmaking process.

PURPOSE: The team should agree upon the overall purpose or theme.

AUDIENCE: The team should adapt the presentation to a specific group of decision makers.

LOGISTICS: The team should be well prepared to adapt to the place where the presentation will be delivered. Special equipment may be needed to enhance the presentation.

CONTENT: The team should make sure that supporting material is recent, consistent, and valid. Sources of information should be credible and unbiased.

ORGANIZATION: The team should plan the introduction, organization, and conclusion for each team member's presentation and for the entire team's presentation.

CREDIBILITY: The team should enhance its credibility by demonstrating its expertise and trustworthiness.

DELIVERY: The team should practice until the team's performance approaches perfection.

Part 10

Speaking in the Classroom

30 Speak to Learn

Effective speaking offers personal, professional, and public benefits. (See section **1a**.) As a college student, those benefits can also enhance your academic success in educational settings.

Oral presentations in college classrooms and training seminars have become an integral part of the learning process in all areas of life. The following list represents only a few of the ways in which in-class presentations influence how and what you learn in a wide variety of academic disciplines.

- **English:** Reviewing/critiquing a book, explaining a literary theory
- **Science:** Reporting individual and group research results; critiquing a study, research methodology, or theory
- **Social Sciences:** Summarizing a literature review, applying a theory or methodology to a particular case or phenomenon

- **Business:** Presenting a business case study, proposing a marketing strategy
- **Technology:** Explaining how to operate a system, promoting a design solution
- **Human Services:** Proposing/evaluating a diagnosis or treatment, demonstrating a best practice
- **Law:** Arguing a case, summarizing/analyzing a series of precedents
- **Education:** Demonstrating a lecture or classroom exercise, explaining the implications of educational research or theories

Classroom presentations do more than demonstrate your subject knowledge and research skills. They also demonstrate your ability to effectively communicate complex ideas and information within the bounds of a discipline-specific, time-limited assignment.

31 Differentiate Written and Oral Reports

Recall the last time that you heard someone read a written report to a class or group of listeners. In all likelihood, the content was either too complicated or just plain boring, the language was formal and impersonal, the sentences were long and complex, and the delivery was uninspired, particularly if the speaker's eyes never left the manuscript. That's because written papers and oral reports differ significantly. Regardless of whether you are presenting a short oral report or major research findings, make sure that you understand *why* and *how* written and oral reports differ.

In section **19b**, we offer advice on how to choose effective words for a presentation. Oral reports require the same kind of oral style. Consider the following tips.

 KEY POINTS

Oral Style for Oral Reports

- Speak the way you talk, not the way you write class papers.
- Use shorter words and sentences.

(continued)

(continued)

- Use more personal pronouns.
- Spice up your oral report by repeating important ideas and using figures of speech to enliven your presentation.
- Strive for brevity *and* eloquence.

31a Organize your report like a speech

Organization is just as essential for an oral report as it is for a major presentation. (See **Part 5**.) If you have written a full report, create a presentation outline from the manuscript for oral delivery. Include an introduction that can capture audience attention and interest. Identify your purpose and give a preview of the key points. Use connectives (transitions, previews, summaries, signposts) to remind audiences where you are in the presentation and where you will be going. Offer interesting examples and stories—even humor.

Remember that audiences have limited attention spans and poor listening habits. Whereas readers can reread a written document, an oral report can't be reviewed later. Rather than including *everything* you would put in a written report, choose the most important ideas for your oral report. Consider using presentation aids or handouts to reinforce your spoken message.

31b Focus on your delivery

Although you may write out your oral report during the preparation process to make sure that it includes the key points and supporting information that you want to cover, don't read it word for word when it comes time to deliver the report.

Be clear and expressive. The tone and energy in your voice can tell an audience which ideas are important. A gesture can direct their attention to a visual. Your posture can communicate intensity or informality. Direct eye contact can connect you with a person who, in your opinion, needs to hear what you are saying in a particular section of your presentation.

Students often jeopardize their grades when they ignore the differences between written and oral reports. An oral presentation in the classroom is a speech, not an oral term paper. *Do not confuse the two.* Do not take the lazy way out and read a report you have written for some other purpose. Use written reports the same way that you use supplementary material—as a rich resource of supporting materials for creating a presentation.

The following example contrasts the beginning of a written essay with a brief presentation outline for an oral report on the same topic.[1]

Documented Written Essay	Presentation Outline for an Oral Report

"I haven't understood a bar of music in my life, but I have felt it" (qtd. in Peter 350). These words were spoken by Igor Stravinsky, who composed some of the most complex and sophisticated music of this century. If the great Stravinsky can accept the elusive nature of music and still love it, why can't we? Why are we analyzing it to try to make it useful?
 	
Ours is an age of information—an age that wishes to conquer all the mysteries of the human brain. Today there is a growing trend to study music's effects on our
	I. Introduction
	  A. <u>Note:</u> Play three selections of music and ask audience to describe what they think and feel when they hear each selection.
	  B. Central Idea: A new brain science threatens to control you by controlling the music that you hear.
	  C. Preview
	    1. New science studies how music affects your brain.
	    2. As a result, scientists can control you by controlling the music that you hear.
	    3. Is resistance futile?

(continued)

(continued)

Documented Written Essay	Presentation Outline for an Oral Report

emotions, behavior, health, and intelligence. Journalist Alex Ross reports how the relatively new field of neuromusicology (the science of the nervous system and its response to music) has been developed to experiment with music as a tool and to shape it to the needs of society. Observations like these let us know that we are on the threshold of seeing music in a whole new way and using music to achieve measurable changes in behavior. However, this new approach carries dangers, and once we go in this direction, there can be no turning back. How far do we want to go in our study of musical science? What effects will it have on our listening pleasure?
 	
    A short history lesson reveals that there has long been an awareness that music affects us, even if the reasons are not clear. Around 900 B.C., David (later King David) played
	II. Body
	    A. Neuromusicology
	        1. Definition (Ross)
	        2. History proves them right. Example: David and Saul in 900 B.C.
	    B. Music and Your Emotions
	        1. Music's positive effects on emotions and behavior. Example: Treating depression
	        2. Music's negative effects on emotions and behavior. Example: Muzak
	
	[Outline would continue to develop each key point and a conclusion.]

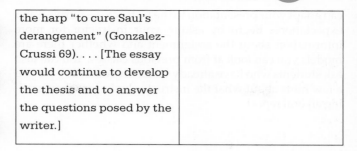

| the harp "to cure Saul's derangement" (Gonzalez-Crussi 69). . . . [The essay would continue to develop the thesis and to answer the questions posed by the writer.] | |

32 Apply the Seven Principles to Classroom Speaking

Depending on the academic discipline or training environment, classroom presentations require making unique decisions about purpose, audience, logistics, content, organization, credibility, and performance. As you begin working on an oral presentation for class, make sure that you understand the requirements of the assignment in terms of the seven basic principles of presentation speaking (see section **2**).

32a Determine the instructor's purpose

Rather than beginning with *your* **purpose** (e.g., master the content, get a good grade), start with questions about the *instructor's* purpose. In other words, what is the instructor's reason for assigning this oral report? Understanding what an instructor wants to achieve can help you make sure that your presentation meets those expectations.

Consider the assignment's purpose   Begin by considering the general purpose of the assignment. Will it be used to assess your knowledge of course content or your ability to apply that content to real-world experiences and contexts? Is the instructor using the assignment to "teach" the class about a concept instead of lecturing or conducting a class discussion about it?

Instructors may not reveal their explicit purpose when they assign an oral presentation. However, the better you understand the reason for the assignment, the better you can adapt your presentation to the instructor's purpose and expectations. Begin by asking your instructor for more information about the assignment and whether there are models you can look at from previous classes. You can also ask students who have already taken the course to give you a few hints about what the instructor looks for when grading an oral report.

Think about thinking In addition to considering the general purpose of the assignment, try to determine the level or type of thinking that best suits the assignment. You can use a tool called **Bloom's Taxonomy** to assess the type of thinking required by the assignment.

Bloom's Taxonomy begins with a basic level of thinking (knowledge) that requires simple information recall and then moves through higher levels of thinking that conclude with making informed judgments (evaluation).[2] Use these levels of thinking to guide how you develop your topic.

For example, if you are asked to critique a piece of literature, research study, or argument, you must do more than describe and summarize what you have studied. Here, analytical thinking (analysis) would be most appropriate. If, however, an assignment asks you to show how a theory operates in a real-world situation (application), you may not do well if you simply describe the theory or recommend using a different theory.

By understanding the level of thinking assumed in the assignment and focusing your attention on that kind of thinking, you are more likely to succeed in meeting the instructor's expectations.

32b Adapt to the classroom audience

As is the case in any audience analysis situation, ask and answer questions about who the members of your audience are, why they are there, what they know, and what their interests and attitudes are. In a classroom setting, you

Bloom's Taxonomy: Levels of Thinking

Levels of Thinking	Thinking Skills	Key Words	Examples
Knowledge	Memorize/recall data and content	Define, describe, outline, list, quote, name, label	Describe the rules or procedures for . . .
Comprehension	Understand and interpret the meaning or nature of a problem	Explain, predict, summarize, compare, translate, estimate, give examples, paraphrase	Explain how to interpret the results of a study
Application	Use methods or concepts in new situations	Apply, demonstrate, show, solve, discover, construct, compute	Solve a problem using a particular method/formula
Analysis	See or organize patterns, flaws, or attributes	Analyze, diagram, illustrate, connect, classify, arrange	Analyze the logical fallacies in an argument
Synthesis	Create new ideas from old ideas	Design, create, combine, change, revise, plan, invent, compose, rewrite	Design a more effective or efficient process for . . .
Evaluation	Make judgements and assess value	Judge, assess, grade, recommend, justify, criticize	Select the best solution, person, or plan for . . .

probably know something about who they are and why they are there. The key to making an effective classroom presentation lies in understanding and adapting to what they know about your topic, whether or not they are interested, and how their attitudes about the topic may affect your ultimate success. There are at least two types of listeners in every classroom audience, and in some cases, there are more.

The instructor   If your presentation is being graded, your instructor may be the most important member of your audience. As we have recommended, understanding the instructor's purpose and the type of thinking required by the assignment is the first step in adapting your presentation. Pay careful attention to the assignment requirements. Are there items that must be included in your presentation? Will you be penalized for speaking less or more than the assigned time limit? Can you adapt your material to what you know about your instructor's interests and attitudes? Be cautious when you analyze your instructor as an audience member. If you analyze the assignment's purpose or requirements incorrectly, adapting to your instructor's personal interests and attitudes may not help you earn the grade you desire.

Classmates   The members of your class are your largest audience. There are several reasons to adapt to the class, even though the instructor is the person evaluating your work. The first is that audience reactions and interaction may be used as criteria for judging your effectiveness. For example, if you are trying to explain and apply a psychological theory to a real-life experience, your instructor may use audience reactions to gauge how well you have achieved your purpose. Or if you are proposing a research methodology or design solution, audience confusion and questions can tell an instructor whether you have succeeded in promoting your solution.

The members of your class can also help enhance your effectiveness as a speaker. An attentive audience can boost your confidence and bolster your credibility as you speak. In turn, you can do the same for other students when it is their turn to present their oral reports.

Outside evaluators In addition to the instructor and students, there is a third type of audience member. In some classroom situations, an instructor may invite an individual or group of outside evaluators to assess and comment on your presentation.

Outside evaluators can include other instructors, working professionals, and even members of the public. For example, senior professors may be invited to a class in which students present a major research study. A marketing professional, attorney, corporate officer, elected official, or service provider may be invited to class to comment on how well students address their areas of expertise. A public audience may be used to assess a sales presentation, an educational lecture, or a public speech. Spending extra time and effort on analyzing and adapting to outside evaluators can impress your guests as well as your instructor and classmates.

32c Adjust to classroom logistics

Classroom logistics can vary from run-down classrooms to state-of-the-art high tech learning centers. As in any presentation, check out the facilities and equipment in advance. If you plan to use a computerized slide presentation, make sure that the necessary equipment will be there and operating. If you have no technical resources, reconsider using the blackboard, securing an overhead projector for transparencies, or bringing a previously prepared flip chart. Even the most well-prepared students can falter in the face of technical problems that could have been avoided.

Pay special attention to the time limit you have been given. Instructors usually schedule presentations well in advance with specified time limits. Although they understand that these limits are difficult to enforce, they are usually less than generous when students abuse and overuse the amount of time they have been given. Respect your class and honor the assignment requirements as you prepare.

In addition to time, pay attention to other requirements. Are you expected to hand in a paper, a bibliography, or copies of your notes and visuals? Is there an accepted dress code? Very often, instructors expect students to dress up for a major presentation, particularly when outside evaluators have been invited.

32d Choose appropriate content

As is the case in all presentations, content is the heart of your message. However, in a classroom presentation, you must consider the nature of the assignment when choosing your content. Go back and reconsider the instructor's purpose and the type of thinking most appropriate for the assignment. Choose your ideas and supporting material to reflect those decisions.

Every time you choose or test an idea, make sure that it helps you achieve your purpose, meets the instructor's expectations, and reflects the kind of thinking required by the assignment.

32e Organize to meet the assignment

Begin by following the advice we offer about organizing and outlining a presentation in **Part 3**. At the same time, however, understand that the organizational pattern you choose should reflect the nature of the assignment. Consider, for example, the following guidelines distributed for an oral book report assignment.

Book Report Assignment

Your oral book report should include these elements:

A. **Title:** What is the book's title?

B. **Author:** Who is the author? What are the author's credentials, degrees, and/or demonstrated area of expertise? Is the author qualified to write this book?

C. **Thesis/Central Idea:** What is the author's thesis or central/main idea?

D. **Major Points:** What key points are used to prove or support the author's thesis?

E. **Evidence:** What evidence or research does the author use to support the thesis and key points of the book?

F. **Application:** What is the practical application/value of the author's claims/advice?

G. **Evaluation:** Summarize the strengths and weaknesses of the book.

1. Are the author's suggestions responsible, useful, and valid?

2. Has the author overstated a simplistic idea or simplified a complex idea?

3. Would you recommend this book to others?

Students are expected to address items A through G in their oral reports. Students who conclude with the application section and fail to summarize the strengths and weaknesses of the book do not earn an *A,* no matter how well they have completed sections A through F of the assignment.

When an assignment is this explicit, consider using the instructor's outline as the basis for your presentation.

32f Enlist your credibility to improve your grade

As you develop your classroom presentation, consider ways to augment the audience's perception of your character and competence. By practicing a delivery style that enhances your level of enthusiasm and confidence, the audience may also perceive you as a charismatic speaker.

You can develop your credibility as a speaker *before* and *during* a presentation. In section **18a**, we advise speakers to know their strengths (and weaknesses), be well prepared, and put as much of themselves into the presentation as possible.

Is there a way that you can use your own experiences as examples in your report? Including information related to your own experiences and expertise can make your report more interesting and memorable.

At the same time, there are cautions to note. If you appear to be bragging about yourself in front of a class, you may be viewed as arrogant, self-centered, and patronizing to your fellow classmates. Don't overdo it. One way to mediate this process is to poke fun at your experiences and even to use failures to illustrate a point. What matters most is that you come across as truthful, sincere, well prepared, and interesting.

32g Use appropriate delivery

Make sure that you know which mode of delivery the instructor expects. In most cases, the mode will be **extemporaneous** (see section **21a**). No manuscript, just notes. Despite its somewhat informal appearance, extemporaneous speaking requires a lot of practice, particularly when you have technical material to cover.

If, however, you decide or are required to use a **manuscript,** practice even more. Memorize the introduction and conclusion so that you can maximize eye contact. As we suggest in sections **19** and **21a**, make sure that the language you use is easy to say and oral in style. Practice with your manuscript until you can maintain eye contact for most of the time when you are speaking.

And if you plan to use visual aids to support your presentation, make sure that they follow the guidelines we recommend in sections **24a–e**.

33　Adapt to Academic Disciplines

The previous section outlines general advice about preparing and presenting an oral report for the classroom. All classes, however, are not alike. A report in an English class will usually be quite different from a report in a physics or marketing class.

Each academic discipline has its own culture. Presentations acceptable for a communication class or a psychology seminar may be inappropriate for science or mathematics settings. Understanding how disciplinary differences can affect your presentation can help you prepare and present an excellent, strategically adapted oral report.

33a　Arts and humanities

All college students are required to take arts and humanities courses. They include English, fine arts, history, philosophy, foreign languages, religion, and communication courses, as well as art, music, and theatre appreciation courses. Because arts and humanities courses are so diverse and are often required in a general education curriculum, instructors may ask students to demonstrate all levels of thinking ability—knowledge, comprehension, application, analysis, synthesis, and evaluation. You may be asked to present a report in which you identify and describe lesser-known painters of a particular historical period. You may be assigned to analyze a poem or group of poems, critique a speech, or apply a philosophical principle to a real-world experience.

Arts and humanities reports may be followed by a class discussion of the topic. These discussions are not high-pressure question-and-answer sessions like those described in section **28b**. Instead, they may encourage the class to provide more examples, share their reactions to the speaker's position, or compare the presentation's content to other reports. Class interaction rather than speaker interrogation is usually the goal of such discussions.

 KEY POINTS

Arts and Humanities Presentations

- Make sure that you understand the instructor's purpose and the thinking style required by the assignment.
- Assess what audience members already know about this topic. What, if anything, can you skip? What aspects need the most time and attention?
- Use interesting and clear examples, vivid descriptions, appropriate visuals, memorable analogies, and well-chosen stories.
- Select a very clear organizational pattern. Use your preview to let listeners know what you are going to tell them and your conclusion to remind them what you have told them. Repeat and emphasize your key points.
- An informal speaking style is usually appropriate for arts and humanities presentations.

33b **Engineering and technology**

Engineering majors specialize in a wide variety of sub-specialties such as chemical, mechanical, electrical, aerospace, and civil engineering. Technology majors are found in a wide array of academic areas ranging from computer science and software engineering to architecture and computer-aided design.

Although speaking ability may appear to be marginal to success in engineering and technology, just the opposite is true. Communication skills are often rated as more important than mathematics, science, and technical skills to student and career success in these fields.[3] Students are often called upon to translate complex technical projects and designs into messages that can be understood and can influence nonengineers and lay audiences. Not only do engineering and technology students make individual presentations of this kind, but they also often work in student teams to prepare and present design projects.

The following guidelines set out five of the unique speaking challenges faced by engineering and technical students.[4]

1. **Keep it simple**   When audience members are not engineers, a simple message may be the only way to achieve your goal.

2. **Sell an idea**   Good ideas and brilliant designs are of little use if you cannot "sell" the idea to others.

3. **Use numbers**   Very often the most valuable, important, and persuasive evidence is numerical. "Real" engineers can show and explain the numbers that go with a project.

4. **Results go first**   Organize your presentation by putting the results first. Explain the outcome; then describe the process or methodology that produced those results.

5. **Use sophisticated visuals**   If anyone should know how to use visuals effectively, it would be a student majoring in engineering or technology. A picture, graph, or diagram can save time and effort when you are explaining a complex process or difficult concept.

The key concepts in this type of presentation are translating technical material for lay audiences, translating designs into visual displays, translating numbers into a results-first structure, and translating design solutions into a "sales pitch."[5]

At first, some of these suggestions may appear contradictory. How can you be simple and also rely on numerical explanations? How can you "sell" an idea if you have to put the results first rather than working up to them? Your decisions on how to resolve these seeming contradictions rest

KEY POINTS

Engineering and Technology Presentations

- Instructors look for presentations in which students demonstrate technical ability and thinking that requires analysis, application, synthesis, and evaluation.

- Assess what audience members know and think about the topic and whether they will comprehend technical information and numerical explanations.

- Given the complex nature of engineering and technology presentations, use the appropriate informative speaking strategies in section **25a** for explaining a complex process. Provide clear key points, use analogies, presentation aids, and connective phrases between sections.

- Use a clear organizational pattern that begins with results and then works through methodologies and processes.

- Review persuasive speaking strategies and select appropriate ways to "sell" your idea.

with how you answer questions about a particular speaking situation. In front of a lay audience, you *must* keep it simple; in front of engineering colleagues, you may rely more on the numbers. The culture of engineering and technology (unlike that of real estate or car sales) expects to see the results first rather than last.

33c Science and mathematics

Science is generally classified into two areas: physical sciences (physics, chemistry, and earth sciences) and natural sciences (biology and medicine). Science reports can range from "term paper" presentations on scientific topics to the presentation of research results. Mathematics at the undergraduate level is less likely to require explanations of complex theories or processes. Instead, students are more likely to demonstrate a solution or methodology in front of the class.

If you are asked to present the results of a research study—either as an individual or as part of a research team—use the organizational elements found in most research studies. Pick up any scientific journal and you will find the basic format in most articles. Generally, a research report contains the following elements:[6]

- **Introductory Section** Summarizes previous research on the topic and states the problem or hypotheses of the study;

- **Methods Section** Describes the research setting and methods that you have chosen;

- **Results Section** Describes the data you have collected. At minimum, several pieces of information are usually included in this section:

  - The statistical method used to analyze the results;

  - The results and the significance of the analysis;

  - The results' impact on the research problem and hypotheses;

- **Analysis Section** Interprets the results, acknowledges limitations that could affect the results, and recommends future research;

- **Concluding Section** Summarizes the critical findings.

Depending on the course and instructor, your report may be much simpler than reporting an entire research study. In some cases, you may be asked to summarize a literature search, explain the methodology used in a study or series of studies, or describe the implications of a study's results. If you are presenting research as part of a team, make sure that you follow the guidelines we offer in section **29d** for team presentations.

 KEY POINTS

Science and Mathematics Presentations

- Determine what kind of thinking is required by the assignment, particularly in the areas of application, analysis, and synthesis.

- Give special attention to audience analysis and adaptation. What does your audience know or think about your topic? If you are speaking to nonscientists or to a lay audience, translate your message into concepts and language that they can understand and appreciate.

- Use the informative speaking strategies discussed in section **25a** for explaining difficult concepts and complex processes.
- Carefully select your supporting material. Use multiple examples and contrast typical examples with atypical ones. Use analogies and metaphors to explain complex concepts.
- Use presentation aids to help your audience visualize a process or principle.
- Select a clear organizational pattern. Use transitions, previews, summaries, and signposts frequently.
- Give the audience time to ask questions.

33d Social sciences

Social science classes include those in psychology, sociology, anthropology, economics, political science, cultural studies, and, in some cases, human communication studies. Reports in the social sciences often share similarities with those in the so-called "hard" sciences. Social scientists, as their name implies, place more emphasis on how their research affects individuals and groups of people. At the same time, they conduct research that uses methods similar to those used by their colleagues in science and mathematics.

In addition to presenting scientific reports, social scientists often look at the implications of their research and develop theories that explain how and why we behave as we do. Whether you are a psychologist or an economist, you are concerned with understanding and predicting human behavior. As a result, instructors often ask students to make presentations that describe or critique an existing theory or that propose a policy or treatment for dealing with a human problem. Oral reports in the social sciences could respond to a whole series of questions such as the following:

What are the most effective treatments for depression?

How do leaders emerge and retain their power?

What strategies are most effective for persuading teenagers to engage in safe sex?

What economic factors have the greatest impact on consumer confidence?

To what extent is communication apprehension a genetic predisposition?

In order to answer such questions, a speaker must do significant research and then decide upon a set of well-organized key points to address the issues inherent in the question.

KEY POINTS

Social Science Presentations

- Determine what kind of thinking is required by the presentation. All six levels of thinking may be required in social science presentations.

- Include a value step (see section **25**) that tells audience members why the information should matter to them and how it can affect their lives.

- Use the informative speaking strategies for explaining difficult concepts. For example, define the concept's essential features and tell how it differs from other concepts, use typical examples, or contrast examples and nonexamples. (See section **25a**.)

- Pose real or rhetorical questions to the audience as a way of generating interest and involvement.

- Use personal stories to link yourself to the topic.

33e Social services

Social services is a term that helps describe a wide range of majors that have not been considered thus far. Students majoring in health care and social work probably come to mind. In a broader sense, so do law enforcement majors and pre-law majors since these professions also serve the public by protecting people from harm and acting as advocates for clients.

KEY POINTS

Social Service Presentations

- Determine what kind of thinking is required by the presentation, particularly in the areas of application, analysis, synthesis, and evaluation.

- Include a value step (see section **25**) that tells audience members why the information should matter to them and how it can affect their lives.

- Use the informative speaking strategies for overcoming confusion and misunderstanding. State the misconception, acknowledge its believability, reject the misconception by providing contrary evidence, and then state and explain the more acceptable and accurate belief. (see section **25a**).

- Open the floor to audience questions as a way of generating interest and involvement.

- Tell stories about your personal involvement in these issues as a way to enhance your credibility and link yourself to the topic.

33f Business

Depending on the institution, business majors often constitute the largest number of college enrollments. Some students are beginning their college careers as business majors while others are returning to college to earn business degrees or to develop specialized expertise in business management principles and techniques.

In **Part 9**, we title section **29** "Learn How to Speak in Business Settings." There we focus on sales presentations, speaking in groups, and team presentations. All three of these types of presentations are also used in business courses. Instructors may expand the sales presentation into the presentation of a marketing plan or corporate strategic plan. The techniques needed to "sell" these proposals are similar. And when a presentation must be made by a group, the same principles apply.

Effective speaking in business settings is critical to professional success. Business students spend years acquiring the knowledge and skills of their professional specialty but devote almost no effort to studying ways to communicate them. Employers rank presentation skills as a top requirement in business settings, but they bemoan the quality of the skills they actually find.[7]

KEY POINTS

Business Presentations

- Identify your purpose as well as the instructor's purpose and the type of thinking required by the assignment. Business presentations often require application, analysis, synthesis, and evaluation.

- Business audiences expect first-class visuals. Use your classroom speaking experiences to develop your skill in creating effective presentation aids using a variety of formats and media.

- Adapt your speaking skills to videoconferences. Pay attention to how you look and keep your message simple but expressive.

- Your success in business depends on your credibility. Use every speaking situation to demonstrate your character, competence, and (if possible) your charisma to an audience.

- Use dramatic supporting material: facts, statistics, testimony, descriptions, and examples.

- Use humor and stories to make a point and to interest your audience. However, make sure that your humorous example or story is linked to the content of your message.

The best time to learn effective presentation speaking skills is while you are in college because on-the-job speech training is both disruptive and difficult. By making classroom presentations in business classes, you begin to develop the knowledge, skills, and confidence that you will need to succeed in the competitive business world.

33g Education

Many would-be teachers begin their teaching careers by giving oral reports in education classes. Others major in discipline areas with a minor in education. Some encounter their first teaching experiences as graduate students assigned to teach freshman courses. Regardless of the route taken, making classroom presentations provides an effective means by which to learn the art and craft of teaching.

Teaching is much more than getting students to learn information. If that were the case, we would not need teachers. Students could learn all they need to know by reading books, consulting the World Wide Web, and experiencing the world around them.

One way to understand the complexity of communicating in the classroom as a teacher involves familiarity with three types of learning: (1) *Knowledge:* mental and intellectual skills such as those included in Bloom's Taxonomy; (2) *Attitude:* feelings and emotions such as appreciation, motivation, and enthusiasm; and (3) *Skills:* physical/psychomotor abilities such as perceiving, imitating, adapting, and creating. Students usually learn more when teachers connect knowledge to attitudes and skills. Teaching a lesson about the Gettysburg Address, for example, will be more successful if the teacher can link the information to an appreciation of the solemn nature of the occasion and the skills that it took to create the speech.

Teachers teach by communicating. They must know how to lecture, conduct class discussions, ask and answer questions, facilitate experiential learning activities, create laboratory experiences, and counsel individual students. Here we can only skim the surface of the communication skills needed by students who learn to teach by making classroom presentations.

 KEY POINTS

Education Presentations

- Determine what kind of thinking is required by the presentation. In many cases, a teacher will apply all levels of thinking to a topic—from knowledge through evaluation.

- Organize your lectures and lessons. Students learn more when information is well organized and clear.

- Adapt to students' learning styles by presenting information in several modes: oral, written, visual, and experiential.

- Use facts, multiple examples, definitions, analogies, descriptions, and stories as supporting material.

(continued)

(continued)

- Include a value step (see section **25**) that tells students why they should learn or how they will benefit from learning about your topic.

- Pose content-based questions to audience students as a way of keeping their attention and determining whether they understand the content of your message.

- Tell stories that motivate listeners to pay attention and remember content.

- Demonstrate that you care about your topic and your students as means of enhancing your credibility and motivating student learning.

34 Classroom Debates

In addition to the many different types of oral reports that you may be assigned to do for a course, one form deserves particular attention: the classroom debate. Instructors use this assignment for many reasons. Debates

- teach students how to think critically about complex issues;

- help students to understand, respect, and adapt to differences of opinion;

- provide a way of comparing and contrasting different theories and viewpoints;

- develop students' ability to create prompt, analytical responses to arguments;

- teach students how to collect and analyze arguments and evidence;

- teach audience members how to listen to and analyze arguments;

- develop presentation skills and student confidence.

A **debate** is a special type of speaking situation in which two sides present arguments designed to help listeners reach a decision. Regardless of which side of the debate you are on, you will have to consider all seven principles of presentation speaking as you prepare your "case." First and foremost, however, make sure that you understand your purpose. Are you affirmative or negative? Do you agree with the topic or disagree? Answers to these basic questions will determine how you make decisions about the other six principles.

Unlike a discussion in which group members confer with one another in order to reach a decision or achieve a goal, a debate relies on an audience or judge to decide who has "won." Lawyers engage in courtroom debates, which are decided by judges and juries. Political candidates engage in public debates after which voters make the final decision.

In the context of a college course, winning or losing a debate is less important than learning. Classroom debates can cover a wide range of topics, depending on the academic discipline.

Classroom Debates

Discipline Area	Debate Topics
Arts and Humanities	**Michelangelo Was the Greatest Artist of All Time.** All students should be required to attend a classical concert, play, or opera each year.
Engineering and Technology	**Software X Is Better than Software Y for _____.** Design flaws led to the collapse of the world trade towers.
Science and Mathematics	**Nanotechnology Will Dominate Twenty-first-Century Science.** Mathematics is the most eloquent academic discipline.
Social Sciences	**Watching Violence on Television Increases the Incidence of Domestic Violence.** Leaders are born, not made.
Social Services	**Cigarette Smoking Should Be Banned in All Public Bars and Restaurants.** The rights of criminals exceed the rights of law-abiding citizens.
Business	**Money Motivates Employees to Work More Productively.** Marketing plan X will increase product sales.
Education	**Intercollegiate Athletics Should Be Abolished at Our College.** Educational vouchers should be provided to all families.

Types of debates   Begin the debate preparation process by making sure that you know what kind of debate your topic requires.

- **Debates About Facts**   The topic "Does money motivate employees?" directs debaters to argue about what is true or not true. Most debates begin with questions about facts and then progress to arguments about values and policies. In a debate about facts, gather and analyze research that has been done in a variety of settings and circumstances. Consider your own and your audience's experiences with, in this example, money as a motivator.

- **Debates About Values**   The topic "Was Michelangelo the greatest of all artists?" directs debaters to justify a belief, attitude, or value. Many debates include questions about values and then progress to arguments about outcomes and plans. Find expert opinions and examples that demonstrate why the object/person in the topic can be judged as right or wrong, good or bad, moral or immoral, or best or worst.

- **Debates About the Future**   The topic "Will nanotechnology dominate twenty-first-century science?" directs debaters to make judgments about the future based on today's facts and values. Make sure that you understand what is happening in the present and seek the opinions of futurist experts who support your position.

- **Debates About Policies**   The topic "Should intercollegiate athletics be abolished at our college?" directs debaters to take a pro or con position on a proposed plan of action. Establish whether there is a significant problem and whether a change is needed to solve the problem or reduce the harms. Consider the implications of change and whether the new policy will result in significant advantages or disadvantages.

Debate strategies   Debate strategies are as numerous as debaters and debate topics. What works in one debate may be ineffective in another, depending on the purpose, audience, logistics, occasion, and topic. At the same time, there are some basic strategies that can be useful in almost any debate situation in which two speakers debate questions about facts, values, the future, and proposed policies.

In order to win, debaters must seek, gather, and select strong evidence to support their argumentative positions.

For example, both sides in a policy debate would have to research a whole series of questions on a topic such as "Intercollegiate athletics should be abolished at our college": How much money is spent on intercollegiate athletics? What percentage of college athletes fail to complete college? How much money is generated by college sports for colleges? Do students choose colleges based on the existence or success of college athletic programs? Would alumni contributions decrease if colleges dropped intercollegiate athletics?

Regardless of whether you take the pro or con position in a debate, you can enlist a variety of argumentative strategies to support your position or to refute arguments made by the opposition. Answering the following questions about an argument's claim, evidence, reasoning, refutation, language, and delivery can help you strengthen your own position and weaken an opponent's case.

1. **Claim:** What is your position on a particular topic or issue? Are you trying to prove that something is true (a claim of fact), that some is worthwhile (a claim of value), that something will happen (a claim about the future), or that something should be changed (a claim of policy)? Can you express your claim in a clear statement?

2. **Evidence:** Can you support your claims with valid evidence? Is the source of the evidence competent, credible, and unbiased? Is the evidence consistent with other evidence? Is the evidence relevant to the argument?

3. **Reasoning:** Have good reasons been given to justify your opponent's claims? Are examples relevant, sufficient in number, and typical? Do alleged causes really produce the effect? Are there other causes that produce the same effect?

4. **Refutation:** What are the weaknesses in your opponent's arguments? Can you deny or minimize the person's claims with valid evidence? Can you demonstrate the disadvantages that will result if your opponent's plan is adopted? Can you suggest a better way to solve the problem?

5. **Language:** Is your opponent's language ambiguous or unclear? Do you or your opponent use loaded, emotionally charged language to establish a point without evi-

dence or proof? Are you or your opponent using big words and fancy phrases to hide poor argumentation?

6. **Delivery:** How persuasive is your speaking style? Are you clear and expressive? Do you appear well prepared and confident?

We debate in our homes, we debate at work, and we analyze public debates to make critical decisions about our communities and nation. Debate is an art and craft that cannot be mastered by memorizing a simple set of rules and questions. Engaging in classroom debate, however, provides a way of learning how to advocate an idea and defend yourself against a challenge. Thus, learning to debate can also help you succeed well beyond the college classroom.

 KEY POINTS

Tips for Debaters

- Clarify your position before you begin developing your "case." What kind of decision or judgment are you seeking from your listeners?

- Search for and use the best evidence you can find to support your position. You can lose a debate if your opponent identifies flaws or biases in your evidence.

- Be prepared to speak impromptu. Try to anticipate what the other debater(s) will say. If, however, your opponent catches you off guard, be prepared to think and respond on your feet.

- Take notes when your opponent speaks and try to respond to each of the arguments you have heard.

- Make sure that you give yourself enough time to reestablish your own arguments after refuting what your opponent has said.

- Always treat your opponent ethically and with extreme courtesy. This is a learning experience, not a war.

Unit 2

Keys to Style, Grammar, and ESL

Part 11

The 5 C's of Style

217

Sometimes listeners may daydream or doze off during a presentation—even when ideas are well researched and well organized. Such reactions may happen when audience members are bored or distracted by inappropriate words, too many words, uninspired words, or sentences constructed without interesting variations in words. As you prepare your presentation, follow the five C's of style to make your presentation more engaging and interesting.

35 The First C: Cut

Most presentations can be improved and even cut to half their original length if you focus on stating your essential ideas and expressing them succinctly. Examine your presentation for any unnecessary material, whether ideas, sentences, phrases, or individual words.

35a Cut wordiness

Say something only once and in the best possible place.

▶ The Lilly Library ~~contains many rare books. The books in the library are~~ carefully preserved, ~~The~~
 s
 ~~library also houses a manuscript collection~~.
 many rare books and manuscripts
 ^

 director of
▶ Stephen Spielberg, ~~who has directed~~ the movie ~~that has been~~ described as the best war movie ever made, ~~is someone who~~ knows many politicians.

 T
▶ ~~What~~ they ~~do is~~ shop.

▶ California residents have voted to abolish bilingual education, ~~The main reason for their voting to abolish bilingual education was that~~ many children
 because
 ^
 were being placed indiscriminately into programs and kept there too long.

In addition, avoid words that simply repeat an idea expressed in another word in the same phrase: *basic* essentials, *true* facts, circle *around*. Steer clear of redundant pairs: *various and sundry, each and every.*

▶ The task took *diligence and* perseverance.

 has
▶ His surgeon *is a doctor* with a great deal of clinical experience. ^

35b Cut formulaic phrases

Replace wordy phrases with shorter or more direct expressions.

FORMULAIC	NOT FORMULAIC
at the present time	now
at this point in time	
in this day and age	
in today's society	

because of the fact that	because
due to the fact that	
are of the opinion that	believe
have the ability to	can
in spite of the fact that	although, despite
prior to	before
concerning the matter of	about

36 The Second C: Check for Action ("Who's Doing What?")

Employ vigorous sentences with vivid, expressive verbs rather than bland forms of the verb *be (be, am, is, are, was, were, being, been)* or verbs in the passive voice (see section **41g**). Use the subject and verb to tell your audience who (or what) is doing what.

36a Ask "Who's doing what?" about subject and verb

Let the subject of your sentence perform the action.

WORDY   **The mayor's approval of the new law was due to the voters' suspicion of the conceal-ment of campaign funds by his deputy.**

Ask "Who's doing what?"

SUBJECT	VERB
the mayor	approved
the voters	suspected
his deputy	had concealed

REVISED   **The mayor approved the new law because the voters suspected that his deputy had concealed campaign funds.**

36b   Use caution in beginning a sentence with *there* or *it*

Recasting a sentence that begins with *there* often makes the sentence leaner and more direct. Revise by using a verb that shows action and a subject that "does" the action.

WORDY   **There was a discussion of the health care system by the politicians.**

Who's doing what here?

REVISED   **The politicians discussed the health care system.**

WORDY   **It is clear that Baker admires Updike.**

REVISED   **Clearly, Baker admires Updike.**

In some languages, an *it* subject can be omitted. It must be included in English.

36c   Avoid unnecessary passive voice constructions

The passive voice tells what is done to the grammatical subject of the sentence ("The turkey *was cooked* too long"). Extensive use of the passive voice can make your style dull and wordy.

PASSIVE   **The problem will be discussed thoroughly by the committee.**

ACTIVE   **The committee will discuss the problem thoroughly.**

The passive voice is used frequently in scientific presentations because listeners are primarily interested in data, procedures, and results, not in who developed or produced them. In a scientific report, you are likely to hear, for example, "The rats were fed," not "The researchers fed the rats." (See section **41g** for more on the passive voice.)

37 The Third C: Connect

Coherent presentations are ones in which information that has been mentioned before is connected to new information in a smooth flow, not a series of grasshopperlike jumps.

37a Apply the principle of consistent subjects

Audiences need to have a way to connect the ideas beginning a sentence with what has gone before. When going from one sentence to the next, avoid jarring shifts of subjects.

JARRING
SHIFT
Memoirs are becoming increasingly popular. _Readers_ all over the continent are finding them appealing.

REVISED
Memoirs are becoming increasingly popular. _They_ appeal to readers all over the continent.

37b Connect with transitional words and expressions

The following words and expressions provide logical connections between sentences and paragraphs.

TRANSITIONAL WORDS AND EXPRESSIONS

Adding an idea: also, in addition, further, furthermore, moreover

Contrasting: however, nevertheless, nonetheless, on the other hand, in contrast, still, on the contrary, rather, conversely

Providing an alternative: instead, alternatively, otherwise

Showing similarity: similarly, likewise

Showing order of time or order of ideas: first, second, third (and so on), then, next, later, subsequently, meanwhile, previously, finally

Showing result: as a result, consequently, therefore, thus, hence, accordingly, for this reason

Affirming: of course, in fact, certainly, obviously, to be sure, undoubtedly, indeed

Giving examples: for example, for instance

Explaining: in other words, that is

Adding an aside: incidentally, by the way, besides

Summarizing: in short, generally, overall, all in all, in conclusion, above all

37c Vary the way you connect and combine your ideas

To express an idea, you have alternatives. Vary the methods you use to show the connections between ideas, as in the following examples:

▶ **Brillo pads work well. I don't give them as gifts.**

▶ **Brillo pads work well, but I don't give them as gifts.**

▶ **Although Brillo pads work well, I don't give them as gifts.**

▶ **Brillo pads work well; however, I don't give them as gifts.**

37d Connect ideas and paragraphs

In the written version of your speech, a new paragraph signals a shift to a new topic but not necessarily to one that is completely different. Use the following strategies to connect your ideas:

1. Read a draft of your presentation aloud. As you finish a paragraph, note what point you made in the paragraph. Then, at the end, check your flow and logic.

2. Refer to the main idea of the previous paragraph as you begin the next. After a paragraph on retirement, the next paragraph might begin like this: *Retirement is not the only reason for saving. Saving also provides a nest egg for the unexpected and the pleasurable.*

3. Use transitions such as *also, too, in addition, however, therefore,* and *as a result* to signal the logical connection between sections of your talk (see section **37b**).

38 The Fourth C: Commit

Audiences usually expect speakers to analyze and question their sources, to commit to an informed and interesting point of view (not necessarily to the dominant view), and to provide convincing reasons why that view is valid. Commitment means researching and considering an issue, assuming a critical stance, taking a position, and persuasively supporting that position. Audiences perceive committed speakers as highly credible because they demonstrate competence and dedication.

38a Commit to critical thinking

Critical thinking does not mean criticizing negatively. It means examining and analyzing information with an open mind. When you think critically, your presentation takes on your own voice, your own stance.

Do the following to develop your critical thinking skills as you prepare your presentation: Observe and remember details; write frequent journal entries on your observations, reading, and ideas; ask questions; look for assumptions and bias in the words of others; try to understand the reasoning behind viewpoints you disagree with; analyze and evaluate how arguments are presented.

38b Commit to a point of view

Use language that shows commitment to the point of view you develop through your critical thinking. When you are trying to persuade your audience to accept your point of view, avoid the language of ambivalence and indecisiveness evident in words and phrases like *maybe, perhaps, might, it could be, it could happen, it might seem,* and *it would appear.* Aim for language that reflects accountability and commitment: *as a result, consequently, of course, believe, need, demand, think, should, must.* Use language of commitment, however, only after you have thoroughly researched your topic and found the evidence convincing.

39 The Fifth C: Choose Vivid, Appropriate, and Inclusive Words

Word choice, or *diction,* contributes a great deal to the effect your presentation has on an audience. Do not give your listeners puzzles to solve.

39a Choose vivid and specific words

Choosing vivid words means avoiding clichés. Avoid sayings that have been heard too often, like *hit the nail on the head, crystal clear, better late than never,* and *easier said than done.* Use words that are vivid, descriptive, and specific. Provide details to create visual images for your listeners. General words such as *area, aspect, certain* ("a certain expression," for example), *circumstance, factor, kind, manner, nature, situation, nice,* and *thing* are vague and do not give an audience much information.

VAGUE
> **The girl in Kincaid's story "Girl" did many things often regarded as women's jobs.**
>
> [*Things* is a vague word.]

SPECIFIC
> **The girl in the story did many household chores often regarded as women's work: She washed the clothes, cooked, swept, set the table, and cleared away dishes.**

39b Avoid slang, regionalisms, and jargon

Slang   When you make a college presentation, your tone and diction can be informal but should not be overly colloquial. Avoid slang expressions such as *folks, guy, OK, okay, pretty good, hassle, kind of interesting/nice, too big of a deal, a lot of, lots of, a ways away.* Do not change your tone to signal to your listeners that you know an expression is inappropriate. Instead, revise.

> disgusting
> ▶ The working conditions were ~~"gross."~~

> well
> ▶ I did ~~real super~~ in my last job.

> defendant
> ▶ The jury returned the verdict that the ~~guy~~ was not guilty.

Regional language   Use regional and ethnic dialects in a presentation only when you are quoting someone directly: "Your car needs fixed," he advised. Otherwise, use standard forms.

> myself
> ▶ I bought ~~me~~ a camcorder.

> be able to
> ▶ She used to ~~could~~ run two miles, but now she's out of shape.

Jargon   Most areas of specialized work and study have their own technical words, which people outside those fields perceive as jargon. A sportscaster talking about baseball will, for instance, refer to *twinight doubleheaders, ERAs,* and *brushbacks.* A linguist discussing language will use terms like *phonemics, kinesics,* and *suprasegmentals.* If you know that your audience is familiar with the technical vocabulary of the field, specialized language is acceptable. Try to avoid jargon when speaking to a more general audience; if you must use technical terms, provide definitions that will make sense to your listeners.

39c Avoid biased and exclusionary language

Do not use divisive terms that reinforce stereotypes or belittle other people. Do not emphasize differences by separating society into *we* to refer to people like you and *they* or *these people* to refer to people different from you. Use *we* only to be truly inclusive of yourself and all your listeners. Be aware, too, of terms that are likely to offend. You don't have to be excessive in your zeal to be PC ("politically correct"), using *underachieve* for *fail,* or *vertically challenged* for *short,* but do your best to avoid alienating your audience.

Gender   The writer of a speech edited the following sentence to avoid gender bias in the perception of women's roles and achievements.

▶ ~~Mrs. John~~ Andrea Harrison, ~~married to a real estate tycoon and herself the bubbly, blonde~~ chief executive of a successful computer company, has expanded the business overseas.

Choice of words can reveal gender bias, too.

AVOID	USE
actress	actor
authoress	author
chairman	chairperson
female astronaut	astronaut
forefathers	ancestors
foreman	supervisor
mailman	mail carrier
male nurse	nurse

man, mankind (meaning any human being)	person, people, our species, human beings, humanity
manmade	synthetic
policeman, policewoman	police officer
salesman	sales representative, salesclerk
veterans and their wives	veterans and their spouses

With the use of pronouns, too, avoid the stereotyping that occurs by assigning gender roles to professions, such as *he* for a doctor or lawyer, and *she* for a nurse or a secretary.

► Before a surgeon can operate, he ^or she^ must know every detail of the patient's history.

However, often it is better to avoid the *he* or *she* issue by recasting the sentence or using a plural noun or pronoun.

► Before operating, a surgeon must know every detail of the patient's history.

► Before surgeons can operate, they must know every detail of the patient's history.

(See section **43c** for more on pronouns and gender.)

Race and place   Name a person's race only when it is relevant.

► Attending the meeting were three doctors and an ~~Asian~~ computer programmer.

Use the names people prefer for their racial or ethnic affiliation. Consider, for example, that *black* and *African American* are preferred terms; *Asian* is preferred to *Oriental.* Be careful, too, with the way you refer to countries and continents; the Americas include both North and South America. Avoid stereotyping people according to where they come from. Some British people may be stiff and formal, but not all are. Not all Germans eat sausage and drink beer; not all North Americans carry cameras and wear plaid shorts.

Age   Avoid derogatory, condescending, or disrespectful terms associated with age. Refer to a person's age or condition neutrally, if at all: not *well-preserved little old lady* but *woman in her eighties* or just *woman*.

Politics   Words referring to politics are full of connotations. The word *liberal*, for instance, has been used with positive and negative connotations in various election campaigns. Take care with words like *radical, left-wing, right-wing,* and *moderate.* Are you identifying with one group and implicitly criticizing other groups?

Religion   An old edition of an encyclopedia referred to "devout Catholics" and "fanatical Muslims." The new edition refers to both Catholics and Muslims as "devout," thus eliminating biased language. Examine your use of words that sound derogatory or exclusionary—such as *cult* or *fundamentalist*—and terms—such as *these people*—that emphasize difference, or even the word *we* when it implies that all your listeners share (or should share) your beliefs.

Health and abilities   Avoid terms like *confined to a wheelchair* and *victim* (of a disease) so as not to focus on difference and disability. Instead, use *someone who uses a wheelchair* and *person with* (a disease). Do not draw unnecessary attention to a disability or an illness.

Sexual orientation   Refer to a person's sexual orientation only if the information is necessary to your content. To say that someone was "defended by a homosexual lawyer" is gratuitous when describing a case of stock market fraud but is more relevant in a case of discrimination against homosexuals. Since you will not necessarily know your audience's sexual orientation, do not assume it is the same as your own, and beware of using terms and making comments that might offend.

The word **normal**   One word to be especially careful about using is *normal*—when referring to your own health, ability, or sexual orientation. Some listeners could justifiably find that offensive.

Part 12

Basic Grammar

229

40   Sentence Snarls

Avoid or edit sentences with structural inconsistencies that
will force your audience to struggle to untangle the meaning.

40a Tangles: Mixed constructions, faulty
comparisons, and convoluted syntax

Mixed constructions   A mixed construction is a sentence with parts incompatible in grammar and meaning.
The sentence begins one way and then veers off in an unexpected direction. Check that the subject and verb in your
sentence are clear and work together. Do not use a pronoun
to restate the subject (see section **47a**).

▶ ~~In the~~ The excerpt by Heilbrun and the story by Gould
are similar.

▶ ~~By~~ Sleeping late can create tension with parents.

▶ Dinah Macy ~~she~~ got Lyme disease when she was ten.

When you start a sentence with an adverb clause (beginning
with a word like *when, if, because,* or *since*), make sure you
follow that clause with an independent clause. An adverb
clause cannot serve as the subject of a verb.

▶ ~~Because she swims~~ Swimming every day does not guarantee she
is healthy.

▶ ~~When~~ Trading a player ~~is traded~~ often causes family
problems.

Faulty comparisons   When you make comparisons,
your audience needs to know clearly what you are comparing to what. (See also section **43a** for faulty comparisons with
personal pronouns.)

FAULTY COMPARISON	**Like Wallace Stevens, her job strikes readers as unexpected for a poet.** [It is not her job that is like the poet Wallace Stevens; her job is like his job.]
REVISED	**Like Wallace Stevens, she holds a job that strikes readers as unexpected for a poet.**

Convoluted syntax   Avoid sentences that ramble on to such an extent that they become tangled. Make sure they have clear subjects, verbs, and connections between clauses.

TANGLED   **The way I feel about getting what you want is that when there is a particular position or item that you want to try to get to do your best and not give up because if you give up you have probably missed your chance of succeeding.**

POSSIBLE   **To get what you want, keep trying.**
REVISION

40b Misplaced modifiers

Keep words, phrases, and clauses that provide adjectival or adverbial information next to the sentence elements that they modify. That is, avoid *misplaced modifiers.*

Take care with words such as **only.**   Place a word such as *only, even, just, nearly, merely,* or *simply* immediately before the word it modifies. The meaning of a sentence can change significantly as the position of *only* changes, so careful placement is important.

▶ *Only* the journalist began to investigate the incident.
   [no one else]

▶ The journalist *only* began to investigate the incident.
   [but didn't finish]

▶ The journalist began to investigate *only* the incident.
   [nothing else]

Place a phrase or clause close to the word it modifies.

MISPLACED   **They sent a present to their mother wrapped in silver paper.** [This sentence gives the impression that the mother was wrapped in silver paper.]

POSSIBLE   **They sent their mother a present wrapped in**
REVISIONS   **silver paper.**

They sent a present wrapped in silver paper to their mother.

Consider the case for splitting an infinitive. You split an infinitive when you place a word or phrase between *to* and the verb. *The New Oxford Dictionary of English* finds the use of split infinitives "both normal and useful," as in "To boldly go where no man has gone before . . ." (*Star Trek*). However, such splitting may irritate your audience, especially when a clumsy sentence is the result.

─── split infinitive *(to inform)* ───

▶ We want to sincerely, honestly, and in confidence

inform you of our plans for expansion.

40c Dangling modifiers

An adjectival modifier that is not grammatically linked to the noun or phrase it is intended to describe is said to *dangle*. An *-ing* or *-ed* modifier beginning a sentence needs to tell about the subject of the sentence.

DANGLING **Walking into the house, the telephone rang.**

[Who was walking? The sentence says it was the telephone.]

REVISED **Walking into the house, we heard the telephone ring.**

While we were walking into the house, the telephone rang.

40d Shifts

Do not shift abruptly from statements to commands.

They should ask
▶ Students need to be more aggressive. ~~Ask~~ more
questions and challenge the professors.

Do not shift from indirect to direct quotation, with or without quotation marks.

▶ The client told us that he wanted to sign the lease

asked us to
and ~~would we~~ prepare the papers.

Do not shift tenses unnecessarily.

▶ Some lawyers advance their careers by honest hard work. Others represented~~ famous clients.

Do not shift point of view. Be consistent in using first, second, or third person pronouns. (See section **43d**.)

▶ We all need a high salary to live in a city because
    we
    ~~you~~ have to spend so much on rent and

    transportation.

40e Faulty predication

Do not use a subject and predicate (verb and object or complement) that do not make logical sense together.

            Building
▶ ~~The decision to build~~ an elaborate extension onto the train station made all the trains arrive late. [It was not the decision that delayed the trains; the building of the extension did.]

▶ According to the guidelines, ~~people in~~ dilapidated buildings will be demolished this year. [The buildings, not people, will be demolished.]

40f Definitions and reasons: Avoiding *is when* and *the reason is because*

When you define a term, avoid using *is when* or *is where* (or *was when, was where*).

▶ A tiebreak in tennis *is ~~where~~* there's a final game to decide a set.

In discussing reasons, avoid *the reason is because.* . . . Grammatically, an adverb clause beginning with *because* cannot follow the verb *be*. Instead, use *the reason is that . . .* or recast the sentence.

FAULTY   *The reason* Venus Williams lost *is because* her opponent was serving so well.

POSSIBLE
REVISIONS   *The reason* Williams lost *is that* her oppo-
            nent was serving so well.

            Williams lost *because* her opponent was
            serving so well.

Note that Standard English requires *the reason (that)* and not
the reason why.

▶ The TV commentator explained the reason ~~why~~
Williams lost.

40g Lack of parallel structures

Balance your sentences by using similar grammatical constructions in each part.

NOT   The results of reform were that class size
PARALLEL   decreased, more multicultural courses,
           and being allowed to choose a pass/fail
           option.

PARALLEL   The results of reform were that class size
           decreased, more multicultural courses were
           offered, and students were allowed to
           choose a pass/fail option.

PARALLEL   The results of reform were a decrease in
           class size, an increase in the number of
           multicultural courses, and the introduction
           of a pass/fail option for students.

Use parallel structures in comparisons with *as* or *than* and in
lists.

     To drive
▶ ~~Driving~~ to Cuernavaca is as expensive as to take the
bus.

     Taking
▶ ~~To take~~ the bus is less comfortable than driving.

▶ Writing well demands the following: (1) planning

                               revising
your time, (2) paying attention to details, (3) ~~the need~~

~~for revision~~, and (4) proofreading.

40h Necessary words in compound structures and comparisons

Do not omit necessary words in compound structures.
If you omit a verb form from a compound verb, the remaining verb form must fit into each part of the compound; otherwise, you must use the complete verb form.

> tried
> ► He has always ‸and will always try to preserve his father's good ‸name in the community. [*Try* fits only with *will*, not with *has*.]

Do not omit necessary words in comparisons.

> as
> ► The volleyball captain is as competitive ‸or even more competitive than her teammates. [The comparative structures are *as competitive as* and *more competitive than*. Do not merge them.]

  Sometimes you create ambiguity for your audience if you omit the verb in the second part of a comparison.

> did
> ► He liked baseball more than his son‸. [Omitting *did* implies that he liked baseball more than he liked his son.]

41 Verbs
Identify a verb by checking that the base form (that is, the form found as a dictionary entry) fits one or more of these sentences. For example, *vary* will fit; *variety* will not.

They want to —————. It is going to —————.
They will —————. It will —————.

Verbs tell listeners what people or things do and are. Changes in form and tense can convey subtle distinctions, so use verbs with care.

41a Verb forms in Standard English

All verbs except *be* and modal verbs such as *must* and *can* (see section **41b**) have five forms. For *regular verbs*, the five forms follow a regular and predictable pattern. Once you know the base form, you can construct all the other forms by using the auxiliaries *be*, *do*, and *have*.

> Base form: the form in a dictionary; used in present tense or after *do* and modal verbs
>
> *-s* form: the third person singular form of the present tense
>
> *-ing* form: also known as the *present participle*; needs auxiliary verbs to form a complete verb phrase; can also appear in a phrase (*Looking* happy, she accepted the award) and as a noun (gerund—*Waiting* is boring)
>
> Past tense form: forms a complete verb; used without auxiliaries
>
> Past participle form: needs auxiliary verbs to form a complete verb phrase (*has selected, was selected*); can appear in a phrase (*the selected gifts; selected for her efficiency*)

For *be, do, have,* and modal verbs, see section **41b**.

REGULAR VERBS

BASE	–s	–Ing PRESENT PARTICIPLE	PAST TENSE	PAST PARTICIPLE
paint	paints	painting	painted	painted
smile	smiles	smiling	smiled	smiled

Irregular verbs do not use *-ed* to form the past tense and the past participle. See the following table for forms of irregular verbs, including the verb *be*.

IRREGULAR VERBS

BASE FORM	PAST TENSE	PAST PARTICIPLE
arise	arose	arisen
be	was/were	been
beat	beat	beaten
become	became	become
begin	began	begun
bend	bent	bent
bet	bet	bet (or betted)
bind	bound	bound
bite	bit	bitten

BASE FORM	PAST TENSE	PAST PARTICIPLE
bleed	bled	bled
blow	blew	blown
break	broke	broken
bring	brought	brought
build	built	built
burst	burst	burst
buy	bought	bought
catch	caught	caught
choose	chose	chosen
cling	clung	clung
come	came	come
cost	cost	cost
creep	crept	crept
cut	cut	cut
deal	dealt	dealt
dig	dug	dug
do	did	done
draw	drew	drawn
drink	drank	drunk
drive	drove	driven
eat	ate	eaten
fall	fell	fallen
feed	fed	fed
feel	felt	felt
fight	fought	fought
find	found	found
flee	fled	fled
fly	flew	flown
forbid	forbad(e)	forbidden
forget	forgot	forgotten
forgive	forgave	forgiven
freeze	froze	frozen
get	got	gotten, got
give	gave	given
go	went	gone
grind	ground	ground
grow	grew	grown
hang*	hung	hung
have	had	had

Hang in the sense of "put to death" is regular: *hang, hanged, hanged.*

BASE FORM	PAST TENSE	PAST PARTICIPLE
hear	heard	heard
hide	hid	hidden
hit	hit	hit
hold	held	held
hurt	hurt	hurt
keep	kept	kept
know	knew	known
lay	laid	laid (see also **41c**)
lead	led	led
leave	left	left
lend	lent	lent
let	let	let
lie	lay	lain (see also **41c**)
light	lit, lighted	lit, lighted
lose	lost	lost
make	made	made
mean	meant	meant
meet	met	met
put	put	put
quit	quit	quit
read	read	read
ride	rode	ridden
ring	rang	rung
rise	rose	risen (see also **41c**)
run	ran	run
say	said	said
see	saw	seen
seek	sought	sought
sell	sold	sold
send	sent	sent
set	set	set (see also **41c**)
shake	shook	shaken
shine	shone	shone
shoot	shot	shot
shrink	shrank	shrunk
shut	shut	shut
sing	sang	sung
sink	sank	sunk
sit	sat	sat (see also **41c**)
sleep	slept	slept

BASE FORM	PAST TENSE	PAST PARTICIPLE
slide	slid	slid
slit	slit	slit
speak	spoke	spoken
spend	spent	spent
spin	spun	spun
spit	spit, spat	spit
split	split	split
spread	spread	spread
spring	sprang	sprung
stand	stood	stood
steal	stole	stolen
stick	stuck	stuck
sting	stung	stung
stink	stank (or stunk)	stunk
strike	struck	struck, stricken
swear	swore	sworn
sweep	swept	swept
swim	swam	swum
swing	swung	swung
take	took	taken
teach	taught	taught
tear	tore	torn
tell	told	told
think	thought	thought
throw	threw	thrown
tread	trod	trodden, trod
understand	understood	understood
upset	upset	upset
wake	woke	waked, woken
wear	wore	worn
weave	wove	woven
weep	wept	wept
win	won	won
wind	wound	wound
wring	wrung	wrung
write	wrote	written

41b Verb forms after auxiliaries

An independent clause needs a *complete verb*. Verb forms such as the *-ing* form and the past participle are not complete because they do not show tense. They need auxiliary verbs to complete their meaning as a verb of a clause.

AUXILIARY VERBS	MODAL AUXILIARY VERBS	
do: does, do, did	will, would	shall, should
be: be, am, is, are, was, were, being, been	can, could	may, might, must
have: has, have, had		

Auxiliary verbs and modal auxiliary verbs can be used in combination. Whatever the combination, the verb form immediately following the final auxiliary or modal verb is fixed: base form, *-ing*, or past participle.

WHICH FORM SHOULD I USE?

1. After *do, does, did,* and the nine modal verbs—*will, would, can, could, shall, should, may, might,* and *must*—use the base form.

   ▶ He *might stay.*   ▶ They *must eat* soon.

   ▶ *Did* she *leave*?   ▶ He *could try.*

2. After *has, have,* and *had,* use the past participle.

   ▶ It *has snowed.*

   ▶ They should *have gone* (not "They should have went").

   ▶ They *had eaten* when I arrived.

   In speech, we run sounds together. In any written version of your speech, however, edit carefully for the word *of* in place of *have.*

           have
   ▶ She should ~~of~~ left that job last year.

   The pronunciation of the contraction *should've* is probably responsible for the nonstandard form *should of.* Edit carefully for the appearance of the word *of* in place of *have* in verb phrases.

3. After *be, am, is, are, was, were,* and *been,* use the *-ing* form for active voice verbs.

   ▶ She *is taking* her driving test.   ▶ You *were watching.*

   ▶ He might have *been driving.*   ▶ They could *be jogging.*

4. After *be, am, is, are, was, were, been,* and *being,* use the past participle for passive voice (see section **41g**).

► They *were taken* to a tropical island for their anniversary.

► The faucet should *be fixed*.

► The passage might have *been plagiarized*.

► The department is *being reorganized*.

41c Verbs commonly confused

You may need to give special attention to the forms of certain verbs that are similar but have different meanings. Some verbs can or should be followed by a direct object; these are called *transitive verbs*. Some verbs, however, can never be followed by a direct object; these are called *intransitive verbs*.

1. *rise:* to get up, ascend (intransitive)

   raise: to lift, to cause to rise (transitive)

BASE	–s	–ing	PAST TENSE	PAST PARTICIPLE
rise	rises	rising	rose	risen
raise	raises	raising	raised	raised

2. *sit:* to be seated (intransitive)

   set: to put or place (transitive)

sit	sits	sitting	sat	sat
set	sets	setting	set	set

3. *lie:* to recline (intransitive)

   lay: to put or place (transitive)

lie	lies	lying	lay	lain
lay	lays	laying	laid	laid

   ► The sun *rose* at 5:55 A.M. today.

   ► She *raised* the blind and peeked out.

   ► He *sat* on the wooden chair.

▶ She *set* the vase in the middle of the shelf.

    lay
▶ I ~~laid~~ down for half an hour.

    lying
▶ I was ~~laying~~ down when you called.

    Lay
▶ ~~Lie~~ the map on the floor.

In addition, note the verb *lie* ("to say something untrue"), which is intransitive:

BASE	*–s*	*–ing*	PAST TENSE	PAST PARTICIPLE
lie	lies	lying	lied	lied

▶ He *lied* when he said he had won three trophies.

41d Verb tenses

Tenses and time are closely related. Verbs change form to indicate present or past time. Auxiliary verbs (*be*, *do*, and *have*) are used with the main verb to convey completed actions (perfect forms), actions in progress (progressive forms), and actions that are completed by some specified time or event and that emphasize the length of time in progress (perfect progressive forms).

Simple present   Use the simple present tense for the following purposes:

1. To make a generalization

   ▶ We *turn* the clocks ahead every April.

2. To indicate an activity that happens habitually or repeatedly

   ▶ He *works* for Sony.

   ▶ They *take* vacations in Puerto Rico.

3. To express future time in dependent clauses (clauses beginning with subordinating words such as *if, when, before, after, until, as soon as*) when *will* is used in the independent clause

   ▶ When they *arrive,* the meeting will begin.

4. To discuss literature and the arts (called the *literary present*) even though the work was written in the past or the author is no longer alive

   ▶ In *Zami,* Audre Lorde *describes* how a librarian *introduces* her to the joys of reading.

   However, in your own narrative, use past tenses to tell about past actions.

   ▶ Then the candidate ~~walks~~ walked up to the crowd and ~~kisses~~ kissed all the babies.

5. To refer to ideas of mental activity, appearance, inclusion and possession

   ▶ They ~~are possessing~~ possess different behavior patterns.

   ▶ She believes in ghosts.

   Do not use progressive (-ing) forms with verbs such as *believe, smell, prefer, understand, possess, seem, want,* and *contain.*

Present progressive Use the present progressive to indicate an action in progress at the moment of speaking or writing.

   ▶ The war *is escalating.*

Present perfect and present perfect progressive Use the present perfect (*has* or *have* followed by a past participle) in the following instances:

1. To indicate that an action that occurred at some unstated time in the past is related to present time

   ▶ They *have worked* in New Mexico, so they know its laws.

2. To indicate that an action that began in the past continues to the present

   ▶ They *have worked* for the same company ever since I have known them.

However, if you state the exact time when something occurred and ended, use the simple past tense, not the present perfect.

▶ They ~~have~~ worked in Arizona four years ago.

3. To report scientific research results in APA style

▶ Feynmann *has shown* that science can be fun.

Use the present perfect progressive when you indicate the length of time an action is in progress up to the present time.

▶ They *have been dancing* for three hours. [This sentence implies that they are still dancing.]

Simple past   Use the simple past tense when you specify exactly when an event occurred or when you illustrate a general principle with a specific incident in the past.

▶ She *married* him last month.

▶ Some bilingual schools offer intensive instruction in English. My sister *went* to a bilingual school where she *studied* English for two hours every day.

When the sequence of past events is indicated with words like *before* or *after,* use the simple past for both events.

▶ She *knew* how to write her name before she *went* to school.

Use past tenses in an indirect quotation introduced by a past tense verb.

▶ Our lawyer *told* us that the meetings *were* over.

Past progressive   Use the past progressive for an activity in progress over time or at a specified point in the past.

▶ He *was lifting* weights when I called.

Past perfect and past perfect progressive   Use the past perfect or past perfect progressive when one past event was completed before another past event occurred.

▶ Ben *had cooked* the whole meal by the time Sam arrived. [Two events occurred: Ben cooked the meal; then Sam arrived.]

▶ He *had been cooking* for three hours when his sister finally offered to help. [An event in progress—cooking—was interrupted in the past.]

▶ The professor announced that she *had revised* the syllabus.

41e Past tense and past participle forms

With regular verbs, both the past tense form and the past participle form end in *-ed*. Your audience, however, will not necessarily hear an *-ed* ending, particularly when it blends into the next sound. Remember to include the ending in a written version of your speech.

▶ They wash~ed~ two baskets of laundry last night.

Standard English requires the *-ed* ending in the following instances:

1. To form the past tense of a regular verb

   ▶ He ask~ed~ about a promotion.

2. To form the past participle of a regular verb for use with the auxiliary *has, have,* or *had* in the active voice or with forms of *be* (*am, is, are, was, were, be, being, been*) in the passive voice (see section **41g**)

   ▶ She has work~ed~ for the mayor for a long time. [Active]

   ▶ The work will be finish~ed~ soon. [Passive]

3. To form a past participle for use as an adjective

   ▶ Put in some chop~ped~ meat.

   ▶ The frighten~ed~ boy ran away.

   ▶ I was surprise~d~ when I read how many awards he had won.

Note: The following *-ed* forms are used after forms of *be*:

concerned, confused, depressed, divorced, embarrassed, married, prejudiced, satisfied, scared, supposed (to), surprised, used (to), worried. You must include the *-d* ending in any written version of your speech. (See also section **46e**.)

d
► He use to play third base; now he pitches.
      ^

d
► They were suppose to call their parents when they
          ^
arrived.

Do not confuse the past tense and past participle forms of irregular verbs. A past tense form occurs alone as a complete verb, and a past participle form must be used with a *have* or *be* auxiliary.

drank
► He ~~drunk~~ too much last night.

did
► She ~~done~~ her best.

gone
► You could have ~~went~~ alone.

rung
► The bell was ~~rang~~ five times.

 41f Verbs in conditional sentences, wishes, requests, demands, and recommendations

Conditions When *if* or *unless* is used to introduce a dependent clause, the sentence expresses a condition. Note the four types of conditional sentences; two refer to actual or possible situations, and two refer to speculative or hypothetical situations. The following box gives examples of the four types of conditional sentences.

KEY POINTS

Verb Tenses in Conditional Sentences

MEANING EXPRESSED	*IF* CLAUSE	INDEPENDENT CLAUSE
1. Fact	Simple present	Simple present

► If people *earn* more, they *spend* more.

(continued)

(continued)

2. Prediction/ possibility	Simple present	*will, can, should, might* + base form

▶ If you *turn* left here, you *will end up* in Mississippi.

3. Speculation about present or future	Simple past *or* subjunctive *were*	*would, could, should, might* + base form

▶ If he *had* a cell phone, he *would use* it.

▶ If she *were* my lawyer, I *might win* the case.

4. Speculation about past	Past perfect (*had* + past participle)	*would have* *could have* *should have* *might have* } + past participle

▶ If they *had saved* the diaries, they *could have sold* them.

Note: In Standard English, use *would* only in the independent clause, not in the conditional clause. However, *would* occurs frequently in the conditional clause in informal conversation.

showed
▶ If the fish fry committee ~~would show~~ more initiative, more people might attend the events.

had
▶ If I ~~would have~~ heard their answer, I would have been angry.

Wishes   For a present wish—about something that has not happened and is therefore hypothetical and imaginary—use the past tense or the subjunctive *were* in the dependent clause. For a wish about the past, use the past perfect: *had* + past participle.

A WISH ABOUT THE PRESENT

▶ I wish I *had* your attitude.

▶ I wish that Shakespeare *were* still alive.

A WISH ABOUT THE PAST

▶ Some of us wish that the strike *had* never *occurred*.

▶ He wishes that he *had bought* a lottery ticket.

Requests, demands, and recommendations After certain verbs such as *request, command, insist, demand, move* (in the sense of "propose"), *propose,* and *urge,* use the base form of the verb, regardless of the person and number of the subject.

▶ I suggest that this rule *be* changed.

▶ He insisted that she *hand in* the report.

41g Passive voice

In the active voice, the grammatical subject is the doer of the action, and the sentence gives a straightforward display of "who is doing what." The passive voice tells what *is done to* the subject of the sentence. The person or thing doing the action may or may not be mentioned but is always implied: "My car was repaired" (by somebody at the garage).

ACTIVE

   ┌── subject ──┐ active voice verb ┌── direct object ──┐
▶ **Alice Walker**   **wrote**   *The Color Purple*.

PASSIVE

                     passive voice
  ┌───── subject ─────┐ ┌── verb ──┐ ┌── doer or agent ──┐
▶ *The Color Purple* **was written** **by Alice Walker.**

To form the passive voice, use a form of the verb *be* followed by a past participle. Do not overuse the passive voice. A general rule is to use the passive voice only when the doer in your sentence is unknown or is unimportant or when you want to keep subjects consistent (see section **37a**).

▶ The puppies are rare. Four of them *will be sold* to a breeder.

Use the passive voice *only* with verbs that are transitive. Intransitive verbs such as *happen* and *occur* are not used in the passive voice.

▶ The ceremony ~~was~~ happened yesterday.

42 Subject-Verb Agreement

In Standard English, singular subjects take singular verbs, and plural subjects take plural verbs.

42a Basic principles

When you use the present tense, the subject and verb must agree in person (first, second, or third) and number (singular or plural). The ending *-s* is added to nouns and verbs in English, but in very different contexts.

 KEY POINTS

Two Key Points About Agreement

1. Follow the *one -s rule.* You can either put an *-s* on the noun to make it plural or put an *-s* on the verb to make it singular (note the irregular forms *is* and *has*). An *-s* added to both subject and verb is not Standard English.

   FAULTY AGREEMENT   **My friends comes over every Saturday.**

   POSSIBLE REVISIONS   **My friend comes over every Saturday.**
   (one friend)

                    My friends come over every Saturday.
   (more than one)

2. Do not drop a necessary *-s*.

   ▶ His sister wear^s gold jewelry.

   ▶ The book on my desk describe^s life in Tahiti.

42b Words between subject and verb

When words come between the subject and the verb, find the verb and ask "Who?" or "What?" about it to determine exactly what the subject is. Ignore any intervening words.

▶ **Her collection of baseball cards is much admired.**

[What is admired? The subject, *collection,* is singular.]

▶ **The government's proposals about preserving the environment cause controversy.**

[What things cause controversy? The subject, *proposals,* is plural.]

Do not be confused by intervening words ending in -*s,* such as *always* and *sometimes.* The -*s* ending still must appear on a present tense verb if the subject is singular.

▶ **His assistant always make mistakes.**

Phrases introduced by *as well as, along with,* and *in addition to* that come between the subject and the verb do not cause a change in the verb.

▶ **His daughter, as well as his two sons, want him to move nearby.**

42c Subject after verb

When the subject comes after the verb in the sentence, the subject and verb must still agree.

1. *Questions*   In a question, the auxiliary verb agrees with the subject, which follows the verb.

   ▶ *Does* **the editor agree to the changes?**

   ┌────────── plural subject ──────────┐
   ▶ *Do* **the editor and the production manager agree to the changes?**

2. *Initial* **here** *or* **there**   When a sentence begins with *here* or *there,* the verb agrees with the subject, which follows the verb.

   ▶ **There** *is* **a reason to rejoice.**
   ▶ **There** *are* **many reasons to rejoice.**

It does not follow the same pattern as *here* and *there*. Sentences beginning with *it* always take a singular verb.

▶ It *is* hundreds of miles away.

3. *Inverted order*   When a sentence begins not with the subject but with a phrase preceding the verb, the verb still agrees with the subject, which follows it.

```
                              plural
  ┌── prepositional phrase ──┐ verb ┌── plural subject ──┐
```
▶ **In front of the library sit two stone lions.**

42d Tricky subjects

1. **Each** *and* **every**   *Each* and *every* may seem to indicate more than one, but grammatically they are singular words used with a singular verb.

   ▶ **Each of the cakes *has* a different frosting.**

   ▶ **Every conceivable type of problem *arises* in the first few weeks.**

2. **-ing** *words*   With a noun formed from an *-ing* verb (called a *gerund*) as a subject, always use a singular verb form.

   ▶ **Playing the piano in front of a crowd *causes* anxiety.**

3. *Singular nouns ending in* **-s**   Some nouns end in *-s* (*news, politics, economics, physics, mathematics, statistics*), but they are not plural. Use them with a singular verb.

   ▶ **Politics *is* dirty business.**   ▶ **The news *has been* bad.**

4. *Phrases of time, money, and weight*   When the subject is regarded as one unit, use a singular verb.

   ▶ **Five hundred dollars *is* too much to pay.**

5. *Uncountable nouns*   An uncountable noun (such as *furniture, money, equipment, food, advice, happiness, honesty, information, knowledge*) encompasses all the items in its class. An uncountable noun does not have a plural

form and is always followed by a singular verb (see section **45a**).

▶ **The information found in the newspapers *is* not always accurate.**

6. **One of** *One of* is followed by a plural noun and a singular verb form.

▶ *One of* **her friends *loves* to tango.**

7. **The number of** The phrase *the number of* is followed by a plural noun (the object of the preposition *of*) and a singular verb form.

▶ **The number of reasons *is* growing.**

However, with *a number of,* meaning "several," use a plural verb.

▶ **A number of reasons *are* listed in the letter.**

8. *A title of a work or a word used to refer to the word itself* Use a singular verb with a title of a work or a word used to refer to the word itself.

▶ <u>Cats</u> *was* **entertaining.**

▶ **In her story, the word <u>yikes</u> *appears* five times.**

42e Collective nouns

Generally, use a singular verb form with a collective noun like *class, government, family, jury, committee, group, couple,* or *team.*

▶ **My family *goes* on vacation every year.**

A plural verb form can be used, though, if you wish to emphasize differences among the individuals or if the group is thought of as individuals.

▶ **The jury *are* from a variety of backgrounds.**

You can also avoid the issue by revising the sentence.

▶ **The members of the jury *are* from a variety of backgrounds.**

However, with collective nouns like *police, poor, elderly,* and *young,* always use plural verbs.

▶ The elderly *deserve* our respect.

42f Compound subjects

With **and** When a subject has two or more parts joined by *and*, treat the subject as plural and use a plural verb form.

▶ His daughter and his son *want* him to move to Florida.

However, if the two joined parts refer to a single person or thing, use a singular verb.

▶ The restaurant's chef and owner *makes* good fajitas.

With **each** *or* **every** When *each* or *every* is used with a subject that has two or more parts joined by *and*, use a singular verb.

▶ Every toy and game *has* to be put away.
▶ Each plate and glass *looks* new.

With **or** *or* **nor** With compound subjects joined by *or* or *nor*, the verb agrees with the part of the subject nearer to it.

▶ Her sister or her parents *plan* to visit her next week.
▶ Neither her parents nor her sister *drives* a station wagon.

42g Indefinite pronouns

Use a singular verb with the following indefinite pronoun subjects:

> someone, somebody, something
> anyone, anybody, anything
> no one, nobody, nothing
> everyone, everybody, everything
> each, either, neither, one

▶ Neither of his parents *knows* where he is.
▶ Someone *has* been sitting in my chair.

▶ **Each computer** *has* **a modem.**

▶ **Everyone** *agrees* **with you.**

For agreement with *one of*, see section **42d**, item 6.

42h Quantity words

Quantity words can be used alone or to modify a noun. Some are singular; some are plural; some can be used to indicate either singular or plural, depending on the noun to which they refer.

WORDS EXPRESSING QUANTITY	
WITH SINGULAR NOUNS AND VERBS	WITH PLURAL NOUNS AND VERBS
much	many
(a) little	(a) few (see p. 299)
a great deal (of)	several
a large amount (of)	a large number (of)
less	fewer
another	both

▶ **Much** *has* **been accomplished.**

▶ **Much progress still** *needs* **to be made.**

▶ **Many** *have* **gained from the recent stock market rise.**

▶ **Many activities** *let* **everyone participate.**

▶ **Few of his fans** *are* **buying his recent book.**

You will hear *less* used in place of *fewer* in informal conversation, but in a formal speech, use only *fewer* to refer to a plural word.

▶ **More** *movies* **have been made this year than last, but** *fewer have* **made money.**

The following quantity words can be used with both singular and plural nouns and verbs: *all, any, half (of), more, most, no, none, other, part (of), some.*

▶ **You gave me some information. More** *is* **necessary.**

▶ **You gave me some facts. More** *are* **needed.**

42i Relative clauses *(who, which, that)*

Determine subject-verb agreement within a relative (adjective) clause by asking whether the antecedent of a subject relative pronoun *(who, which, that)* is singular or plural.

▶ **The book that *has been* at the top of the bestseller list for weeks gives advice about health.** [*Book* is the antecedent of *that*.]

▶ **The books that *have been* near the top of the bestseller list for a few weeks give advice about making money.**

[*Books* is the antecedent of *that*.]

For more on relative pronouns, see section **43e**.

43 Pronouns

A pronoun is a word that refers to or replaces a noun.

▶ **Jack's hair is so long that *it* hangs over *his* collar.**

[*It* refers to *hair*; *his* refers to *Jack*.]

43a Personal pronouns

Personal pronouns have different forms to express person (first, second, or third), number (singular or plural), and function in a clause (case).

KEY POINTS

Forms of Personal Pronouns

	SUBJECT	OBJECT	POSSESSIVE (BEFORE A NOUN)	POSSESSIVE (WITH NO FOLLOWING NOUN)
First person singular	I	me	my	mine
First person plural	we	us	our	ours
Second person singular and plural	you	you	your	yours
Third person singular	he	him	his	his
	she	her	her	hers
	it	it	its	its *(rare)*
Third person plural	they	them	their	theirs

With an infinitive   Use an object pronoun after a verb used with an infinitive. When a sentence has only one object, this principle is easy to apply.

▶ The dean wanted *him* to lead the procession.

Difficulties occur with compound objects.

　　　　　　　　　him and me
▶ The dean wanted ~~he and I~~ to lead the procession.

In a compound subject or object with and: I *or* me; he *or* him?   To decide which pronoun form to use with a compound subject or object, mentally recast the sentence with only the pronoun in the subject or object position.

　　　　　　I
▶ Jenny and ~~me~~ went to the movies.

　　[If *Jenny* is dropped, you would use *I went to the movies,* not *me went to the movies.* Here you need the subject form, *I.*]

　　　　　　　　　　　　　　me
▶ They told my brother and *I* to wait in line.

　　[If *my brother* is dropped, you would want *They told me to wait in line.* You need the object form, *me.*]

After a preposition   After a preposition, use an object form.

　　　　　　　me
▶ Between you and *I*, the company is in serious trouble.

After a linking verb   Use the subject form of the pronoun after a linking verb, such as *be.*

　　　　　　　　　　　　　　　　　　he
▶ Sam confessed that the cause of trouble was ~~him~~.

　　[Many would choose to revise this sentence to sound less formal: "Sam confessed that he was the cause of the trouble."]

In appositive phrases   When using a pronoun in an appositive phrase (one that gives more specific information about a preceding noun), determine whether the noun to which the pronoun refers functions as subject or as object.

▶ The supervisor praised only two employees, Ramon
and ~~I~~.
  me

▶ Only two employees, Ramon and ~~me,~~ received a
bonus.
  I

We *or* **us** *before a noun*   Use *us* when the noun phrase is
the direct object of a verb or the object of a preposition, *we*
when it is the subject.

▶ The singer waved to ~~we~~ fans.
  us

▶ ~~Us~~ fans have decided to form a club.
  We

In comparisons   In comparisons with *than* and *as*, decide
on the subject or object form of the pronoun by mentally
completing the comparison.

▶ She is certainly not more intelligent than I. [. . . than I
am.]

▶ Jack and Sally work together; Jack sees his boss more
than she.   [. . . more than she does.]

▶ Jack and Sally work together; Jack sees his boss more
than her.   [. . . more than he sees Sally.]

Possessive pronoun before an **-ing** *form*   Generally,
use a possessive pronoun before an *-ing* verb form used as a
noun (a *gerund*).

▶ We appreciate *your* participating in the auction.

▶ *Their* winning the marathon surprised us all.

Sometimes, though, the *-ing* form is not used as a noun.
In that case, the pronoun preceding the *-ing* form should be
the object form.

▶ We saw *them* giving the runners foil wraps.

No apostrophe with possessive pronouns   Even
though possessive in meaning, the pronouns *yours, ours,
theirs, his, hers,* and *its* (Note: *It's* is an abbreviation for
it is or *it has.*) should never be used with an apostrophe.

Use an apostrophe only with the possessive form of a noun.

▶ That coat is *Maria's*.

▶ That is *her* coat.

▶ That coat is *hers*.

43b Clear reference

A pronoun refers to or replaces a noun, a noun phrase, or a pronoun already mentioned, known as its *antecedent*.

▶ **Because the Canadian skater practiced daily, *she* won the championship.** [*She* refers to *skater*.]

State a specific antecedent. Avoid using a pronoun such as *they, this,* or *it* without an explicit antecedent.

NO SPECIFIC ANTECEDENT | **When Rivera applied for a loan, they outlined the procedures.**

[The sentence does not have a clear antecedent for the pronoun *they*.]

REVISION | **When Rivera applied for a loan, bank officials outlined the procedures.**

Do not make a pronoun refer to a possessive noun or to a noun within a prepositional phrase.

George Orwell
▶ **In ~~George Orwell's~~ "Shooting an Elephant," ~~he~~ reports an incident that shows the evil effects of imperialism.**

Avoid an ambiguous reference. Your audience should never be left wondering which *this, they,* or *it* is being discussed.

AMBIGUOUS REFERENCE | **He faced having to decide whether to move to California. This was not what he wanted to do.**

[We do not know what *this* refers to: having to decide? moving to California?]

REVISION   He faced having to decide whether to move to California. This decision was not one he wanted to make.

43c Agreement with antecedent

A plural antecedent needs a plural pronoun; a singular antecedent needs a singular pronoun.

▶ Listeners heard *they* could win free tickets. The ninth caller learned *she* was the winner.

Note: Demonstrative pronouns *this* and *that* are singular. *These* and *those* are the plural forms.

A generalized (generic) antecedent Generic nouns describe a class or type of person or object, such as *a student* meaning "all students." Do not use *they* to refer to a singular generic noun, and make sure that you use *he* and *she* without gender bias (see section **39c**).

FAULTY   When *a student* is educated, *they* can
AGREEMENT   go far in the world.

POSSIBLE   When *a student* is educated, *he or she*
REVISIONS   can go far in the world.

              When *students* are educated, *they* can
              go far in the world.

Often, a plural noun is preferable as it avoids clumsy repetition of *he or she*. (See section **39c**.)

▶ We should judge ~~a person~~ people by who ~~he or she is~~ they are, not by the color of ~~his or her~~ their skin.

A collective noun Refer to a collective noun like *class, family, jury, committee, couple,* or *team* with a singular pronoun.

▶ The committee has not yet completed *its* report.

However, when the members of the group named by the collective noun are considered to be acting individually, use a plural pronoun.

▶ The committee began to cast *their* ballots in a formal vote.

An indefinite pronoun   Indefinite pronouns, such as *one, each, either, neither, everyone, everybody, someone, some-body, something, anyone, anybody, anything, no one, nobody,* and *nothing,* are generally singular in form (see section **42g**). A singular antecedent needs a singular pronoun to refer to it. For many years, the prescribed form in Standard English was *he,* as in sentences such as *Everyone needs his privacy* or *Each person needs his privacy.* Now, however, such usage is regarded as biased—*he or she* is clumsy, and *they,* although sometimes used informally, is regarded as ungrammatical. Use a plural noun and pronoun instead.

NOT APPROPRIATE   *Everyone* picked up *his* [*his or her; their*] marbles and went home.

REVISED   *The children* picked up *their* marbles and went home.

43d   Appropriate use of *you*

Do not use *you* for general reference—to mean "people generally." Use *you* only to address the audience directly, as in "If you look at the next slide, you will find. . ."

                   teenagers   their
▶ While growing up, ~~you~~ face arguments with ~~your~~ parents.

43e   *Who, whom, which, that*

When to use **who, which,** *or* **that**   Use *who* (or *whom*) to refer to human beings; use *which* or *that* to refer to animals, objects, or concepts.

              who
▶ The teacher ~~which~~ taught me algebra was strict.

When to use who *or* whom   *Whom* is an object pronoun. You will often hear *who* in its place, but some listeners may prefer the standard form.

▶ **Whom [informal *who*] did Romeo love?**

Whom used as a relative pronoun can often be omitted.

▶ **The players [whom] the team honored invited everyone to the party.**

Do not use *whom* in place of *who.*

▶ **The dancer ~~whom~~ is doing the tango is a scientist.**

who

When to use which *or* that   Generally, use *that* rather than *which* in restrictive clauses (ones that provide necessary rather than extra information). When *that* is the object of its clause, you can omit it. Use *which* when you provide extra information.

▶ **The book [*that*] you gave me was fascinating.**
  [restrictive]

▶ **War and Peace , *which* you gave me, was fascinating.**
  [nonrestrictive]

Note that *what* cannot be used as a relative pronoun.

▶ **Everything ~~what~~ she does receives praise.**

that

---

44 Adjectives and Adverbs

Adjectives describe, or modify, nouns or pronouns. They do not add *-s* or change form to reflect number or gender.

▶ **He tried three *different* approaches.**

Adverbs modify verbs, adjectives, and other adverbs as well as whole clauses.

▶ **She settled down *comfortably*.**

44a Correct forms of adjectives and adverbs

Check your dictionary for information on adjective and adverb forms not covered here.

Many adverbs are formed by adding *-ly* to an adjective: *intelligent/intelligently.*

In a written version of your presentation, form an adverb from an adjective ending in *-ic* by adding *-ally (basic, basically; artistic, artistically).* Note the exception of *public, publicly.*

Irregular adverb forms   Certain other adjectives do not add *-ly* to form an adverb:

ADJECTIVE	ADVERB
good	well
fast	fast
hard	hard

▶ He is a *good* cook.   ▶ He *cooks* well.

Note: *Well* can also function as an adjective, meaning "healthy" or "satisfactory."

▶ A *well* baby smiles often.   ▶ She feels *well* today.

44b When to use adjectives and adverbs

In informal conversation, adjectives (particularly *good, bad,* and *real*) are often used to modify verbs, adjectives, or adverbs. In a formal speech, use adverbs instead.

          clearly   really well
▶ She speaks very ~~clear.~~   ▶ I sing ~~real good.~~

After linking verbs like *be, seem, appear,* and *become,* use an adjective (as a complement).

▶ She seems *pleasant.*

Some verbs, such as *appear, look, feel, smell,* and *taste,* are sometimes used as linking verbs and sometimes as action verbs. If the modifier tells about the subject, use an adjective. If the modifier tells about the action of the verb, not the subject, use an adverb.

ADJECTIVE   She looks *confident* in her new job.

ADVERB   She looks *confidently* at all the assembled partners.

ADJECTIVE   The steak smells *bad*.

ADVERB   The chef smelled the lobster *appreciatively*.

44c Compound adjectives

Note the forms when a compound adjective is used: no noun plural endings, *-ed* endings where necessary, and in a written version of your speech, hyphens.

▶ The executive contributed a *hundred-dollar* bill. [He contributed a hundred dollars.]

▶ They have a *five-year-old* daughter. [Their daughter is five years old.]

▶ He is a *left-handed* pitcher. [He pitches with his left hand.]

Many compound adjectives use the *-ed* form: *flat-footed, barrel-chested, broad-shouldered, old-fashioned, well-dressed, left-handed.*

44d Avoiding double negatives

Although some languages and dialects allow more than one negative to emphasize an idea, Standard English uses only one negative in a clause. Words like *hardly*, *scarcely*, and *barely* are considered negatives. The contraction *-n't* stands for the adverb *not*. Avoid double negatives.

DOUBLE NEGATIVE   We do*n't* have *no* excuses.

REVISED   We do*n't* have any excuses.

We have *no* excuses.

DOUBLE NEGATIVE   They ca*n't hardly* pay the rent.

REVISED   They can *hardly* pay the rent.

44e Comparative and superlative forms

Adjectives and adverbs have *comparative* and *superlative* forms that are used for comparisons. Use the comparative form when comparing two items, people, places, or ideas; use the superlative form when comparing more than two.

SHORT ADJECTIVES		
	COMPARATIVE (COMPARING TWO)	SUPERLATIVE (COMPARING MORE THAN TWO)
short	shorter	shortest
pretty	prettier	prettiest
simple	simpler	simplest
fast	faster	fastest

LONG ADJECTIVES AND *-LY* ADVERBS		
	COMPARATIVE	SUPERLATIVE
intelligent	more intelligent	most intelligent
carefully	more carefully	most carefully

If you cannot decide whether to use an *-er/-est* form or *more/most*, consult a dictionary. If there is an *-er/-est* form, the dictionary will say so.

Note: Do not use the *-er* form with *more* or the *-est* form with *most*.

▶ The first poem was ~~more~~ better than the second.

▶ Boris is the ~~most~~ fittest person I know.

Irregular forms

	COMPARATIVE	SUPERLATIVE
good	better	best
bad	worse	worst
much/many	more	most
well	better	best
badly	worse	worst

44f Avoiding faulty and incomplete comparisons

Make sure that you state clearly what items you are comparing. Some faulty comparisons may give your audience the wrong idea.

► He likes the parrot better than his wife. [Does the speaker really mean he likes the parrot better than he likes his wife?]

does

► Williams's poem gives a more objective depiction of the painting than Auden. [To compare Williams's poem with Auden's poem, you need to include an apostrophe; otherwise, you compare a poem to the poet W. H. Auden.]

's

Part 13

For Multilingual Speakers (ESL)

267

If English is not your native language, you will probably make some errors as you speak and write, especially when you are grappling with new subject matter and difficult topics. For a guide to the specific types of errors commonly made by speakers of different languages, visit our web site at www.cengage.com/english (click on *Pocket Keys for Speakers,* and then on "ESL center"). This web site also provides you with links to sites specifically designed for multilingual students.

45 *A, An,* and *The*

To decide whether to use *a, an, the,* or no article at all before a noun, first determine the type of noun you have.

45a What you need to know about nouns

Nouns fall into two categories.

Proper nouns A proper noun names a unique person, place, or object and begins with a capital letter: *Walt Whitman, Lake Superior, Grand Canyon, Vietnam Veterans Memorial.*

Common nouns   A common noun does not name a unique person, place, object, or idea: *bicycle, furniture, plan, daughter, home, happiness*. Common nouns can be further categorized into two types, countable and uncountable.

- A *countable noun* can have a number before it (*one, two,* and so on); it has a plural form. Countable nouns frequently add *-s* to indicate the plural: *picture, pictures; plan, plans.* Singular countable nouns can be used after *a, an, the, this, that, each, every.* Plural countable nouns can be used after *the, these, those, many, a few, both, all, some, several.*

- An *uncountable noun* has no plural form: *furniture, equipment, advice, information.* Uncountable nouns can be used after *the, this, that, much, some, any, no, a little, a great deal of,* or a possessive such as *my* or *their.* They can never be used after a number or a plural quantity word such as *several* or *many.* Never use an uncountable noun after *a* or *an.*

  ▶ **My country has a̶ lovely scenery.**

Note: You can use an uncountable noun in a countable sense—that is, indicate a quantity of it—by adding a word or phrase that indicates quantity, but the noun itself always remains singular: three pieces of *furniture,* two bits of *information,* many pieces of *advice.*

  Some nouns can be countable in one context and uncountable in another.

▶ **He loves *chocolate.***

  [All chocolate, applies to the class: uncountable]

▶ **She gave him *a chocolate.***

  [One piece of candy from a box: countable]

45b   Articles: Four basic questions

Ask four basic questions about a noun to decide whether to use an article and, if so, which article to use.

KEY POINTS

Articles at a Glance: Four Basic Questions

1. PROPER OR COMMON NOUN?
   ↓
   Singular: no
      article (zero article)
   Plural: *the*

   2. SPECIFIC OR NONSPECIFIC REFERENCE?
      ↓
      the (see section **45d**)

      3. UNCOUNTABLE OR COUNTABLE NOUN?
         ↓
         no article OR
         some, much, a little, etc.

         4. PLURAL OR SINGULAR?
            ↓
            no article OR
            some, many, a few, etc.

                           a/an

Using the questions: a sample   Answering the four questions can help you decide which article, if any, to use with the noun *jacket* in the following sentence:

▶ **The motorcyclist I saw on the street was carrying ___?___**
   jacket and wearing black leather pants.   article

1. *Jacket* is a common noun.
2. *Jacket* is not identified in the text as one specific jacket in the same way that *motorcyclist* is (the one seen on the street).
3. *Jacket* is a countable noun.
4. *Jacket* is singular and begins with a consonant sound (*a* is used before a consonant sound, *an* before a vowel sound as in *an egg, an honest man*).

   ▶ **The motorcyclist I saw on the street was carrying *a* jacket and wearing black leather pants.**

45c Basic rules for articles

1. Use *the* whenever a reference to a common noun is specific and unique for speakers and listeners or you and your audience (see section **45d**).

   ▶ He loves ^the house that she bought.

2. Do not use *a/an* with plural countable nouns.

   ▶ They cited ~~a~~ reliable surveys.

3. Do not use *a/an* with uncountable nouns.

   ▶ He gave ~~a~~ helpful advice.

4. To make generalizations about countable nouns, do one of the following:
   - Use the plural form: *Lions are majestic.*
   - Use the singular with *a/an*: *A lion is a majestic animal.*
   - Use the singular with *the* to denote a classification: *The lion is a majestic animal.*

5. A countable singular noun can never stand alone. Make sure that a countable singular noun is preceded by an article or by a demonstrative pronoun *(this, that)*, a numeral, a singular word expressing quantity (see section **42h**), or a possessive.

   ▶ ^A (Every, That, One, Her) nurse ~~Nurse~~ has a difficult job.

6. In general, though there are many exceptions, use no article with a singular proper noun *(Mount Everest)*, and use *the* with a plural proper noun *(the Himalayas)*.

45d *The* for a specific reference

When you use a common noun that both you and the audience know refers to one or more specific persons, places, things, or concepts, use the article *the*. The reference can be specific in two ways: outside the text of your speech or inside it.

Specific reference outside your text

▶ I study the earth, the sun, and the moon. [The ones in our solar system]

▶ **She closed the door.** [Of the room she was in]

▶ **Her husband took the dog out for a walk.** [The dog belonging to the couple]

Specific reference inside your text

▶ *The* **kitten that her daughter brought home had a distinctive black patch above one eye.** [The kitten is identified as a specific one.]

▶ **Her daughter found** *a* **kitten. When they were writing a lost-and-found ad that night, they realized that** *the* **kitten had a distinctive black patch above one eye.**

[The second mention is to a specific kitten identified earlier—the one her daughter found.]

▶ **He bought** *the most expensive* **bicycle in the store.**

[A superlative makes a reference to one specific item.]

46 Infinitive, – *ing*, and – *ed* Verb Forms

46a Verb followed by an infinitive

Some verbs are followed by an infinitive (*to* + base form): *His father wanted to rule the family.* Verbs commonly followed by an infinitive include these:

agree	choose	fail	offer	refuse
ask	claim	hope	plan	venture
beg	decide	manage	pretend	want
bother	expect	need	promise	wish

Note any differences between English and your own language. In Spanish, for example, the word for *refuse* is followed by the equivalent of an *-ing* form.

       to criticize
▶ He refused ~~criticizing~~ the system.

Position of a negative In a verb + infinitive pattern, the position of the negative affects meaning. Note the difference in meaning that the position of a negative *(not, never)* can create.

▶ **He did** *not* **decide to buy a new car. His wife did.**

▶ **He decided** *not* **to buy a new car. His wife was disappointed.**

Verb + noun or pronoun + infinitive Some verbs are followed by a noun or pronoun and then an infinitive.

▶ The librarian *advised me to use* a better database.

Verbs that follow this pattern are *advise, allow, ask, encourage, expect, force, need, order, persuade, cause, command, convince, remind, require, tell, urge, want, warn.*

Languages such as Spanish and Russian use a *that* clause after verbs like *want*. In English, however, *want* is followed by an infinitive, not by a *that* clause.

　　　　　　　　her son to
▶ Rose *wanted* ~~that her son would~~ become a doctor.

Make, let, *and* ***have*** After these verbs, use a noun or pronoun and a base form of the verb (without *to*).

▶ He *made his son practice* for an hour.

▶ They *let us leave* early.

▶ She *had me wash* the car.

46b Verb followed by -*ing* (gerund)

▶ I can't help *singing* along with Paul Simon.

The -*ing* form of a verb used as a noun is known as a *gerund*. The verbs that are systematically followed by an -*ing* form make up a relatively short and learnable list:

admit	consider	enjoy	miss	resist
appreciate	delay	finish	postpone	risk
avoid	deny	imagine	practice	suggest
be worth	discuss	keep	recall	tolerate
can't help	dislike			

　　　　　　inviting
▶ We considered ~~to invite~~ his parents.

　　　　reading
▶ He dislikes ~~to read~~ in bed.

Note that a negation comes between the verb and the -*ing* form:

▶ During their vacation, they enjoy *not* getting up early every day.

46c Verb followed by a preposition + *-ing*

After a preposition, use the *-ing* form that functions as a noun (the gerund).

▶ **They congratulated him** *on winning* **the prize.**

▶ **He ran three miles** *without stopping.*

▶ **The cheese is the right consistency** *for spreading.*

Note: Take care not to confuse *to* as a preposition with *to* used in an infinitive. When *to* is a preposition, it is followed by a noun, a pronoun, a noun phrase, or an *-ing* form, not by the base form of a verb.

▶ **They want** *to adopt* **a child.**   [infinitive]

▶ **They are looking forward** *to adopting* **a child.**
   [preposition + *-ing*]

See Glossary of Usage, page 295, for forms used after *used to* and *get used to*.

46d Verb followed by an infinitive or *-ing*

Some verbs can be followed by either an infinitive or an *-ing* form (a gerund) with almost no discernible difference in meaning: *begin, continue, hate, like, love, start.*

▶ **She loves** *cooking.*   ▶ **She loves** *to cook.*

   With a few verbs, however *(forget, remember, try, stop)*, the infinitive and the *-ing* form signal different meanings:

▶ **He remembered** *to mail* **the letter.**   [intention]

▶ **He remembered** *mailing* **the letter.**   [past act]

46e *-ing* and *-ed* forms as adjectives

Adjectives can be formed from both the present participle *-ing* form and the past participle form of verbs (*-ed* ending for regular verbs). Each form has a different meaning: The *-ing* adjective indicates that the word modified produces an effect; the past participle adjective indicates that the word modified has an effect produced on it.

▶ The *boring* cook served baked beans yet again.

[The cook produces boredom. Everyone is tired of baked beans.]

▶ The *bored* cook yawned as she scrambled eggs.

[The cook felt the emotion of boredom as she did the cooking, but the eggs could still be appreciated.]

PRODUCES AN EFFECT	HAS AN EFFECT PRODUCED ON IT
amazing	amazed
amusing	amused
annoying	annoyed
confusing	confused
depressing	depressed
disappointing	disappointed
embarrassing	embarrassed
exciting	excited
interesting	interested
satisfying	satisfied
shocking	shocked
worrying	worried
surprising	surprised

Note: In a written version of a speech, do not drop the *-ed* ending from a past participle. Sometimes in speech it blends with a following *t* or *d* sound, but in writing the *-ed* ending must be included.

▶ I was surprise to see her wild outfit.

[d inserted above]

▶ They were annoy that the speech was so long.

[ed inserted above]

47 Sentence Structure and Word Order

47a Basic rules of order

• Always include the subject of a clause, even a filler subject *it* or *there*.

▶ The critics hated the movie because ^it^ was too

sentimental.

▶ When the company lost money, ^there^ were

immediate effects on share prices.

- Do not use a pronoun to restate the subject.

    ▶ The adviser who was recommended to me ~~she~~
    was very helpful.

- Do not put an adverb or a phrase between the verb and its object.

    ▶ The quiz show host congratulated

    | many times | the winner |.

    ▶ He saw | yesterday | the movie |.

- Position a long descriptive phrase after, not before, the noun it modifies.

    ▶ I would go to | known only to me | places |.

- Stick to the order of subject-verb-direct object.

    ▶ ~~Good grades received~~ ^E^very student in the
    received good grades.
    class ^,^

- Do not include a pronoun that a relative pronoun has replaced.

    ▶ The house that I lived in ~~it~~ for ten years has
    been sold.

47b Direct and indirect object

Some verbs can be followed by both a direct object and an indirect object. (The indirect object is the person or thing to whom or to what, or for whom or for what, something is done.) *Give, send, show, tell, teach, find, sell, ask, offer, pay, pass,* and *hand* are some verbs that take indirect objects. The indirect object follows the verb and precedes the direct object.

▶ He gave his mother some flowers.

▶ He gave her some flowers.

    An indirect object can also be replaced with a prepositional phrase that *follows* the direct object.

▶ He gave some flowers to his mother.

Note: Some verbs—such as *explain, describe, say, mention,* and *open*—are never followed by an indirect object. However, they can be followed by a direct object and a prepositional phrase with *to* or *for*.

▶ She explained ~~me~~ the election process. *to me*

▶ He described ~~us~~ the menu. *to us*

47c Direct and indirect questions

When a direct question is reported indirectly, it loses the quotation marks, the word order of a question, and the question mark. Sometimes changes in tense are also necessary after an introductory verb in the past tense (see section **41d**).

DIRECT QUESTION	The buyer asked, "*Are the goods* ready to be shipped?"
INDIRECT QUESTION	The buyer asked if *the goods were* ready to be shipped.

DIRECT QUESTION	"Why *did you send* a letter instead of a fax?" my boss asked.
INDIRECT QUESTION	My boss asked why *I [had] sent* a letter instead of a fax.

Use only a question word or *if* or *whether* to introduce an indirect question. Do not use *that* as well.

▶ My boss wondered ~~that~~ why I had left early.

Avoid shifts between direct and indirect quotations (See section **40d**).

47d *Although* and *because* clauses

In some languages, a subordinating conjunction (such as *although* or *because*) can be used along with a coordinating conjunction *(but, so)* or a transitional expression *(however, therefore)* in the same sentence. In English, only one is used.

FAULTY:	*Although* he loved his father, *but* he did not visit him.
POSSIBLE REVISIONS:	*Although* he loved his father, he did not visit him.
	He loved his father, *but* he did not visit him.
	He loved his father. *However,* he did not visit him.
FAULTY:	*Because* she loved children, *therefore* she became a teacher.
POSSIBLE REVISIONS:	*Because* she loved children, she became a teacher.
	She loved children, *so* she became a teacher.
	She loved children; *therefore,* she became a teacher.

Endnotes

▶ Part 1

[1]Significant portions of *Pocket Keys for Speakers* are based on and adapted from Engleberg, I. & Daly, J. (2001). *Presentations in Everyday Life: Strategies for Effective Speaking* Boston: Houghton Mifflin.

[2]Business–Higher Education Forum (1997). *Spanning the chasm: Corporate and academic cooperation to improve work-force preparation.* Washington, DC: Business–Higher Education Forum, in affiliation with the American Council on Education.

[3]National Association of Colleges and Employers, Job Outlook, 2000. See <http://www.jobweb.org/pubs/pr/pr)1180.htm>.

[4]See <http://www.natcome.org/about NCA/Policies/Platform.html>.

▶ Part 3

[1]These cultural dimensions are based on the work of Geert Hofstede. See Hofstede, G., (1984) *Culture's Consequences: International Differences in World-Related Values.* (Beverly Hills: Sage; Hofstede, G., 1991.) *Culture and Organizations: Intercultural Cooperation and Its Implications for Survival: Software of the Mind* (London: McGraw-Hill.) Also see Lustig, M. W., and Koester, J., (1999). *Intercultural Competence: Interpersonal Communication Across Cultures* (3rd ed.). (New York: Longman.)

▶ Part 8

[1]See Rowan, K. E. (1995). A new pedagogy for explanatory public speaking: Why arrangement should not substitute for invention. *Communication Education, 44,* 236–250.

[2]The presentation outline on page 134 is based on an address by Candace Corlett that appeared in *Vital Speeches of the Day, 66* (1), October 15, 1999, pp. 24–27. As a subsidiary of WSL Strategic Retail, 50+ Marketing Directions specializes in marketing to target audiences over age fifty. The World Research Group sponsors business conferences which often specialize in marketing.

[3]See Petty, R., & Cacioppo, J. (1986). *Communication and persuasion: Central and peripheral routes to attitude change.* New York: Springer-Verlag.

[4]See Maslow, A. H. (1954). *Motivation and personality.* New York: Harper & Row.

[5]See Schutz, W. C. (1958). *FIRO: A three-dimensional theory of interpersonal behavior.* New York: Holt, Rinehart, & Winston.

[6]See Monroe, A. H. (1935). *Principles and types of speech.* Chicago: Scott, Foresman.

[7]This presentation appeared in *Vital Speeches of the Day, 65* (20), August 1, 1999, pp. 633–634.

▶ Part 9

[1]29C Speaking in Groups and 29D Team Presentations are based on Engleberg, I. & Wynn, D. (2003). *Working in Groups: Communication principles and strategies,* 3rd ed. Boston: Houghton Mifflin.

▶ Part 10

[1]The sample paper using MLA style is taken from Raimes, A. (2002). *Keys for writers: A brief handbook,* 3rd ed. Boston: Houghton Mifflin, pp. 152–158.

[2]See Bloom, B. S., and Krathwohl, D. A. (1956). *Taxonomy of educational objectives: The classification of educational goals by a committee of college and university examiners. Handbook I: Cognitive domain.* New York: Longman, Green. For web-based information on Bloom's Taxonomy, see <http://faculty.washington.edu/krumme/guides/bloom.hrml> and <http://www.nwlink.com/~donclark/hrd/bloom.html>.

[3]Daniels, D. P. (2002). Communication across the curriculum and in the disciplines: Speaking in engineering. *Communication Education, 51,* 254–268.

[4]Daniels, pp. 259–263.

[5]Daniels, pp. 263–264.

[6]Keyton, J. (2001). *Communication research: Asking questions, finding answers.* Boston: McGraw Hill, pp. 315–323.

[7]Leech, T. (1993). *How to prepare, stage, and deliver winning presentations: New and updated edition.* New York: AMACOM, p. 3.

Part 14

Glossaries and Index

281

48 Glossary of Speaking Terms

4R's of Organization   A series of critical thinking steps (review, reduce, regroup, refine) that can be used to find an effective organizational pattern for a speech. **13a.**

acceptance speech   A typically brief speech expressing gratitude as a speaker receives an honor or award. **27.**

active listening   Listening very carefully in order to gain information and understanding. **4.**

active listening process   Preparing yourself to listen and listening effectively. **4.**

aerobic exercise   Physical activity that increases one's heart rate and respiration and that, as a result, reduces tension. **3c.**

alliteration   Beginning words with the same sound and placing them closely together to gain attention and reinforce an idea. **19b.**

analogy   Identifies similarities in things that are alike or comparable in function and highlights similarities in things that don't initially seem alike. **10a.**

anecdotes   Brief stories that provide concrete examples of an idea or a concept. **10a.**

antithesis   Placing together two images that have sharply contrasted meanings.

appropriateness   The degree to which information can be understood and appreciated by an audience.

argument(s)   A series of ideas, each one supported by materials, used to advance a particular position about an issue.

articulation   The manner in which one produces individual sounds in words and phrases. **22b.**

assertion   A claim that one advances with an insistence that it is truthful.

attention span   The typical amount of time one can remain focused and attentive.

audience adaptation   Connecting one's message to the interests and needs of the audience at a level appropriate to their knowledge and experience and in a style that they find comfortable.

audience analysis   The ability to understand, respect, and adapt to audience members before and during a presentation. **8a.**

audience attitudes A measure of whether audience members agree or disagree with a speaker's purpose. **8.**

audience centered Focused on one's audience—on their characteristics, needs, and well-being.

audience-centered communication Thinking about one's audience throughout the process of communication, from topic selection to message delivery.

bar graph A graph in which a series of bars depicts comparative numbers of certain features or elements.

belonging needs The need to be loved, accepted, and wanted by others.

biased A source whose opinion is so slanted or self-serving that it may not be objective or fair. **6a.**

brainstorming The process of thinking creatively and imaginatively, temporarily suspending critical judgments about what is produced.

captive audience An audience whose members see no special reason to attend to the speaker.

cause-and-effect arrangement An organizational format that identifies a situation, object, or behavior and then describes the results of that situation, object, or behavior. **13c.**

central idea A sentence or thesis statement that summarizes the key points in a speech. **13b.**

character A component of speaker credibility that relates to a speaker's honesty and goodwill. **18.**

charisma A component of speaker credibility that relates to a speaker's level of energy, enthusiasm, vigor, and/or commitment; a speaker's dynamic qualities. **18.**

chronological pattern An organizational pattern in which ideas are arranged in a logical time order.

circumlocutions The use of an unnecessarily large number of words to express an idea.

claim The conclusion or position a speaker is advocating.

clarity The quality of being instantly intelligible to an audience.

cliché An expression that is trite and overused.

communication apprehension The feeling of anxiety that a speaker feels before and/or during a public presentation.

comparison-contrast arrangement An organizational format that uses the similarities and differences between two things or concepts as a method of arranging major ideas. **13c.**

competence A component of speaker credibility that relates to a speaker's experience and ability. **18.**

comprehension questions Questions asked of an audience by a speaker during a presentation as a way of assessing and enhancing their understanding. **8a.**

conclusion The ending of a speech, in which a speaker can summarize what has been covered and can attempt to create a lasting impression of what has been offered in the speech.

connectives Devices that link key points, remind the audience of the speaker's direction, and preview or summarize major sections of a presentation. **15.**

constraints Anything that limits or otherwise affects what one can or should say in a given situation.

contention A statement or claim advanced as a main idea in an argument.

context The situational factors and setting in which one speaks.

credibility The extent to which audience members believe a speaker is competent, trustworthy, and/or dynamic. **2f, 18.**

cumulative ethos The audience's accumulating perceptions of a speaker's credibility.

databases A categorized grouping of data stored in electronic form on a computer or on a computer disk such as a CD-ROM.

deductive reasoning Applying a generally accepted premise to a specific situation or person.

deep breathing Expanding the diaphragm to increase one's intake of air. Doing so helps one to relax and to have good vocal support.

definition A statement that explains or clarifies the meaning of a word, phrase, or concept. **10a.**

delivery The manner in which one presents a speech.

description A statement that creates a mental image of a scene, concept, event, object, or person. **10a.**

descriptive statistics Observable numerical data.

dynamism Audience's perception of a speaker's enthusiasm, energy, and genuine interest in the issues being discussed.

effectiveness   The degree to which the speaker and the audience benefit from a message.

eloquence   The ability to phrase a thought or feeling in a way that makes it clear, appropriate for the occasion, and memorable. **19b.**

empty words   Words that add length but no additional meaning.

entertainment speech   A presentation designed to amuse, interest, divert, or "warm-up" an audience. **7a.**

ethical emotional appeals   An appeal that seeks an emotional response while simultaneously providing good reasons to justify the reaction sought.

ethical listeners   People who listen open-mindedly to a speaker before making any pronouncements about the integrity and value of the speaker's message.

ethical norms   A common code for what is and for what is not ethical behavior.

ethical speaking   Speaking honestly and truthfully, with a thoughtful and genuine concern for the well-being of the audience and the community.

ethics   A set of behavioral standards deemed to be good or desirable.

ethos   The speaker's character, intelligence, and goodwill, as perceived by the audience.

eulogy   A speech of tribute to honor one who has died and to comfort those who mourn. **27g.**

evidence   Fact and opinion used to support a particular perspective about a subject.

example   A reference to a specific case or instance. Examples are often items, facts, or instances that represent an entire group. **15a.**

expert testimony   The views of someone who is well informed on a particular subject.

expressiveness   The vitality, variety, and sincerity that speakers put into their delivery of a speech. **20.**

extemporaneous speaking   A carefully prepared presentation delivered from an outline or a minimal set of notes so as to achieve a less formal, more direct, audience-centered delivery. **21a.**

eye contact   The establishment and maintenance of direct visual contact with individual members of one's audience. **23a.**

facial expression   The expressive use of one's face to convey emotion. **23a.**

fact   A verifiable observation, experience, or event known to be true. **10a.**

fallacies   Various types of arguments that contain flawed reasoning.

feedback   Nonverbal and verbal reactions to another's message.

figures of speech   Special uses of language that heighten the beauty of expression to make it clearer, more meaningful, and more memorable.

flexibility   The degree to which one can adapt one's speechmaking to new elements within a speaking situation.

formal argument   A position one advances as one leads from a premise to evidence to a claim or conclusion.

formal outline   A comprehensive written framework for a presentation that follows established conventions of content and style. **14b.**

forum period   The question-and-answer period following a speech that allows a dialogue between the speaker and the audience.

freespeaking   Thinking aloud as one tries to explain something or work through a problem.

freewriting   Writing creatively and freely about something one wishes to explain or figure out while temporarily suspending a critique of its quality.

full-sentence outlines   An outline in which ideas are articulated completely and precisely.

general purpose   What the speaker hopes to give the audience as well as what the person hopes to obtain by speaking.

gestures   The expressive use of one's hands. **23a.**

groupthink   A negative outcome that occurs when a group's critical appraisal of ideas and willingness to express concerns are hindered by its desire for consensus.

identify   What one brings to a speaking situation and who one is in relation to it.

immediate audience   Those who constitute a speaker's audience at the speaking event.

impromptu speaking   A presentation for which the speaker has little or no time to prepare or practice. **21a, 28.**

inferential statistics Numerical data used to calculate a probability.

informative report A brief, informative presentation made to assist a group's performance or decision making.

informative speech A presentation designed to instruct, explain, describe, demonstrate, or clarify. **7a, 25.**

internal preview A connective phrase or sentence that introduces the key points in a speech or tells an audience what will be covered in what order. **15a.**

internal summary A connective phrase or sentence that concludes a major section of a speech, summarizes key points, or reinforces important ideas and information before the speaker moves on to the next area of the speech. **15a.**

interpersonal communication Communicative exchange with one, two, or a similarly small number of individuals.

irony The use of language to imply a meaning that is totally opposite from the literal meaning of a work or expression.

isometric exercise Tensing a muscle and holding it for a short time, followed by complete relaxation of the muscle.

key points The most important issues or the main ideas that a speaker wants an audience to understand and remember during and after a presentation. **13a.**

key word outline An abbreviated outline that serves as a speaker's notes while the person is speaking.

lay testimony Testimony offered by ordinary people that is based upon their experiences and beliefs.

lectern A stand that serves as a support for a speaker's notes.

line graph A graph in which one or more lines depict a trend or trends over time.

listening The ability to understand, analyze, respect, and respond to the meaning of another person's spoken and nonverbal messages. **4.**

listening critically Analyzing what is being said in terms of whether it is accurate, reasonable, fair, and of good consequence.

listening purposefully Listening respectfully with the goal of gaining something from the message and responding appropriately to it.

logistics The strategic planning, arranging, and use of people, facilities, equipment, and time relevant to a presentation. **9.**

logos   Logical content that influences people's beliefs or actions.

long-range purpose   The ultimate goal a speaker hopes to accomplish as a result of presenting a series of speeches on a particular topic.

mannerisms   Vocal habits and conventions that clutter a person's speaking and might distract listeners.

manuscript speaking   A presentation written out in advance and delivered word for word from a prepared text. **21a.**

margin of error   Possible error or slight miscalculation associated with inferential statistics.

mean   A mathematical average calculated by adding a set of numbers and dividing the total by the number of figures that have been added to obtain the sum.

median   A number that is halfway between the largest and smallest number in a particular set of numbers.

memorized presentation   A presentation for which the speaker memorizes a manuscript and then delivers it without notes. **21a.**

memory aids arrangement   An organizational format that uses easily remembered letters, words, or common phrases to arrange the key points of a speech. **13c.**

mental argument   Mentally formulating rebuttals to the speaker's ideas and, in the process, losing track of the speaker's message as a whole.

metaphor   A figure of speech that makes a comparison between two things or ideas without directly connecting the resemblances with words such as *like* or *as*. **19b.**

mind mapping   An organizational technique for discovering the key points and connections among the ideas for a presentation without forcing a predetermined organizational scheme on them. **13.**

mode   A numerical figure that occurs most frequently in a particular set of numbers.

motivated sequence   A pattern of organization for a speech to actuate that engages the audience's emotions. **26d.**

motive   What compels a speaker to speak to an audience.

movement   The expressive use of one's body. **23a.**

noise   Any interference that distorts or interrupts message flow.

nonverbal communication   Facial expressions, vocal qualities, and physical movements that reinforce or contradict one's verbal messages.

nonverbal messages   Facial expressions, vocal qualities, and physical movements that reinforce or contradict one's verbal messages.

note taking   A type of active listening that, if done correctly, can assist the comprehension and retention of a message.

objectivity   Audience's perception of a speaker's openness and fair-mindedness in considering diverse points of view.

occasion   The reason that an audience assembles at a particular place and time. **9.**

oral practice   Practicing one's speech aloud in conditions that simulate the actual speaking environment.

organization   A strategy or method that determines what to include in a presentation as well as how to arrange the ideas and information in an effective way. **13.**

overarching purpose   A speaker's main reason for speaking and overall goal for a speech.

oxymoron   An expression that presents, in combination, seemingly contradictory terms.

panel discussions   Public discussions in which participants interact spontaneously under the guidance of a moderator.

parallelism   The use of similar language constructions to signify the equality of ideas.

pathos   Emotional content that influences people's beliefs or actions.

performance   The effective vocal and physical delivery of a presentation. **2.**

personal testimony   Testimony based upon one's own personal experiences and beliefs.

personification   A description of an inanimate form or thing as if it were human.

persuasive speech   A presentation designed to change or influence the audience's opinion and/or behavior. **7a, 26.**

physiological needs   The need to be physically secure. **26c.**

physiological reactions to anxiety   Bodily responses that accompany communication apprehension.

pictograph   A graph that relies upon a set of self-explanatory icons to depict the growth or decline of an item over time.

pie graph   A graph in the shape of a circle, in which segments of the circle (cut into slices like those of a pie) depict the relative size of a particular feature or element within the whole. **24b.**

plagiarism   Presenting as new and original an idea derived from another source.

podium   An elevated platform on which a speaker stands.

preliminary outline   An initial planning outline that puts the major pieces of a speech in a clear and logical order. **14a.**

premise   An acceptable generalization for a particular context or audience.

presentation aids   Visual or audiovisual materials that help clarify, support, and/or strengthen the verbal content of a speech. **24.**

presentation outline   A brief outline including key points and references to supporting material that can be used as speaker notes during a presentation. **14c.**

prestige testimony   The views of a popular, famous person who, though not an expert on the subject being addressed, expresses a genuine commitment to a cause.

pretending to listen   Simulating listening behaviors but not paying attention to the speaker's message.

preview   A glimpse of the major areas or points one will be treating in a speech or in a section of a speech.

priming   A heightened sensitivity to relevant materials as a result of being attuned to a given subject.

probability   The extent to which people can predict something based upon past experiences or observations.

problem-solution arrangement   An organizational format that describes a situation that is harmful (the problem) and then offers a plan to solve the problem (the solution). **13c.**

productive anxiety   Nervous energy that can be utilized to make a more dynamic speech.

pronunciation   The manner in which a word is produced, in terms of sounds and accents. **22b.**

proposal presentations   Persuasive presentations typically delivered to a small group of decision makers and seeking their endorsement of what is being proposed.

protocol The expected format of a ceremony or the etiquette observed at a particular type of ceremony or event. **9a.**

purpose The outcome one is seeking as a result of making a speech. Purpose answers the question "What do I want my audience to know, think, feel, or do as a result of my presentation?" **2, 6.**

purpose statement A sentence that clearly states the specific, achievable, and relevant goal of a presentation. **6.**

rate The degree of quickness or slowness in one's vocalizations.

recency The degree to which information is current and up to date.

reliability The degree to which an information source can be considered credible.

repetition Repeating, word for word, key elements presented in a message.

restatement Restating, with slightly different language and/or sentence construction, key elements presented in a message.

revision Critiquing one's own writing and modifying it by adding, deleting, or altering material.

rhetorical question A question posed by a speaker that is intended to stimulate thought and interest rather than an actual oral response.

safety needs The need to have a safe and predictable environment. **26c.**

self-actualization needs The desire to achieve to the full extent of one's capabilities. **26c.**

self-analysis The evaluation of potential topics in terms of one's capabilities, limitations, and personal characteristics.

self-effacing humor The ability to direct humor at oneself. **20c.**

self-expectations The expectations people have for themselves in terms of their performance, including the extent to which they demand perfection from themselves.

self-inventory A list of topics that a person cares about and knows something about.

sensory appeals Language that encourages sensory sensations.

setting   The immediate environment in which a speech is presented.

sexist language   Language that demeans an individual or group on the basis of sex or gender.

signposts   Words or short phrases that tell or remind an audience of the speaker's current place in the organizational scheme of a presentation. **15b.**

simile   A figure of speech that makes a direct comparison between two things or ideas, usually by using words such as *like* or *as*. **19b.**

situational distractions   Disturbances in the environment or medium that challenge people's ability to listen.

sound bites   Brief excerpts of a longer message offered as a substitute for the longer message.

source credibility   The degree to which a source of information is perceived as reputable.

space arrangement   An organizational format that arranges ideas, objects, events, people, and/or places in a physical pattern, location, or space. **13c.**

speaker credibility   The extent to which an audience believes a speaker. **18.**

speaker's purpose   What a speaker hopes to accomplish by speaking.

specific examples   A real-life case or instance.

specific purpose   A precise statement of how the speaker wants the audience to respond to his or her message. It serves to direct the research and construction of the speech.

speech of demonstration   A speech intended to teach an audience how something works or how to do something.

speech of description   An informative speech intended to provide a clear picture of a place, event, or person.

speech of explanation   A speech intended to help an audience understand complicated, abstract, or unfamiliar concepts or subjects.

speech of inspiration   A speech intended to inspire and motivate listeners to pursue worthy goals or embrace lofty values.

speech of tribute   A speech in praise of a significant person or event.

speech to actuate   A persuasive speech in which the speaker attempts to get the audience to take specific, overt action.

speech to convince   A persuasive speech in which the speaker attempts to secure audience agreement with his or her point of view.

speech to entertain   A speech intended to stimulate enjoyment by the audience while advancing a meaningful theme.

speech to stimulate   A speech intended to reinforce ideas and beliefs already held by the audience members and to intensify their feelings.

statistics   A system of organizing, summarizing, and analyzing numerical data that have been collected and measured, in order to display or suggest such factors as typicality, cause to effect, and trends. **10a.**

stereotyping   Making assumptions about someone based upon such factors as race or gender without considering the person's individuality. **8a.**

stories   Accounts or reports about some things that have happened. **10a.**

strategy   A plan that attempts to identify the best steps for achieving one's goals.

structure   The organization and arrangement of ideas and materials within a speech.

style   A speaker's choice of language.

subsidiary purpose   Minor goals for speaking, in comparison with a speaker's overarching purpose for a speech.

suitable language   Language choices that are precise, clear, interesting, and appropriate to audience and purpose.

summary   A brief account of what was presented in a speech to refresh audience members' memories and to reinforce the various points that have been made.

summary table   An analysis of raw data that is presented in the format of a table.

supporting material   Ideas, opinions, and information that help explain and/or advance a presentation's key points and purpose. **10.**

target audience   Those whom the speaker would most like to influence with the message.

technical language   Any language that has a very precise meaning within a particular field of endeavor.

temporal context   Previous, current, and anticipated events that affect what can or should be said and how it might be received.

testimony   Statement or opinions someone has said or written. **10a.**

thesis statement   A single sentence that expresses the principal idea of a speech.

time arrangement   An organizational format that orders ideas and information according to time or calendar dates. **10c.**

toast   A typically short, abbreviated speech of tribute and celebration. **27e.**

topic   The subject matter of a speech. **7.**

topical arrangement   An organizational format that divides a large topic into smaller subtopics. **13c.**

transitional language   Words and phrases that signal movement and direction within a speech.

transitional statement   A single sentence that reviews what the speaker has just covered and previews the next area to be covered.

transitions   A connective in the form of a word, phrase, number, or sentence that helps a speaker move from one key point or section to another. **15b.**

trustworthiness   Audience's perception of a speaker's reliability, honesty, sincerity, and goodwill.

typicality   The degree to which a particular example is normal.

values   Those things that we consider good and desirable.

variety   The degree to which a speaker varies his or her voice to add expressiveness to vocalizations.

verbal messages   Messages created via language or code.

visualization technique   A technique in which a speaker anticipates good things transpiring before a speech during a speech, and as a result of giving a speech.

vocal clarity   The degree to which a speaker's vocalization can be readily understood.

volume   The degree of softness or loudness in a speaker's vocalizations.

working outline   Early drafts of a speech outline, representing the work in progress.

49   Glossary of Usage

accept, except, expect   *Accept* is a verb: *She accepted the salary offer. Except* is usually a preposition: *Everyone has gone home except my boss. Expect* is a verb: *They expect to visit New Mexico on vacation.*

adapt, adopt   *Adopt* means "to take into a family" or "to take up and follow": *The couple adopted a three-year-old child. The company adopted a more aggressive policy. Adapt* means "to adjust" and is used with the preposition *to: We need some time to adapt to work after college.*

advice, advise   *Advice* is a noun: *Take my advice and don't start smoking. Advise* is a verb: *He advised his brother to stop smoking.*

affect, effect   In their most common uses, *affect* is a verb, and *effect* is a noun. To *affect* is to have an *effect* on something: *Pesticides can affect health. Pesticides have a bad effect on health. Effect,* however, can be used as a verb meaning "to bring about": *The administration hopes to effect new health care legislation. Affect* can also be used as a noun in psychology, meaning "a feeling or emotion."

all ready, already   *All ready* means "totally prepared": *The students were all ready for their final examination. Already* means "by this time": *He has already written the report.*

all right, alright   *Alright* is nonstandard. *All right* is standard.

all together, altogether   *Altogether* is an adverb meaning "totally," often used before an adjective: *His presentation was altogether impressive. All together* is used to describe acting simultaneously: *As soon as the boss appeared, the managers spoke up all together.*

allude, elude   *Allude* means "to refer to": *She alluded to his height. Elude* means "to avoid": *He eluded her criticism by leaving the room.*

allusion, illusion   *Allusion* means "reference to": *Her allusions to his height made him uncomfortable. Illusion* means "false idea": *He had no illusions about being Mr. Universe.*

almost, most   Do not use *most* to mean *almost: Almost* (not *Most*) *all my friends are computer literate.*

a lot, alot, lots   *Alot* is nonstandard. *A lot of* and *lots of* are regarded by some as informal for *many* or *a great deal of: They have performed a lot of research studies.*

ambiguous, ambivalent *Ambiguous* is used to describe a phrase or act with more than one meaning: *The ending of the movie is ambiguous; we don't know if the butler really committed the murder. Ambivalent* describes lack of certainty and the coexistence of opposing attitudes and feelings: *The committee is ambivalent about the proposal for restructuring the company.*

among, between Use *between* for two items, *among* for three or more: *I couldn't decide between red or blue. I couldn't decide among red, blue, or green.*

amount, number *Number* is used with countable plural expressions: *a large number of people, a number of attempts. Amount* is used with uncountable expressions: *a large amount of money, work,* or *information.*

anyone, any one *Anyone* is a singular indefinite pronoun meaning "anybody": *Can anyone help me? Any one* refers to one from a group and is usually followed by *of* + plural noun: *Any one* (as opposed to any two) *of the suggestions will be considered acceptable.*

anyplace The standard *anywhere* is preferable.

anyway, anywhere, nowhere; anyways, anywheres, nowheres *Anyway, anywhere,* and *nowhere* are standard forms. The others, ending in *-s,* are not.

apart, a part *Apart* is an adverb: *The old book fell apart.* But *I'd like to be a part of that project.*

as, as if, like See *like, as, as if.*

ask Use Standard English pronunciation (not "aks").

as regards, in regard to See *in regard to, as regards.*

at Avoid including *at* at the end of a question: *Where's the library?* not *Where's the library at?*

awful, awfully Avoid using these words to mean "bad" (*It's an awful story*) or "very" (*They are awfully rich*).

a while, awhile *While* is a noun: *a while ago; in a while. Awhile* is an adverb meaning "for some time": *They lived awhile in the wilderness.*

bad, badly *Bad* is an adjective, *badly* an adverb. Use *bad* after linking verbs (such as *am, is, become, seem*); use *badly* to modify verbs: *They felt bad after losing the match. They had played badly.*

because, because of *Because* is used to introduce a dependent clause: *Because it was raining, we left early. Because of* is followed by a noun: *We left early because of the rain.*

being as, being that   Avoid. Use *because* instead: *Because* (not *Being as*) *I was tired, I didn't go to class.*

belief, believe   *Belief* is a noun: *She has radical beliefs. Believe* is a verb: *He believes in an afterlife.*

beside, besides   *Beside* is a preposition meaning "next to"; *besides* is a preposition meaning "except for": *Sit beside me. He has no assistants besides us. Besides* is also an adverb meaning "in addition": *I hate horror movies. Besides, there's a long line.*

better   See *had better.*

between   See *among.*

breath, breathe   The first is a noun, the second a verb: *Take three deep breaths. Breathe in deeply.*

can't hardly   This expression is nonstandard. See *hardly.*

cite, site, sight   *Cite* means "to quote or mention"; *site* is a noun meaning "location"; *sight* is a noun meaning "view": *She cited the page number in her paper. They visited the original site of the abbey. The sight of the skyline from the plane produced applause from the passengers.*

complement, compliment   As verbs, *complement* means "to complete or add to something," and *compliment* means "to make a flattering comment about someone or something": *The wine complemented the meal. The guests complimented the hostess on the fine dinner.* As nouns, the words have meanings associated with the verbs: *The wine was a fine complement to the meal. The guests paid the hostess a compliment.*

compose, comprise   *Compose* means "to make up"; *comprise* means "to include." *The conference center is composed of twenty-five rooms. The conference center comprises twenty-five rooms.*

conscience, conscious   *Conscience* is a noun meaning "awareness of right and wrong." *Conscious* is an adjective meaning "awake" or "aware." *Her conscience troubled her after the accident. The victim was still not conscious.*

continual, continuous   *Continual* implies repetition; *continuous* implies lack of a pause. *The continual interruptions made the lecturer angry. Continuous rain for two hours stopped play.*

could care less   This expression used without a negative is not standard. In formal English, use it only with a negative: *They couldn't care less about their work.*

custom, customs, costume   *Custom* means "habitual practice or tradition." *Customs* refers to a government agency that collects taxes on imports or to the procedures for inspecting items entering a country. A *costume* is a style of dress: *a family custom, go through customs at the airport, a Halloween costume.*

dairy, diary   The first is associated with cows and milk, the second with daily journal writing.

desert, dessert   *Desert* can be pronounced two ways and can be a noun with the stress on the first syllable *(the Mojave Desert)* or a verb, pronounced the same way as the noun *dessert: When did he desert his family?* As a noun, *desert* means "a dry, often sandy, environment." As a verb, *desert* means "to abandon." *Dessert* (with the stress on the second syllable) is the sweet course at the end of a meal.

different from, different than   Standard usage is *different from: She looks different from her sister.* However, *different than* appears frequently in speech and informal writing, particularly when *different from* would require more words: *My writing is different than* (in place of *different from what*) *it was last semester.*

disinterested, uninterested   *Disinterested* means "impartial or unbiased": *The mediator was hired to make a disinterested settlement. Uninterested* means "lacking in interest": *He seemed so uninterested in his job that his boss wondered what to do about him.*

due to   Use *due to,* not *because of,* after a noun plus a form of *be: The Yankees' win was due to Wells's pitching.* See also *because, because of.*

due to the fact that, owing to the fact that   Wordy. Use *because* instead: *They stopped the game because* (not *due to the fact that*) *it was raining.*

each, every   These are singular pronouns; use them with a singular verb. See also **42d** and **42g**.

each other, one another   Use *each other* with two, *one another* with more than two: *The twins love each other. The triplets all love one another.*

effect   See *affect.*

e.g.   In the body of a formal text, use *for example* or *for instance* in place of this Latin abbreviation.

elicit, illicit   *Elicit* means "to get or draw out": *The police tried in vain to elicit information from the suspect's accomplice. Illicit* is an adjective meaning "illegal": *Their illicit deals landed them in prison.*

elude   See *allude, elude.*

emigrate, immigrate   *Emigrate from* is "to leave a country"; *immigrate to* is "to move to another country": *They emigrated*

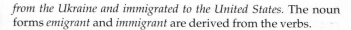

from the Ukraine and immigrated to the United States. The noun forms *emigrant* and *immigrant* are derived from the verbs.

eminent, imminent *Eminent* means "well known and noteworthy": *an eminent lawyer; imminent* means "about to happen": *an imminent disaster.*

etc. This abbreviation for the Latin *et cetera* means "and so on." Do not let a list trail off with *etc.* Rather than *They took a tent, a sleeping bag, etc.,* write *They took a tent, a sleeping bag, cooking utensils, and a stove.*

every, each See *each, every.*

everyday, every day *Everyday* as one word is an adjective meaning "usual": *Their everyday routine is to break for lunch at 12:30. Every day* is an adverbial expression of frequency: *I get up early every day.*

except, expect See *accept, except, expect.*

explicit, implicit *Explicit* means "direct": *She gave explicit instructions. Implicit* means "implied": *A tax increase is implicit in the proposal.*

farther, further Both can apply to distance: *She lives farther (further) from the campus than I do.* But only *further* is used to mean "additional" or "additionally": *The management offered further incentives. Further, the union proposed new work rules.*

female, male Use these words as adjectives, not as nouns replacing *man* and *woman: There are only three women* (not *females*) *in my class. We are discussing female conversational traits.*

few, a few Use *a few* for *some;* use *few* for *hardly any: She has a few days off to relax. She has few friends and is lonely.*

fewer, less Formal usage demands *fewer* with plural countable nouns (*fewer holidays*), *less* with uncountable nouns (*less money*). However, in informal usage, *less* with plural nouns commonly occurs, especially with *than: less than six items, less than ten miles, fifty words or less.* In formal usage, *fewer* is preferred.

get married to, marry These expressions can be used interchangeably: *She will marry her childhood friend next month. He will get married to his fiancée next week.* (The noun form is *marriage: Their marriage has lasted thirty years.*)

had better Include the *had* in standard English, although it is often omitted in advertising and in speech: *You had better* (not *You better*) *try harder.*

hardly   This is a negative word. Do not use it with another negative: *He could hardly walk* (not *He couldn't hardly walk*) *after the accident.*

hisself   Nonstandard; use *himself.*

illicit, elicit   See *elicit, illicit.*

illusion, allusion   See *allusion, illusion.*

immigrate, emigrate   See *emigrate, immigrate.*

imminent, eminent   See *eminent, imminent.*

implicit   See *explicit, implicit.*

imply, infer   *Imply* means "to suggest in an indirect way": *He implied that further layoffs were unlikely. Infer* means "to guess" or "to draw a conclusion": *I inferred that the company was doing well.*

incredible, incredulous   *Incredible* means "difficult to believe": *The violence of the storm was incredible. Incredulous* means "skeptical, unable to believe": *They were incredulous when he told them about his daring exploits in the whitewater rapids.*

in regard to, as regards   Use one or the other. Do not use the nonstandard *in regards to.*

irregardless   Avoid this nonstandard form and use *regardless* instead: *He selected history as a major regardless of the preparation it would give him for a career.*

it's, its   The apostrophe in *it's* signals not a possessive but a contraction of *it is* or *it has. Its* is the possessive form of the pronoun *it: The city government agency has produced its final report. It's available upon request.*

kind, sort, type   In the singular, use with *this* and a singular noun. Use in the plural with *these* and a plural noun: *this kind of book, these kinds of books.*

kind of, sort of   Do not use these words to mean "somewhat" or "a little": *The pace of the baseball game was somewhat* (not *kind of*) *slow.*

lend, loan   *Lend* is a verb, but *loan* is ordinarily used as a noun: *Our cousins offered to lend us some money, but we refused the loan.*

less, fewer   See *fewer, less.*

like, as, as if   *As* and *as if* introduce a dependent clause with a subject and verb: *She walks as her father does. She looks as if she could eat a big meal. Like* is a preposition followed by a noun or pronoun, not by a clause: *She looks like her father.* In speech, however, *like* is often used where formal usage dictates *as* or *as*

if: She walks like her father does. He looks like he needs a new suit.
Formal usage requires *He looks as if he needs a new suit.*

loan See *lend, loan.*

loose, lose *Loose* is an adjective meaning the opposite of *tight:*
This jacket is comfortable because it is so loose. Lose is a verb, with
the past tense and past participle form *lost: Many people lose their
jobs in a recession.*

lot, alot, lots See *a lot, alot, lots.*

marital, martial *Marital* is associated with marriage, *martial*
with war.

may be, maybe *May be* consists of a modal verb followed by
the base form of the verb *be; maybe* is an adverb meaning "perhaps." If you can replace the expression with *perhaps,* make it one
word: *They may be there already, or maybe they got caught in traffic.*

most, almost See *almost, most.*

myself Use only as a reflexive pronoun (*I told them myself*) or
as an intensive pronoun (*I myself told them*). Do not use *myself* as
a subject pronoun; use *My sister and I won* (not *My sister and myself won*).

nowadays All one word. Make sure you include the final *-s.*

nowhere, nowheres See *anyway.*

number, amount See *amount, number.*

of a Do not use *of a* after an adjective. Omit *of: She's not that
good a player* (not *She's not that good of a player*).

off, off of Use only *off,* not *off of: She drove the car off the road*
(not *off of*).

OK, O.K., okay Reserve these forms for informal speech and
writing. Choose another word in a formal context: *Her performance was satisfactory* (in place of *Her performance was OK*).

one another See *each other, one another.*

owing to the fact that See *due to the fact that.*

passed, past *Passed* is a past tense verb form: *They passed the
deli on the way to work. He passed his exam. Past* can be a noun (*in
the past*), an adjective (*in past times*), or a preposition (*She walked
past the bakery*).

plus Do not use *plus* as a coordinating conjunction or a transitional expression. Use *and* or *moreover* instead: *He was promoted
and* (not *plus*) *he received a bonus.* Use *plus* as a preposition meaning

"in addition to": *His salary plus his dividends placed him in a high tax bracket.*

precede, proceed *Precede* means "to go or occur before": *The Roaring Twenties preceded the Great Depression. Proceed* means "to go ahead": *After you have paid the fee, proceed to the examination room.*

pretty Avoid using *pretty* as an intensifying adverb. Omit it or use a word like *really, very, rather,* or *quite: The stew tastes very* (not *pretty*) *good.*

principal, principle *Principal* is a noun *(the principal of a school)* or an adjective meaning "main": *His principal motive was greed. Principle* is a noun meaning "standard or rule": *He always acts on his principles.*

quite, quiet Do not confuse the adverb *quite,* meaning "very," with the adjective *quiet* ("still" or "silent"): *We felt quite relieved when the audience became quiet.*

quote, quotation *Quote* is a verb. Do not use it as a noun; use *quotation: The quotation* (not *quote*) *from Walker tells the reader a great deal.*

real, really *Real* is an adjective; *really* is an adverb. Do not use *real* as an intensifying adverb: *She acted really* (not *real*) *well.*

reason is because Avoid *the reason is because.* Instead, use *the reason is that* or rewrite the sentence. See **40f**.

regardless See *irregardless.*

respectable, respectful, respective *Respectable* means "presentable, worthy of respect": *Wear some respectable shoes to your interview. Respectful* means "polite or deferential": *Parents want their children to be respectful to adults. Respective* means "particular" or "individual": *The friends of the bride and the groom sat in their respective seats in the church.*

should (could, might, etc.) of Nonstandard for *should have* tried, *might have* seen.

since Use only when time or reason is clear: *Since you insist on helping, I'll let you paint this bookcase.* Unclear: *Since he got a new job, he has been happy.*

site, sight, cite See *cite, site, sight.*

sometimes, sometime, some time *Sometimes* means "occasionally": *He sometimes prefers to eat lunch at his desk. Sometime* means "at an indefinite time": *I read that book sometime last year.* The expression *some time* is the noun *time* modified by the quantity word *some: I worked for Honda for some time—about five years, I think.*

sort, type, kind See *kind, sort, type.*

sort of, kind of See *kind of, sort of.*

stationary, stationery *Stationary* means "not moving" *(a stationary vehicle);* you use *stationery* when you write letters.

than, then *Then* is a time word; *than* must be preceded by a comparative form: *bigger than, more interesting than.*

their, there, they're *They're* is a contracted form of *they are; there* indicates place or is used as a filler in the subject position in a sentence; *their* is a pronoun indicating possession: *They're over there, guarding their luggage.*

theirself, theirselves, themself Nonstandard; use *themselves.*

to, too, two Do not confuse these words. *To* is a sign of the infinitive and a common preposition; *too* is an adverb; *two* is the number: *She is too smart to agree to report to two bosses.*

uninterested, disinterested See *disinterested, uninterested.*

used to, get (become) used to These expressions share the common form *used to.* But the first, expressing a past habit that no longer exists, is followed by a base form of the verb: *He used to wear his hair long.* (Note that after *not,* the form is *use to: He did not use to have a beard.*) In the expression *get (become) used to, used to* means "accustomed to" and is followed by a noun or an *-ing* form: *She couldn't get used to driving on the left when she was in England.*

way, ways Use *way* to mean "distance": *He has a way to go. Ways* in this context is nonstandard.

weather, whether *Weather* is a noun; *whether* is a conjunction: *The weather will determine whether we go on the picnic.*

whose, who's *Whose* is possessive: *Whose goal was that? Who's* is a contraction of *who is* or *who has: Who's the player whose pass was caught?*

your, you're *Your* is a pronoun used to show possession. *You're* is a contraction for *you are: You're wearing your new shoes today, aren't you?*

50 Glossary of Grammatical Terms

active voice Attribute of a verb when its grammatical subject performs the action: *The dog ate the cake.* **41g.** See also *passive voice.*

adjective　A word that describes or limits (modifies) a noun or pronoun: A *happy* child. The child is *happy*. **44**. See also *comparative, coordinate adjective, superlative*.

adjective clause　See *relative clause*.

adverb　A word that modifies a verb, an adjective, or another adverb. Many adverbs end in *-ly:* She ran *quickly*. He is *really* successful. The children were *well* liked. **44**. See also *comparative, superlative*.

adverb clause　A dependent clause that modifies a verb, an adjective, or an adverb and begins with a subordinating conjunction: He left early *because he was tired.*

agreement　The grammatical match in person, number, and gender between a verb and its subject or a pronoun and the word it refers to (its *antecedent*): The *benefits continue; they are* pleasing. The *benefit continues. It is* pleasing. **42, 43c**.

antecedent　The noun that a pronoun refers to or replaces: My sons found a *kitten. It* was black and white. **43b, 43c**.

appositive phrase　A phrase occurring next to a noun and used to describe it: His father, *a factory worker,* is running for office. **43a**.

article　*A, an* (indefinite articles), or *the* (definite article). **45** ESL.

auxiliary verb　A verb that joins with another verb to form a complete verb. Auxiliary verbs are forms of *do, be,* and *have* as well as the modal auxiliary verbs. **41a, 41b**. See also *modal auxiliary verb*.

base form　The form of a verb with no endings; the dictionary form, used in an infinitive after *to: see, eat, go, be.* **41a**.

clause　A group of words that includes a subject and a verb. See also *independent clause, dependent clause*.

cliché　An overused, predictable expression: *as cool as a cucumber.* **39a**.

collective noun　A noun naming a group of people, places, objects, or ideas that are regarded as a unit: *society, jury, family.* **42e, 43c**.

comma splice　An error caused by connecting two independent clauses with only a comma.

common noun　A noun that does not name a unique person, place, or thing. **45a** ESL. See also *proper noun*.

comparative   The form of an adjective or adverb used to compare two people or things: *bigger, more interesting.* **44e**.

complement   A *subject complement* is a word or group of words used after a linking verb to refer to and describe the subject: Harry looks *happy.* An *object complement* is a word or group of words used after a direct object to complete its meaning: They call him a *liar.* **44b**.

complete verb   A verb that shows tense. Some verb forms, such as present *(-ing)* participles and past participles, require an auxiliary verb or verbs to make them complete verbs. *Going* and *seen* are not complete verbs; *are going* and *has been seen* are complete. **41a**.

compound adjective   An adjective formed of two or more words, used as one unit, and often connected with hyphens: a *well-constructed* house. **44c**.

compound subject   Two subjects with the same predicate and with the parts of the subject joined by words such as *and, or,* and *nor: My uncle and my aunt* are leaving soon. **42f**.

conditional clause   A clause introduced by *if* or *unless,* expressing conditions of fact, prediction, or speculation: *If we earn more,* we spend more. **41f**.

conjunction   A word or words like *and* and *because* joining sentences or sentence elements. See also *coordinating conjunction, subordinating conjunction.*

coordinating conjunction   The seven coordinating conjunctions are *and, but, or, nor, so, for,* and *yet.* They connect sentence elements that are parallel in structure: He couldn't call, *but* he wrote a letter.

countable noun   A common noun that has a plural form and can be used after a plural quantity word (*many, three,* and so on): one *book,* three *stores,* many *children.* **45a** ESL.

dangling modifier   A modifier that does not clearly modify the noun or pronoun it is intended to modify: *Turning the corner,* the lights went out. (Corrected: *Turning the corner, we* saw the lights go out.) **40c**.

demonstrative pronoun   *This, that, these,* or *those: That* is my glass. **43c**.

dependent clause   A clause that cannot stand alone as a complete sentence and needs to be attached to an independent clause. A dependent clause begins with a subordinating word such as *because, if, when, although, who, which,* or *that: When it rains,* we can't take the children outside. **37c**.

diction   Choice of appropriate words and tone. **39**.

direct object   The person or thing that receives the action of a verb or verb form: They ate *cake* and *ice cream.* **47b** ESL.

direct quotation   A person's words, reproduced exactly by a writer and placed in quotation marks: *"I won't be home until noon,"* she said. **40d, 47c** ESL.

double negative   Using two negative words in the same sentence is nonstandard usage: I do *not* know *nothing.* (Corrected: I do not know anything.) **44d**.

dummy subject   See *filler subject.*

faulty predication   A construction in which subject and verb do not fit logically: The *decrease* in stolen cars *has diminished* in the past year. (Corrected: The *number* of stolen cars *has decreased* in the past year.) **40e**.

filler (or dummy) subject   *It* or *there* used in the subject position of a clause, followed by a form of *be: There are* two elm trees on the corner. **36b, 42c**.

first person   The person speaking or writing: *I* or *we.* **43a**.

fragment   A group of words that is punctuated as a sentence but is grammatically incomplete because it lacks a subject or a complete verb or lacks an independent clause: *Because it was a sunny day.*

fused sentence   See *run-on sentence.*

gender   Classification of a noun or pronoun as masculine *(Uncle John, he),* feminine *(Ms. Torez, she),* or neuter *(book, it).* **39c, 43c**.

generic noun   A noun referring to a general class or type of person or object: A *student* has to write many papers. **45c**.

gerund   A form, derived from a verb, that ends in *-ing* and functions as a noun: *Walking* is good for your health. **42d, 43a, 46b** ESL, **46c** ESL.

helping verb   See *auxiliary verb.*

indefinite pronoun   A pronoun that refers to a nonspecific person or object: *anybody, something.* **42g**.

independent clause   A clause containing a subject and a complete verb, not introduced by a subordinating word. An independent clause stands alone grammatically: *Birds sing. The old* *man was singing a song.* Hailing a cab, *the woman used a silver whistle.*

indirect object   The person or thing to whom or what, or for whom or what, an action is performed. It comes between a verb and a direct object: He gave his *sister* some flowers. **47b** ESL.

indirect question   A question reported by a speaker or writer, with no quotation marks: They asked *if we would help them.* **47c** ESL.

indirect quotation   A presentation or paraphrase of the words of another speaker or writer, integrated into a writer's own sentence: He said *that they were making money.* **40d**.

infinitive   The base form, or dictionary form, of a verb, preceded by *to: to see, to steal.* **46a** ESL, **46d** ESL.

intransitive verb   A verb that is not followed by a direct object: Exciting events *have occurred.* He *fell.* **41c, 41g**. See also *transitive verb.*

irregular verb   A verb that does not form its past tense and past participle with *-ed: sing, sang, sung.* **41a**.

linking verb   A verb connecting a subject to its complement. Typical linking verbs are *be, become, seem,* and *appear:* He *seems* angry. A linking verb is intransitive; it does not take a direct object. **43a, 44b**.

mental activity verb   A verb not used in a tense showing progressive aspect: *prefer, want, understand:* He *wants* to leave (*not* He *is wanting*). **41d**.

misplaced modifier   An adverb (particularly *only* and *even*) or a descriptive phrase or clause positioned in a sentence in such a way that it appears to modify the wrong word or words: She showed the doll to her sister *that her aunt gave her.* **40b**.

mixed structure   A sentence with two or more types of structures that do not match grammatically: *By doing* her homework at the last minute *caused* Meg to make many mistakes. **40a**.

modal auxiliary verb   An auxiliary verb used with the base form of the main verb. Modal auxiliaries are seldom used alone and do not change form. The modal auxiliaries are *will, would, can, could, shall, should, may, might,* and *must.* **41b**.

modifier   A word or words that describe a noun, verb, phrase, or whole clause: He is a *happy* man. He is smiling *happily.* **40b, 44**.

mood The mood of a verb tells whether it states a fact (*indicative:* She *goes* to school), gives a command (*imperative: Come* back soon), or expresses a condition, wish, or request (*subjunctive:* I wish you *were* not leaving). **41f**.

nonrestrictive phrase or clause A phrase or clause that adds nonessential information to a sentence. It is set off with commas: His report, *which he gave to his boss yesterday,* received enthusiastic praise. Also called *nonessential phrase* or *clause*. **43e**.

noun A word that names a person, place, thing, or idea. Nouns can be proper or common and, if common, countable or uncountable. **45a** ESL. See also the following entries on the various types of nouns: *collective noun, common noun, compound noun, countable noun, generic noun, proper noun, uncountable noun.*

number The indication of a noun or pronoun as singular (one person, place, thing, or idea) or plural (more than one). **42a, 43a**.

object of preposition A noun or pronoun (along with its modifiers) following a preposition: on *the beach.* **46c** ESL**.**

paragraph A group of sentences, usually on one topic, set off in a text. **37d**.

parallelism The use of coordinate structures that have the same grammatical form: She likes *swimming* and *playing* tennis. **40g**.

participle phrase A phrase beginning with a present participle (*-ing*) or a past participle: The woman *wearing a green skirt* is my sister. *Baffled by the puzzle,* he gave up. **40c, 41e**.

passive voice Attribute of a verb when its grammatical subject is the receiver of the action that the verb describes: The book *was written* by my professor. **36c, 41g**. See also *active voice.*

past participle A form of a verb, ending in *-ed* for regular verbs and having various forms for irregular verbs. The past participle needs an auxiliary verb or verbs in order to function as a complete verb of a clause: *has chosen, was cleaned, might have been told.* It can also function alone as an adjective. **41a, 41e, 41g, 46e** ESL.

perfect progressive verb tense forms Verb tenses that show actions in progress up to a specific point in present, past, or future time. For active voice verbs, use a form of the auxiliary *have been* followed by the *-ing* form of the verb: *has/have been living, had been living, will have been living.* **41d**.

perfect verb tense forms   Verb tenses that show actions completed by present, past, or future time. For active voice verbs, use forms of the auxiliary *have* followed by the past participle of the verb: *has/have arrived, had arrived, will have arrived.* **41d.**

person   The form of a pronoun or verb that indicates whether the subject is doing the speaking (first person, *I* or *we*), is spoken to (second person, *you*), or is spoken about (third person, *he, she, it,* or *they*). **43a, 43b.**

phrase   A group of words that does not contain a subject and verb but that functions as a noun, verb, adjective, or adverb: *under the tree, to work hard.* See also *absolute phrase, appositive phrase,* and *participle phrase.*

possessive   The form of a noun or pronoun that indicates ownership. Possessive pronouns include *my, his, their,* and *theirs.* The possessive form of a noun is indicated by an apostrophe or an apostrophe and *-s: Mario's* car, the *children's* nanny, the *birds'* nests. **43a.**

predicate   The part of a sentence that contains the verb and its modifiers and that comments on or makes an assertion about the subject. **40e.**

preposition   A word used before a noun or pronoun to indicate time, space, or some other relationship (such as *in, to, for, about, during*). **46c ESL.**

present participle   The *-ing* form of a verb, showing an action in progress or as continuous: They are *sleeping.* Without an auxiliary, the *-ing* form cannot be a complete verb, but it can be used as an adjective: *searing* heat. **41a.**

progressive verb tense forms   Verb tenses that show actions in progress at a point or over a period of time in past, present, or future time. They use a form of *be* + the *-ing* form of the verb: They *are working;* he *will be writing.* **41b, 41d.**

pronoun   A word used to represent a noun or a noun phrase. Pronouns are of various types: personal *(I, they),* possessive *(my, mine, their, theirs),* demonstrative *(this, that, these, those),* intensive or reflexive *(myself, herself),* relative *(who, whom, whose, which, that),* interrogative *(who, which, what),* and indefinite *(anyone, something).* **42g, 43, 47a ESL.**

pronoun reference   The connection between a pronoun and its antecedent. Reference should be clear and unambiguous: The *lawyer* picked up *his* hat and left. **43b.**

proper noun   The capitalized name of a specific person, place, or thing: *Golden Gate Park, University of Kansas*. **45a** ESL.

quantity word   A word expressing the idea of quantity, such as *each, several, some, many,* or *much*. Subject-verb agreement is important with quantity words: *Each* of the students *has* a different assignment. **42h**. See also *agreement*.

reflexive pronoun   A pronoun ending in *-self* or *-selves* and referring to the subject of a clause. Standard forms are *himself* and *themselves*. See *hisself* in Glossary of Usage, page 300.

regular verb   Verb with *-ed* in past tense and past participle forms. **41a**.

relative clause   Also called an *adjective clause,* a relative clause is a dependent clause beginning with a relative pronoun *(who, whom, whose, which,* or *that)* and modifying a noun or pronoun: The writer *who won the prize* was elated. **42i, 43e**.

relative pronoun   Pronoun that introduces a relative clause: *who, whom, whose, which, that*. **42i, 43e**.

restrictive phrase or clause   A phrase or clause that provides information necessary to the identity of the word or phrase it modifies. A restrictive phrase or clause is not set off with commas: The book *that is first on the bestseller list* is a memoir. Also called *essential phrase or clause*. **43e**.

run-on sentence   Two independent clauses not separated by a conjunction or by any punctuation. Also called *fused sentence: The dog ate the meat the cat ate the fish.* (Corrected: *The dog ate the meat; the cat ate the fish.*)

second person   The person addressed: *you*. **43a, 43d**.

shifts   Inappropriate switches in grammatical structure, such as from one tense to another or between statement and command or between indirect and direct quotation: Joan asked *whether I was warm enough* and *did I sleep well*. (Corrected: *... and slept well*.) **40d**.

split infinitive   An infinitive with a word or words inserted between *to* and the base form of the verb: *to successfully complete*. Some readers may object to this structure. **40b**.

Standard English   "The variety of English that is most widely accepted as the spoken and written language of educated speakers in formal and informal contexts and is characterized by generally accepted conventions of spelling, grammar, and vocabulary while admitting some regional differences, especially in pronunciation and vocabulary."—*American Heritage Dictionary*.

subject   The noun or pronoun that performs the action of the verb in an active voice sentence or receives the action of the verb in a passive voice sentence. Every sentence needs a subject and a verb. **36a, 37a, 40c, 40e, 42**.

subjunctive   See *mood*.

subordinate clause   See *dependent clause*.

subordinating conjunction   A word used to introduce a dependent adverb clause, such as *because, if, when, although, since, while*.

superlative   The form of an adjective or adverb used to compare three or more people or things: *biggest, most unusual, least effectively*. **44e**.

tense   The form of a verb that indicates time. Verbs change form to distinguish present and past time: He *goes*; he *went*. Auxiliary verbs indicate progressive and perfect actions. **41d**. See also *perfect, progressive,* and *perfect progressive verb tense forms*.

third person   The person or thing spoken about: *he, she, it, they,* or nouns. **43a**.

transitional expression   A word or phrase used to connect two independent clauses. Typical transitional expressions are *for example, however,* and *similarly*: We were able to swim today; *in addition,* we took the canoe out on the river. A semicolon frequently occurs between the two independent clauses. **15b, 37b**.

transitive verb   A verb that has an object, a person or thing that receives the action (in the active voice): Dogs *chase* cats. Transitive verbs can be used in the passive voice (in which case the subject receives the action of the verb): Cats *are chased* by dogs. **41c, 41g**. See also *intransitive verb*.

uncountable noun   A common noun that cannot follow a plural quantity word (such as *several* or *many*), is never used with *a* or *an*, is used with a singular third person verb, and has no plural form: *furniture, happiness, information*. **42d, 42h, 45a** ESL, **45b** ESL, **45c** ESL.

verb   A word that expresses action or being and that tells what the subject of the clause is or does. A complete verb of a clause might require auxiliary or modal auxiliary verbs to complete its meaning. **41**. See also the following entries for more specific information.

active voice	*linking verb*	*perfect verb tense*
agreement	*mental activity*	*forms*
auxiliary verb	*verb*	*predicate*
base form	*modal auxiliary*	*present participle*
complete verb	*verb*	*progressive verb*
compound	*mood*	*tense forms*
predicate	*passive voice*	*regular verb*
infinitive	*past participle*	*tense*
intransitive verb	*perfect progres-*	*transitive verb*
irregular verb	*sive verb tense*	*voice*
	forms	

voice Transitive verbs (those followed by an object) can be used in the active voice *(He is painting the door)* or the passive voice *(The door is being painted)*. **41g**.

zero article The lack of an article *(a, an,* or *the)* before a noun. Uncountable nouns are used with the zero article when they make no specific reference. **45b** ESL, **45c** ESL.

Index

Note: An asterisk (*) refers to a page number in the Glossaries of Speaking and Grammatical Terms

Common Correction and Editing Marks

Note: Numbers refer to sections in the book.

Abbreviation	Meaning
ab or abbr	abbreviation
adj	adjective, **44**
adv	adverb, **44**
agr	agreement
art	article, **45**
awk	awkward
bias	biased language
case	case, **43a**
cap (t̲o̲m)	use a capital letter
comp̲	comparison, **40a, 44e, 44f**
coord	coordination
cs	comma splice
dic	diction, **39**
db neg	double negative, **44d**
dm	dangling modifier, **40c**
doc	documentation, **12a**
-ed	error in -*ed* ending, **41e, 46e**
frag	sentence fragment
fs	fused sentence
hyph	hyphenation
inc	incomplete
ind quot	indirect quotation, **40d, 41d, 47c**
-ing	-*ing* error, **46**
ital	italics/underlining
jar	jargon, **39b**
lc (M̸e)	use a lowercase letter
mix or mixed	mixed construction, **40a**
mm	misplaced modifier, **40b**
ms	manuscript form
num	faulty use of numbers
p	punctuation error
pass	ineffective passive voice, **36c, 41g**

Abbreviation	Meaning
pron	pronoun error, **43**
quot	quotation error
ref	pronoun reference error, **43b**
rel cl	relative clause, **42i, 43e,**
rep	repetitive
-s	error in -*s* ending, **42a**
shift	needless shift, **40d**
sp	spelling
s/pl	singular/plural error, **42a, 45a**
sub	subordination
sup	superlative, **44e**
s-v agr	subject-verb agreement, **42**
trans	transition, **15b, 37b**
und	underlining/italics
usg	usage error, **49**
vb	verb error, **41**
vt	verb tense, **41d**
wdy	wordy, **35**
wo	word order, **47**
ww	wrong word, **39**

Symbol	Meaning
??	unclear
¶ or par	new paragraph
no ¶	no new paragraph
//	parallelism
⌒	close up space
#	add space
∧	insert
∧	delete
∽	transpose
×	obvious error
⊙	needs a period
stet	do not change

Table of Contents